35

ANNUAL EXHIBITION

PHOTOGRAPHY
AND
ILLUSTRATION

COMMUNICATION ARTS

*Communication Arts (ISSN 0010-3519) is published eight times a year
by Coyne & Blanchard, Inc., 410 Sherman Avenue, Palo Alto, California 94306
Copyright 1994 by Coyne & Blanchard, Inc.*

Patrick Coyne, editor and designer; Jean A. Coyne, executive editor; Stephanie Steyer-Coyne, consulting editor and designer; Anne Telford, managing editor; Jane McCampbell, designer; Scott Perry, production manager; Ron Niewald, Scott Teaford, production; Michael Krigel, advertising and circulation director; Art Carbone, retail sales; Nancy Hagemann, administrative assistant; Sue Garibaldi, editorial assistant; Jason Jackson, subscription manager; Gloria Rosario, Priscilla Solera, subscriptions; Lisa Marie Perez, traffic manager; Richard Coyne, founder

Cover: © 1994 RJ Muna

This special issue is a combination of the July (Illustration) and August (Photography) issues published exclusively for distribution by RotoVision SA, 9, Route Suisse, Ch-1295 Mies, Switzerland Phone (022) 755 30 55, Fax (022) 755 40 72, Telex 419 246 rovi ch.

INTRODUCTION

Welcome to the international edition of the 35th annual Photography and Illustration Exhibition sponsored by *Communication Arts*. The images on the following pages represent the finest examples of creativity in the service of commerce as well as self-promotion and previously unpublished work.

Considered one of the most prestigious creative competitions in the world, we received over 18,000 entries this year. Two distinguished juries—comprised of respected creative professionals—selected only 643 for inclusion in this exclusive volume.

The competition is extremely important to photographers and illustrators because *Communication Arts* reproduces their images with an unprecedented commitment to quality. More than 60,000 design and advertising professionals worldwide will see the selected images, in the United States and international versions of this annual, guaranteeing important exposure for the creators of this outstanding work.

This year's volume contains the work of talented artists and photographers who expand the infinite spectrum of human creativity in visual communications. Enjoy this book as an invaluable inspirational resource and as a celebration of creative excellence.

Patrick Coyne
Editor/Designer

ご挨拶

このインターナショナル版には、「コミュニケーション・アーツ」主催、第35回写真イラストレーション・コンペティションの入賞作品が掲載されています。以下の作品は、セルフ・プロモーションや以前に出版されたことのない作品としてと同様,コマーシャル業において、卓越したクリエイティビティを代表するものばかりです。

世界で最も権威あるクリエイティブ分野のコンペティションの一つとして、今年は18,000点以上の応募がありました。その中から、プロとして活躍中の著名で権威ある2人の審査員により選ばれた643作品をご紹介します。

入賞作品は、「コミュニケーション・アーツ」が最高のクオリティで再現するので、このコンペティションは写真家やイラストレーターにとって大変有意義なものになっています。この毎年恒例の米国版とインターナショナル版で、世界中の60,000人ものデザイン・広告関係者に入賞作品は紹介されるのです。卓越した作品のクリエーター達にとって自分の作品を他に知ってもらうのに、またとない機会となることは間違いありません。

今年度版には、ビジュアル・コミュニケーション分野で、人類の無限の創造性を一歩押し進めた才能あるアーチストや写真家の作品が掲載されています。インスピレーションを生む貴重な参考資料として、そしてクリエイティビティの素晴らしさを称えるものとして、本書をお楽しみ下さい。

パトリック・コイン
編集者/デザイナー

INTRODUCCIÓN

Bienvenido a la edición internacional de la 35ª exhibición anual de Fotografía e Ilustración patrocinado por *Communication Arts*. Las siguientes páginas muestran las mejores imágenes producidas para revistas, periódicos, libros, publicidad, afiches, empaque y autopromoción, escogidas por su excelencia creativa en el servicio de las artes publicitarias.

Nuestro concurso de expresión creativa es considerado como uno de los de mayor prestigio en el mundo. Este año recibimos más de 18,000 muestras, de las cuales nuestros dos distinguidos jurados, conformado por artistas profesionales de renombre, seleccionó 643 imágenes para incluir en este ejemplar exclusivo.

Este certamen es de suma importancia para fotógrafos e ilustradores dado que la revista *Communication Arts* reproduce sus obras de inigualable calidad y distribuye este libro entre 60,000 profesionales de diseño y publicidad en los Estados Unidos y el mundo entero, asegurando a los ganadores que sus obras se darán a conocer.

La edición de este año reúne las obras de artistas nuevos dedicados a la creación artística en el mundo de la fotografía y la ilustración. Lo invitamos a gozar de este libro que representa una referencia invaluable del estado actual de la comunicación visual, y un baluarte de la excelencia creativa.

Patrick Coyne
Redactor/Diseñador

PART ONE

35

PHOTOGRAPHY
ANNUAL

CATEGORIES

7
ADVERTISING

....

32
BOOKS

....

46
EDITORIAL

....

87
FOR SALE

....

88
INSTITUTIONAL

....

104
SELF-PROMOTION

....

125
UNPUBLISHED

....

THE JURY

CHRISTOPHER AUSTOPCHUK

is vice president of creative services for Sony Music/East Coast and design consultant for *Parade* magazine. He is also a professor at The School of Visual Arts in New York. He has worked for Condé Nast Publications, *Rolling Stone* and Pushpin Studios, Inc., as well as Random House, Mobil and the Limited Editions Club. Chris has received over 300 awards for his design and art direction.

MICHELE CLEMENT

a New Jersey native, moved to Southern California where she attended Art Center College and studied graphic design. While working on design projects at night, she assisted several fashion and advertising photographers during the day, until she opened her own San Francisco photography studio in 1980. She has created images for Polaroid, Royalton Sheets, Lotus, Physician's Formula, Jenny Craig and Baby Guess. Michele's photo-illustrations and celebrity portraits have appeared in *Newsweek*, *Movieline*, *Rolling Stone* and the *New York Times* as well as on Capitol, Electra, Windham Hill and Geffen Record covers.

DIANA LAGUARDIA

is the design director of *Condé Nast Traveler* in New York. LaGuardia began her career at a small newspaper in Maine, after which she designed Francis Ford Coppola's magazine *City* (of San Francisco). She was the art director of the *New York Times Magazine* for two years and joined the staff of *Traveler* in February of 1988. Diana currently serves ex officio on the board of directors of the Society of Publication Designers after three years as president. In 1991, she received the National Magazine Award for Design.

TOM MCCONNAUGHY

is chairman and chief creative officer of the Chicago-based McConnaughy Stein Schmidt Brown advertising agency. Tom holds a BFA in advertising design from Ohio University and began his advertising career as a television art director at Ketchum, MacLeod & Grove in Pittsburgh. McConnaughy joined Ogilvy & Mather, Chicago, when the office opened in 1976, and was elected senior vice president in 1980. In 1986, he became senior vice president, executive creative director of Bozell/Chicago. McConnaughy formed his own agency in 1986.

ROBIN RICKABAUGH

is a principal and partner with his wife, Heidi, in the Portland, Oregon, graphic design firm, Principia Graphica. The firm has received international recognition for its work from all of the design publications as well as the New York Art Directors Club, the AIGA and the Council for Advancement & Support of Education. Robin studied at Portland's Museum Art School from 1963 to 1967 and worked in the New York offices of Robert Miles Runyan Associates and deMartin Marona Associates before returning to Portland. One well-remembered project of the Rickabaughs is the 1976 magazine, *Oregon Rainbow*, dedicated to design excellence and superior photography.

1

2

ADVERTISING

1 (series)
Craig Cutler, photographer
Barb Paulini, art director
Hoffman York & Compton, ad agency
Weather Shield Manufacturing Company, Visions 2000, client

Ads for vinyl windows. Headline for each ad: Some of the more common natural materials found in today's homes.

2
Antony Nagelmann, photographer
Dan Vendetti, art director/designer
Condé Nast Vanity Fair, client

Ad for the magazine. Headline: Splendors of Spring.

3
Pete McArthur, photographer
Patty H.P. Mi, art director
Ogilvy & Mather Direct, ad agency
Microsoft, client

Product brochure showing ten reasons to switch to Microsoft. Reason number five.

4
Andreas Heumann, photographer/art director
Harvey Nichols, client

Ad headline: Take the stairway, lifts or escalator to heaven this Christmas.

1

8 PHOTOGRAPHY ANNUAL 1994

Advertising

1 (series)
Ivo von Renner, photographer
Daniele Cima, art director
Impact Italia, ad agency
Arimo, client

Ad campaign. Headline: Let's try to make the Italians as beautiful as Italy is.

Advertising

1
Trevor Ray Hart, photographer
Paul West/Paula Benson, art directors
Form, design firm
Beechwood Record Co., client

Compilation's record "Independent 20."

2
Chris Sheehan, Parallel Productions,
  photographer
Larae Netten, art director
Colle & McVoy, Inc., ad agency
SmithKline Beecham Animal Health, client

Trade ad headline: Giving sulfas several times a day is a major cause of pillitis.

3 (series)
Malcolm Venville, photographer
Stuart Buckley, art director
BMP DDB Needham Worldwide, Ltd., ad agency
British Gas, client

Ad headlines: Spot the boiler. Now your central heating can have a schedule as busy as yours. A Combi boiler could save you this much space.

COMMUNICATION ARTS 11

1

Advertising

1 (series)
Scott Morgan, photographer
Bill Thorburn, art director
Dayton Hudson, Department Store Division, client

Series of invitations and posters with the theme of world culture and dance for fashion shows throughout the United States.

2
David Katzenstein, photographer
Stacy Drummond, art director
Sony Music, client

CD cover for Schooly D, "Welcome to America."

Advertising

1
Nadav Kander, photographer
Kevin Redman, art director
Gap Advertising, ad agency
Gap Boots USA, client

Consumer ad.

2 (series)
Lars Topelmann, photographer
Kurt Reifschneider, art director
Brett Borders, writer
Left Brain Creative, ad agency
Paws, client

Posters for animal adoption agency. Headlines: Scooter turned and froze. Damn the cursed paparazzi, would their incessant quest to capture him in a compromising position never cease? Nicole's thoughts drifted into the future, to a time when the entire kingdom would be hers and she'd drink from any toilet she fancied. Not long after overcoming yet another law of physics, Barney returned to shore and proceeded to lick himself with abandon.

COMMUNICATION ARTS *15*

Advertising

1
Hans Neleman, photographer
Kevin Redman, art director
Gap, Inc., design
Gap Shoes, client

Store display.

2 (series)
David Allan Brandt, photographer
Kinson Chan, art director
Live Communications, Ltd., ad agency
Jeffery West Footwear, client

Ad headlines: Search for a Higher Ground.

COMMUNICATION ARTS *17*

1

2

18 PHOTOGRAPHY ANNUAL 1994

Advertising

1
Richard Mummery, photographer
Philip Forster, art director
Carmel Said, set designer
Collett, Dickenson, Pearce & Partners, ad agency
Benson & Hedges, client

One from an ad campaign. Headline: Washing up nightmare?

2
Chuck Kuhn, photographer
Chuck Kuhn/Bob Breno, art directors
Mintz & Hoke Inc., ad agency
Centerline, client

Software ad.

3 (series)
Gary Hush, photographer
Joe Shands, art director
David Baldwin, writer
Cole & Weber, ad agency
London Underground International, client

Campaign to create highly stylized product images. Dr. Martens 3-Eyelet Gibson; Dr. Martens Kid's 5-Eyelet Boot; Dr. Martens Women's Mary Jane.

1

2

20 PHOTOGRAPHY ANNUAL 1994

Advertising

1
Bob Miller, photographer
Rick McQuiston, art director
Wieden & Kennedy, ad agency
Nike, Inc., client

Consumer ad.

2
Peter Seaward, photographer
Russell Ramsey, art director
Bartle Bogle Hegarty, ad agency
Audi, client

Ad headline: Three brains decide how hard the Audi brakes. Only one of them is the driver's.

3
Ed Nielsen, photographer
Tim Morgan, art director
Michael Kerbow, Imagic, designer/illustrator
Dazai Advertising, ad agency
Advanced Computer Communications, client

Ad for a router.

4
Nadav Kander, photographer
Kevin Redman, art director
Gap Advertising, ad agency
Gap Boots USA, client

Consumer ad.

Advertising

1
Bob Krist, photographer
Monte Halis, art director
Rich Russo, creative director
Halis/Russo, design firm
Ogilvy & Mather, ad agency
Travel & Leisure, client

Promotional ad for the magazine. Headline: Traveling isn't a reward for working. It's homework for living.

2 (series)
Sue Bennett, photographer
Steve Hall, art director/designer
Rumrill Hoyt, ad agency
Du Pont, client

Ad campaign for a herbicide. Headline: The people who go no-till, go Extrazine II.

COMMUNICATION ARTS 23

Advertising

1 (series)
Miles Lowry, photographer
Scott Pettit, art director
Rhea & Kaiser, ad agency
Rhône-Poulenc, client

Direct mail brochure for cotton growers.

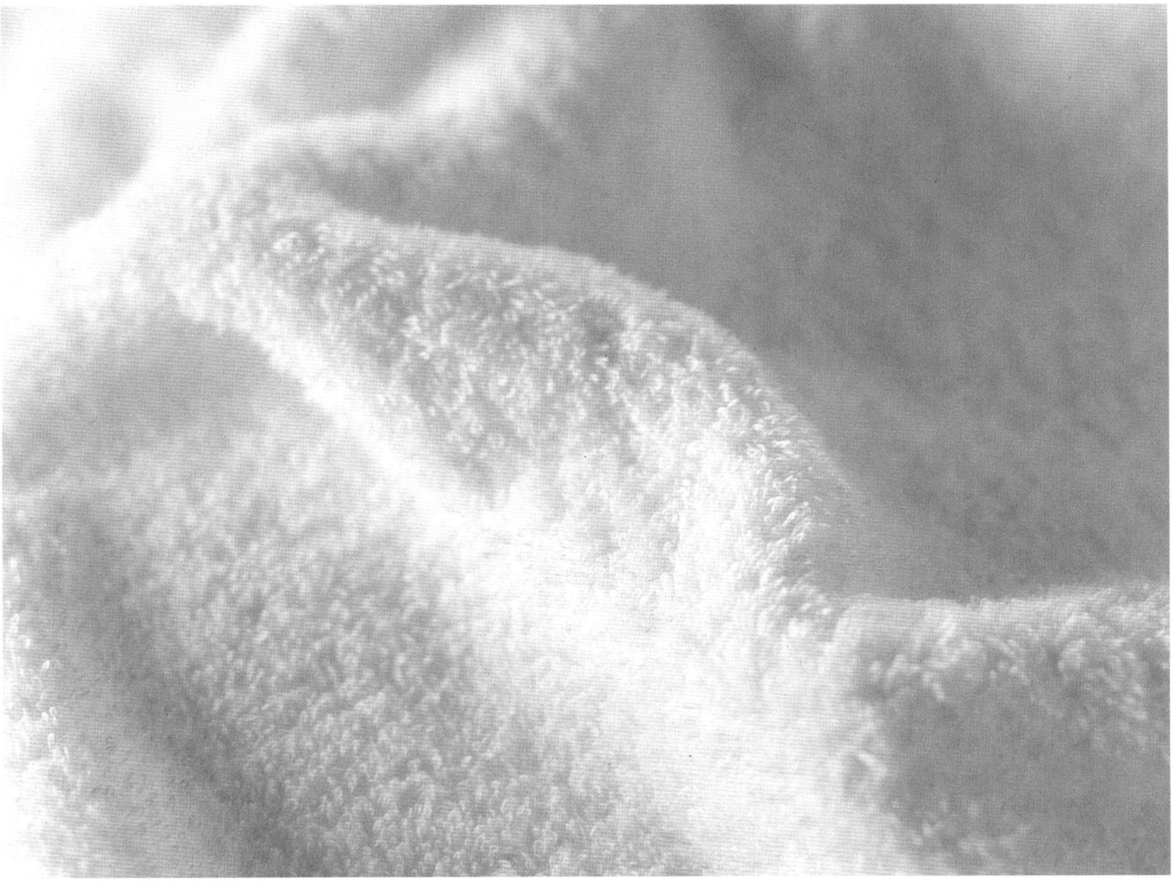

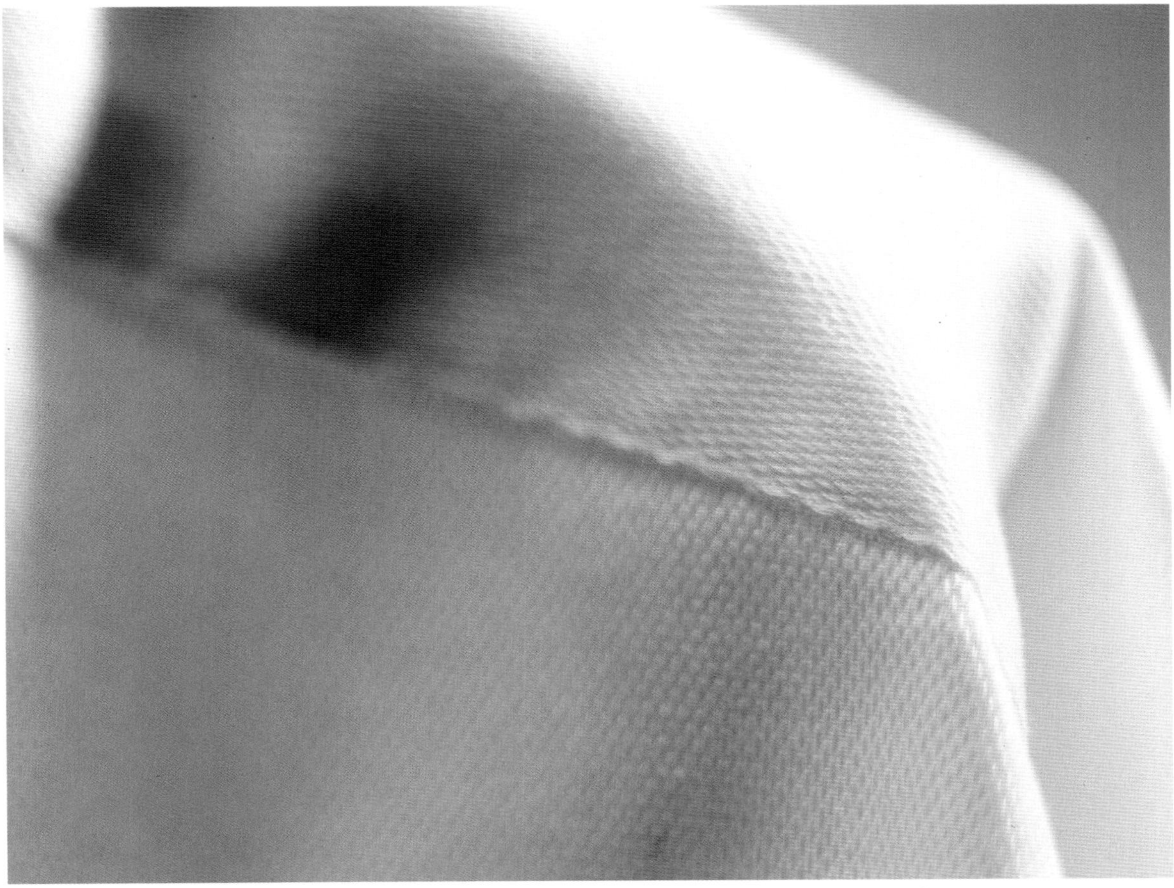

ADVERTISING

1 (series)
Joanne Dugan, photographer
Ann Lemon, designer
Ann Lemon Design, design firm
Postcards, client

Instruments of jazz masters shot for inside CD covers of this New York-based jazz label. Musicians include Reggie Workman, Gary Peacock, Paul Bley, Ralph Simon and Allen Pasqua.

COMMUNICATION ARTS 27

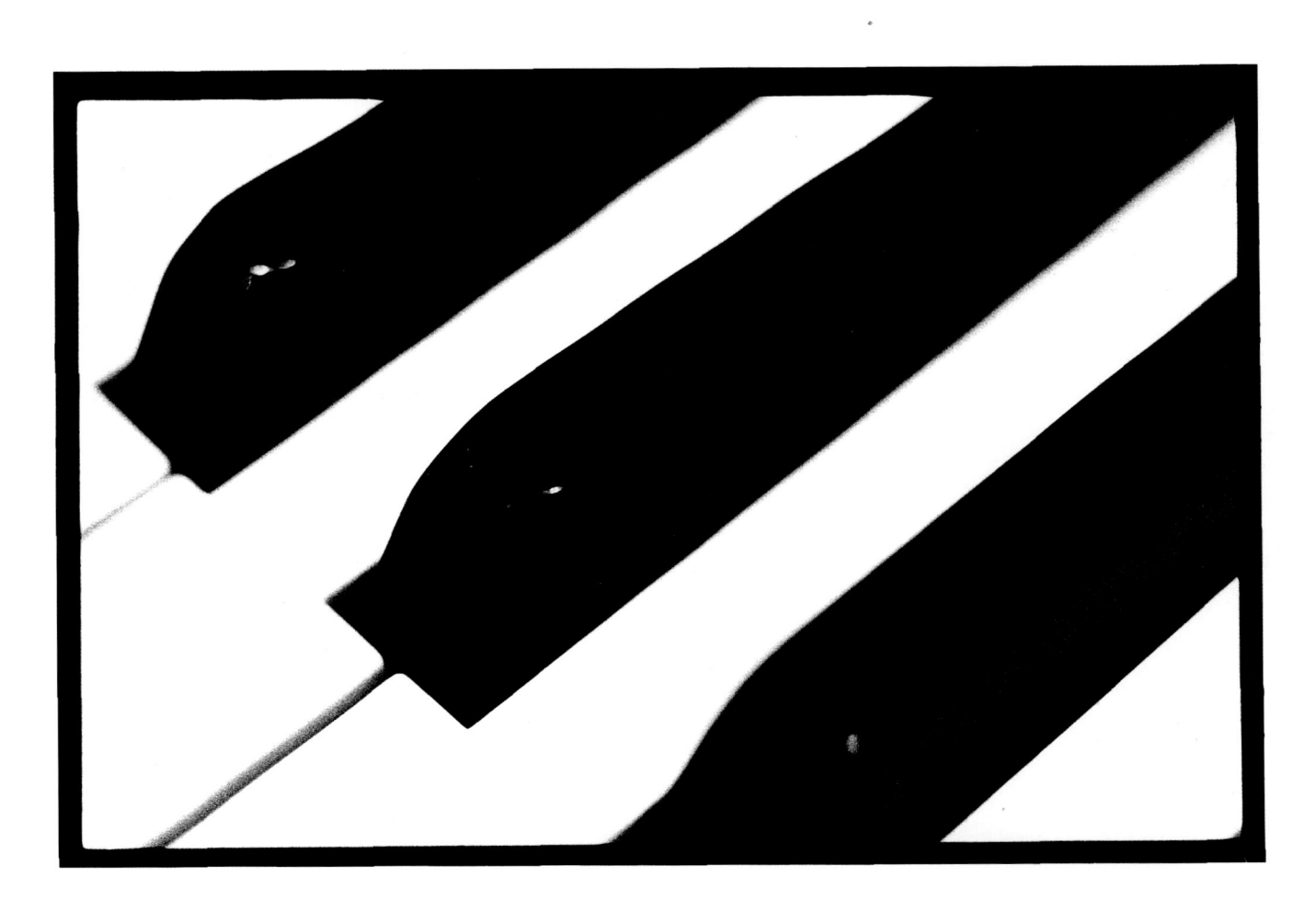

1

2

Advertising

1
Lars Topelmann, photographer
Mike Sheen/Joe Shands, art directors
David Baldwin, writer
Cole & Weber, ad agency
London Underground International, client

Ad headline: As it turns out, Dr. Martens has been making running shoes for over 30 years.

2
Andreas Heumann, photographer
Terence Stevens, art director
The Leith Agency, ad agency
Gala Bingo Clubs, client

Poster "Two Fat Ladies," relates to the number 88 in the game of bingo.

3 (series)
Ron Fehling, photographer
Duncan Bruce, art director
Philippe Garneau, writer
Chiat/Day/Toronto, ad agency
Toshiba of Canada Ltd., client

Ads to demonstrate the durability of the computers. Headlines: Next Monday morning around 345 Canadians will pour themselves a nice hot cup of coffee they will never get to enjoy. In the course of a business day 56% of all executives will forget at least one important thing they were supposed to do. This summer over 145 backyard home runs will find a home.

Advertising

1
David Gaz, photographer
Patrick Lamboy, art director
Ariane Lecourt, designer
Green Art, agency/design/client

Ad for a chain of florist's shops

2 (series)
Nadav Kander, photographer
Warren Eakins, art director
Wieden & Kennedy-Amsterdam,
  ad agency
Nike International, client

To be able to dive to the bottom of a twenty-foot pool on a single breath in a white maillot on vacation in the tropics and emerge like Venus without a gasp. That is not why you have been working out. But it's certainly a pleasing result.

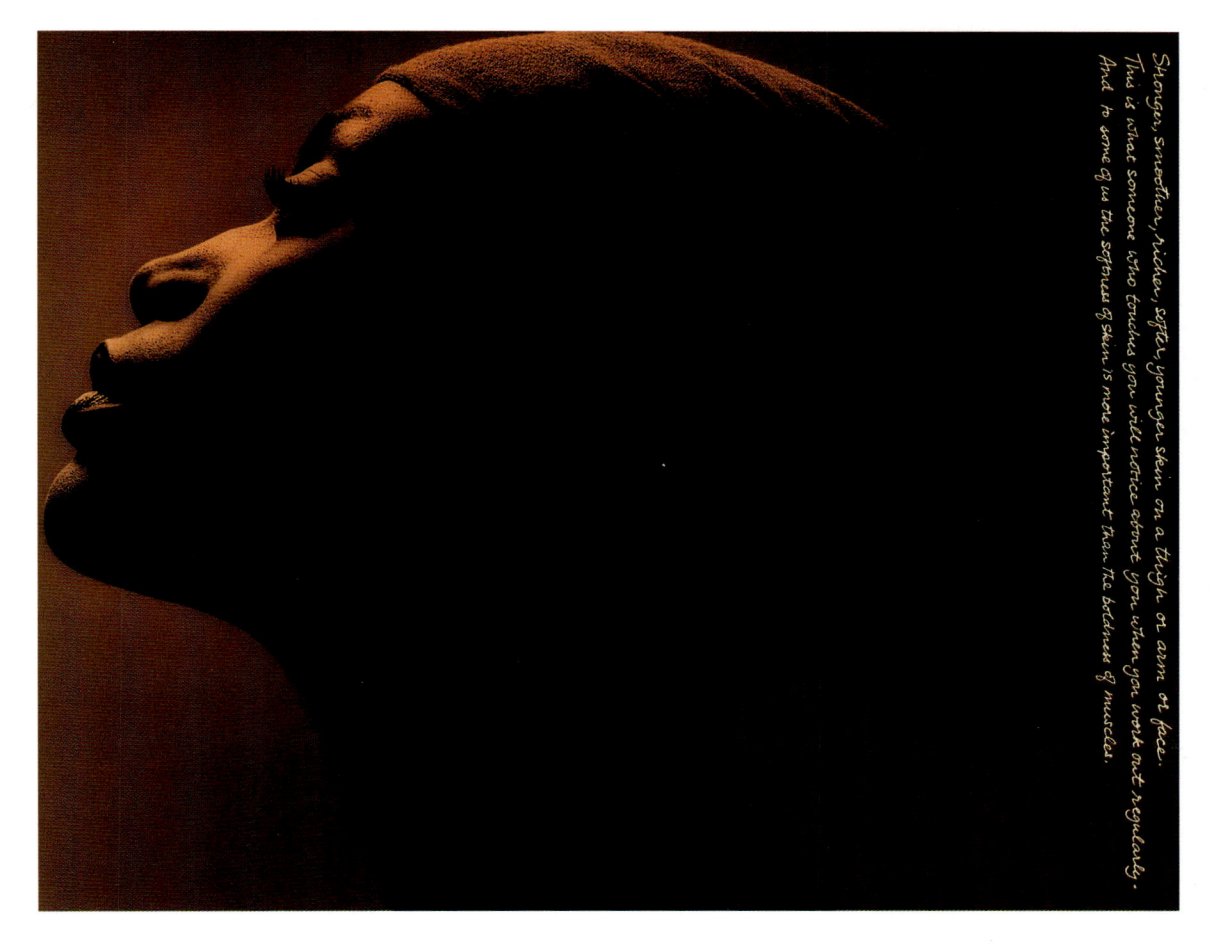

Stronger, smoother, richer, softer, younger skin on a thigh or arm or face. This is what someone who touches you will notice about you when you work out regularly. And to some of us the softness of skin is more important than the boldness of muscles.

COMMUNICATION ARTS 31

Advertising

1
Sean M. Smith, photographer/art director/designer
RCA Records/Cowboy Junkies, clients

Trade ad for album "Pale Sun, Crescent Moon," promoting single selection "Anniversary Song."

2
Paul Aresu, photographer
Al Conner, art director
Adler Boschetto Peebles & Partners, ad agency
The Nashville Network, client

Promotion for "Music City Tonight" program.

3
Will van Overbeek, photographer
Terry Rietta/Wade Devers, art directors
Pagano, Schenck & Kay, Inc., ad agency
PC Magazine, client

Ad headline: Things media planners rarely see.

Books

4
Frans Lanting, photographer
Lucille Tenazas, art director/designer
Tenazas Design, design firm
Chronicle Books, client

Selection from *Okavango, Africa's Last Eden*.

3

4

COMMUNICATION ARTS *33*

1

34 PHOTOGRAPHY ANNUAL 1994

Books

1 (series)
Steven Rothfeld, photographer
Lia Camara, designer
Workman Publishing Company, Inc., client

French Dreams is an impressionistic view of France, using the Polaroid transfer process. Arcade, Paris; Statue, Versailles; Château, Le Buisson; Roses, Regagnac; Dappled landscape, Île-de-France.

Books

1 (series)
Mark Edward Atkinson, photographer/art director
William Owen, designer
Otto Visual Arts, design firm
Operation Smile International, client

A Smile is the Beginning chronicles the work of Operation Smile, a volunteer medical organization that performs free cranial, facial and burn scar surgeries on children worldwide.

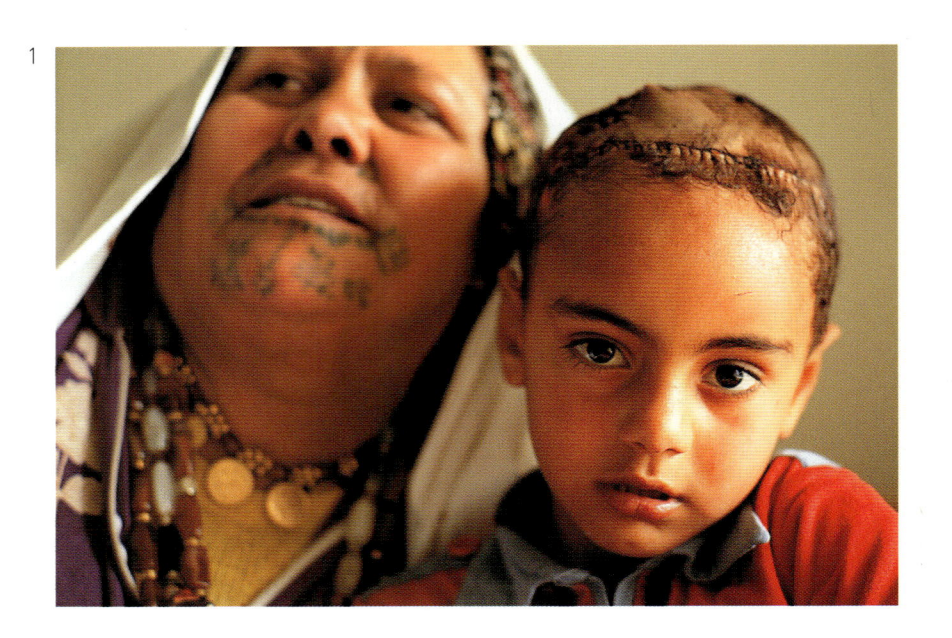

COMMUNICATION ARTS 37

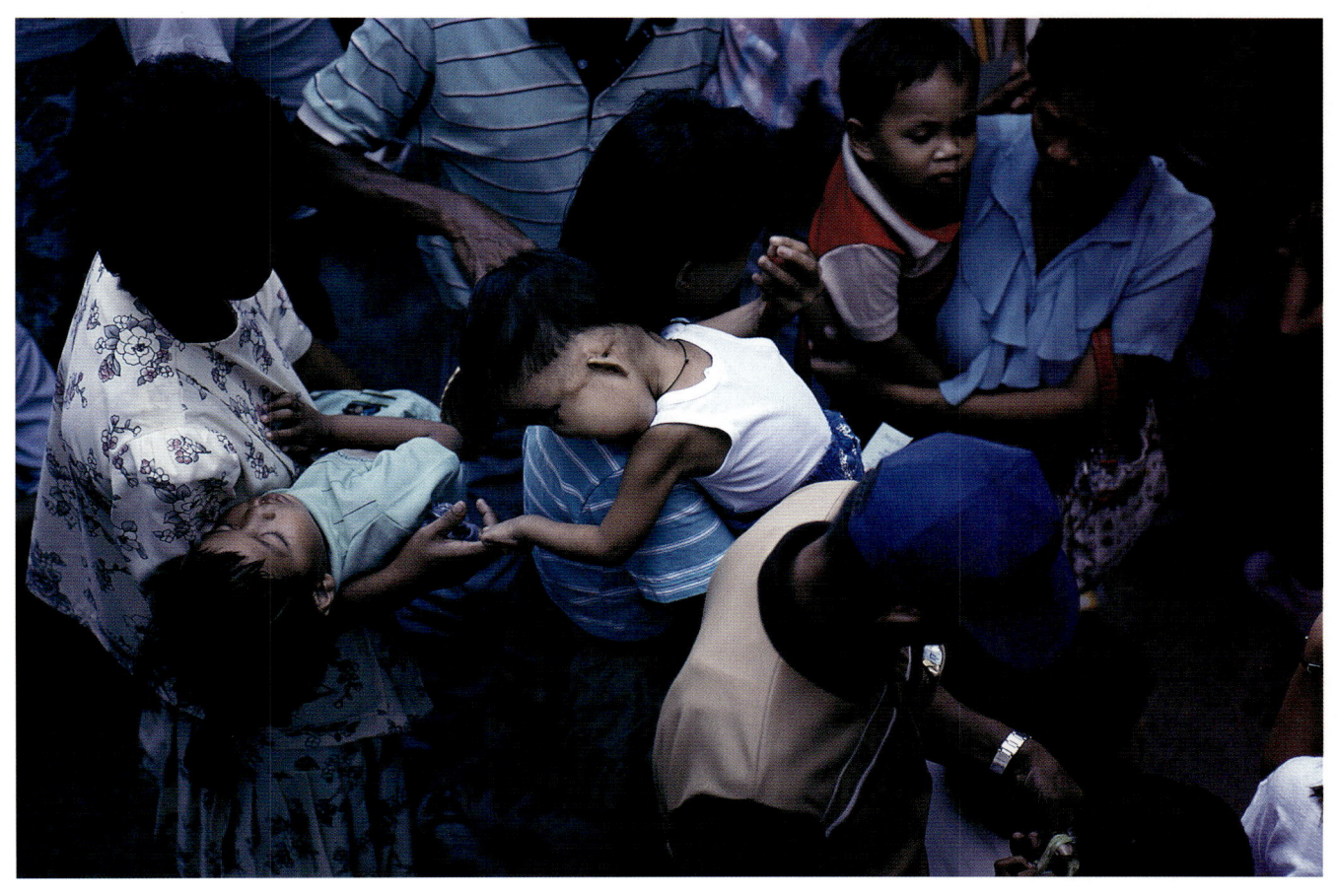

1

Books

1 (series)
Chip Cooper, photographer
Laura Woelfel-Madison, art director/designer
Laura Woelfel-Madison Design, design firm
CKM Press, publisher
The University of Alabama, Division of Student Affairs, client

Used as a fund raiser for Student Affairs, *Silent in the Land* depicts styles and periods of Southern architecture. Whether abandoned, declining or maintained, the houses speak volumes about the history of the countryside, even though these mute structures are silent in the land.

1

40 PHOTOGRAPHY ANNUAL 1994

Books

1 (series)
Eric Lawton, photographer
Phil Cousineau, editor
Detta Penna, designer
HarperSan Francisco, division of HarperCollins
  Publisher, client

Photographs from around the world are paired with eclectic passages by diverse thinkers for *The Soul of the World, A Modern Book of Hours:* Zabriskie Point, Death Valley, California; Temple Pond, Suzhou, China; Yangshuo, China; Machapuchare, Nepal; Taos Pueblo, New Mexico.

1

Books

1 (series)
Kathryn Kleinman, photographer
Kathryn Kleinman/Michaele Thunen, art directors
Jennifer Barry, designer
Michaele Thunen, stylist
CollinsPublishers San Francisco, client

A garden-inspired book, *Souvenirs*, illustrates nature's gifts gathered and presented throughout the seasons.

Books

1
Walter Iooss, Jr., photographer
Michael McMillan, art director
John Vieceli, designer
McMillan Associates, design firm
CollinsPublishers San Francisco, client

Cover of *Rare Air*, a photographic autobiography by Michael Jordan.

2 (series)
Rodney Smith, photographer
Leslie Smolan, art director
Jennifer Domer, designer
Carbone Smolan Associates, design firm
Nan A. Talese, Doubleday, client

Interior photographs from *The Hat Book*.

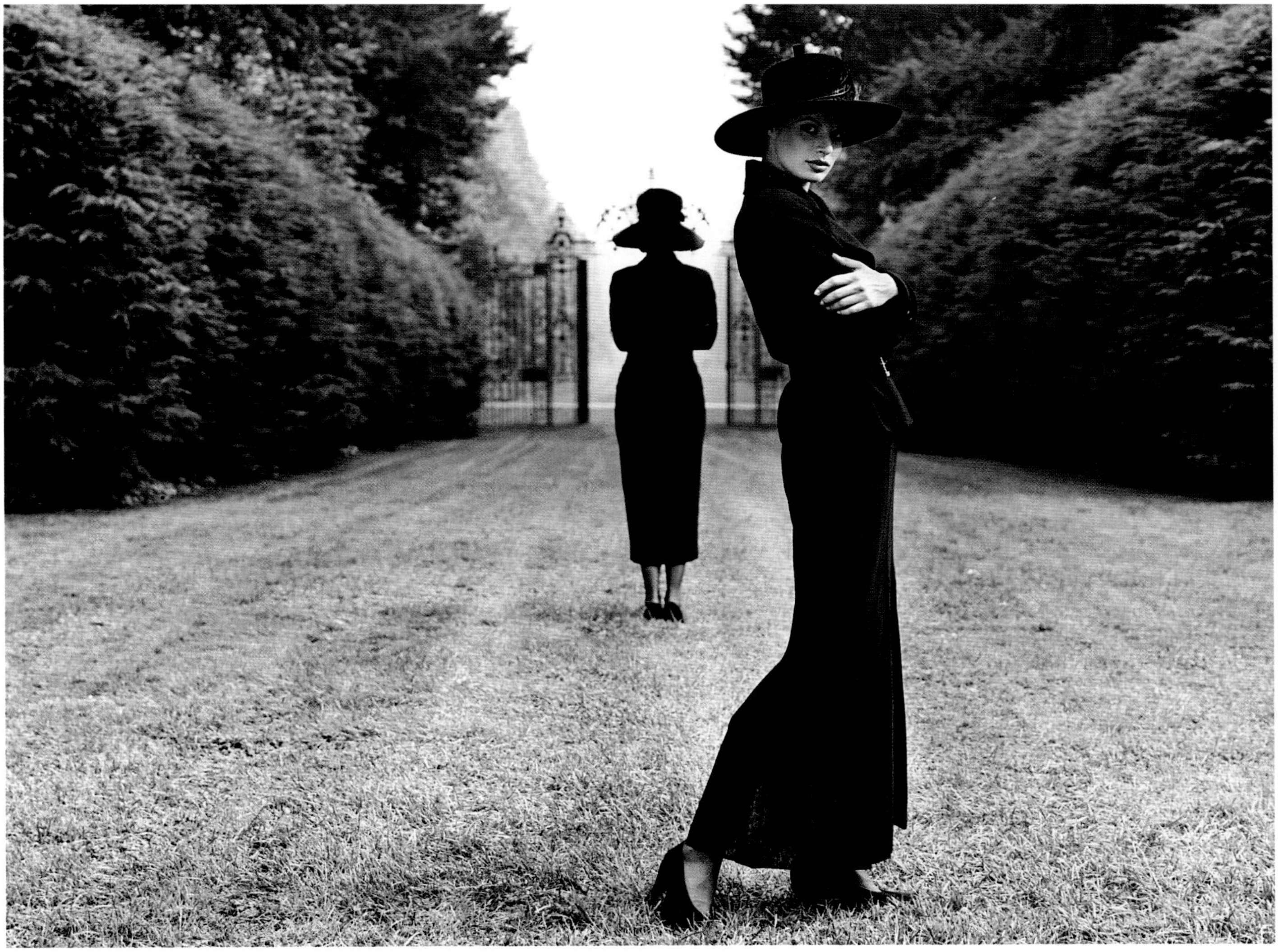

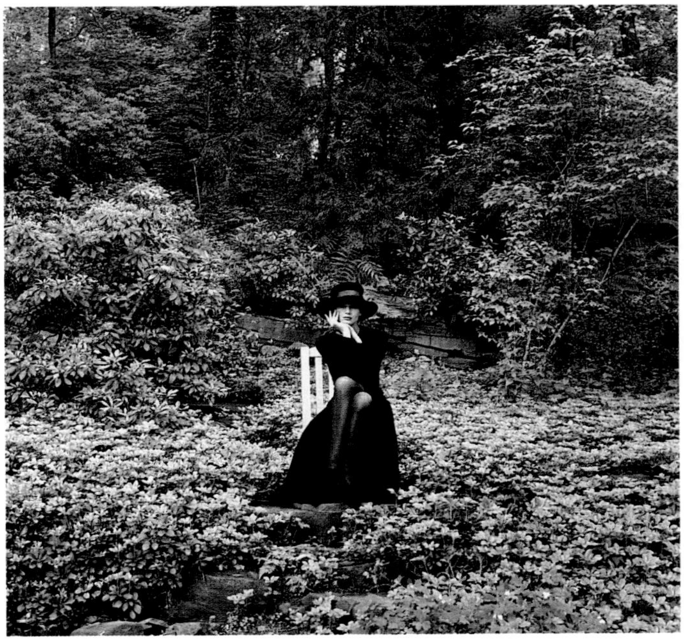

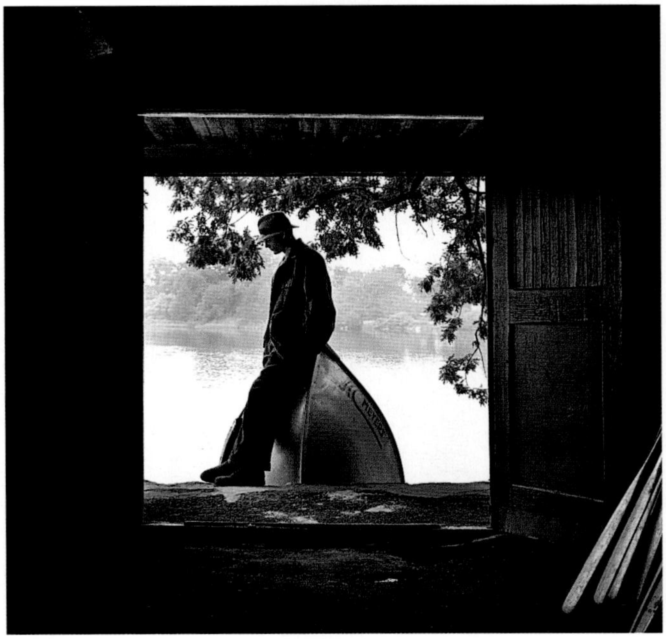

EDITORIAL

1 (series)
Larry C. Price, Contact Press Images, photographer
Bert Fox, art director/designer
Philadelphia Inquirer Magazine, client

Romania's abandoned children fend for themselves, "Throwaways."

46 PHOTOGRAPHY ANNUAL 1994

COMMUNICATION ARTS 47

48 PHOTOGRAPHY ANNUAL 1994

Editorial

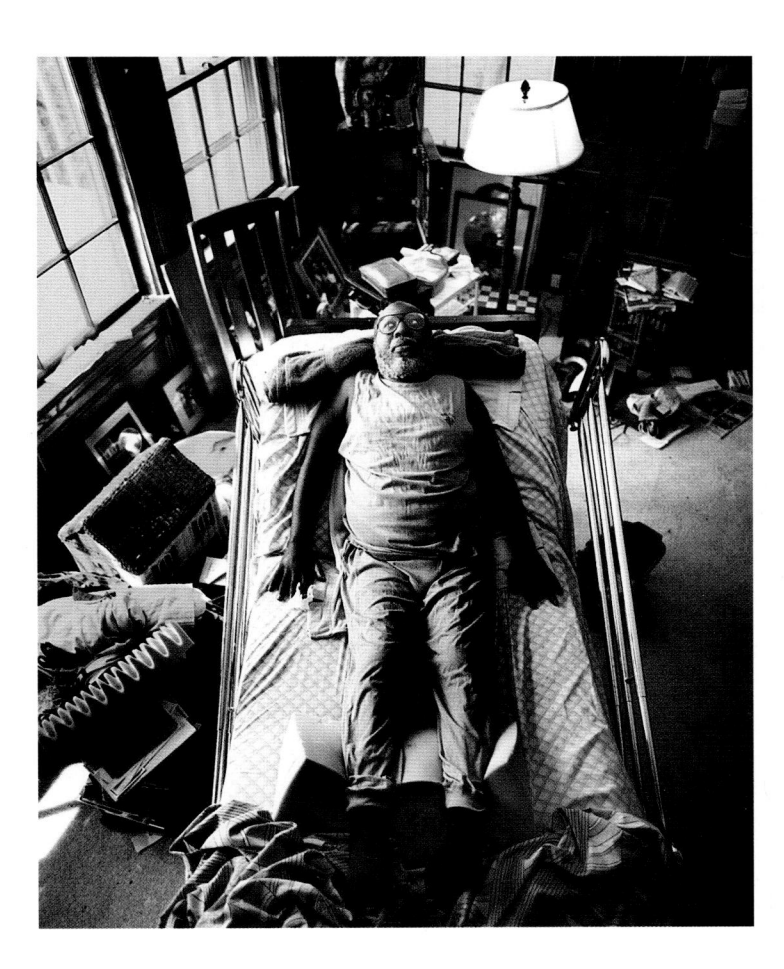

1
Amy Guip, photographer
David Armario, art director/designer
Discover, client

"Death at the Corners." A spate of sudden deaths in the Southwest has revealed a new viral villain.

2
Dan Borris, photographer
Fred Woodward, art director
Rolling Stone, client

"Technopop, Civilizing Cyberspace," an interview with Mitch Kapor, the founder of Lotus software.

3
Bob Sacha, photographer
Lou DiLorenzo, art director
Bill Black, director of photography
Stephanie Syrop, picture editor
Margaret Staats Simmons, editor-in-chief
Travel Holiday, client

The gateway arch glitters in the sun, "St. Louis."

4 (series)
Mark Seliger, photographer
Fred Woodward, art director
Rolling Stone, client

"A Lasting Impression," an interview with Curtis Mayfield.

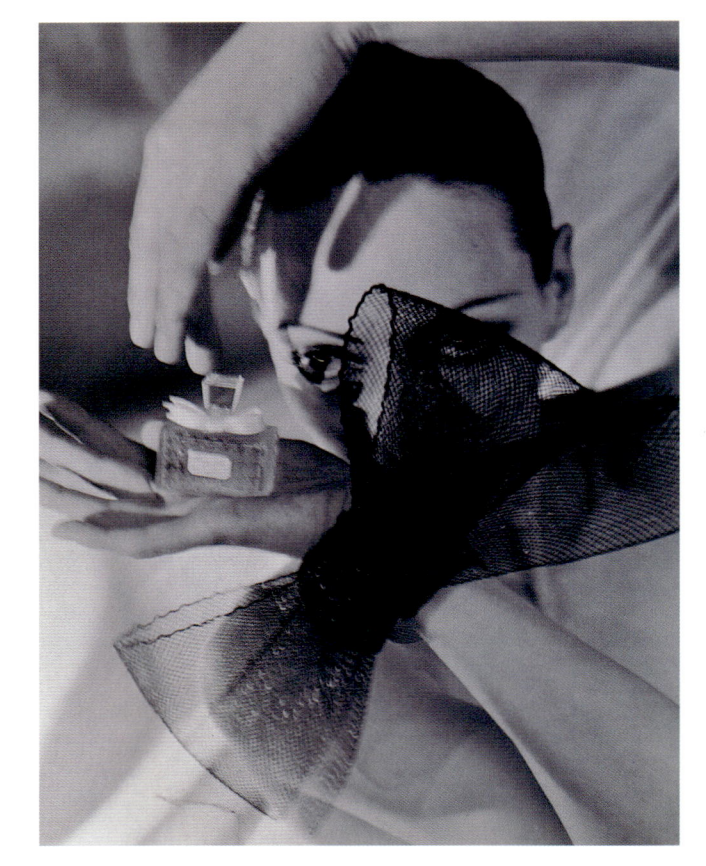

1

Editorial

1 (series)
Don Freeman, photographer
Antoine Keiffer, art director
French Vogue, client

"Dressed Up Scents." The photographs convey the floral ingredients as well as the shapes of the bottles.

2
Mark Richards, photographer
Diane Ooka, art director
Tripp Mikich, photo editor
Lisa Hilgars, designer
Parenting, client

"Coping With Colic."

EDITORIAL

1 (series)
Ruven Afanador, photographer
David Armario, art director/designer
Discover, client

For ten years, two zealous, self-appointed investigators of scientific fraud made headlines and enemies, "Science Police."

2
Antonin Kratochvil, photographer
Lou DiLorenzo, art director
Bill Black, director of photography
Stephanie Syrop, picture editor
Margaret Staats Simmons, editor-in-chief
Travel Holiday, client

The Prater Park ferris wheel, built for the 1896 world exhibition in Vienna.

3
William Mercer McLeod, photographer
Mary Dunn, photography director
Entertainment Weekly, client

Portrait of mystery writer Peter Straub.

2

3

1

Editorial

1 (series)
Pat Crowe, photographer
Craig Winkelman, art director
Outdoor & Travel Photography, client

Magazine essay on the people of Ireland, "Irish Eyes."

1

2

56 PHOTOGRAPHY ANNUAL 1994

Editorial

1
Limor Inbar, photographer
Paul Lussier, associate art director
Michele Stephenson, picture editor
Mary Worrell, assistant picture editor
Time, client

"Gay Parents: Under Fire and on the Rise."
Lesbian parents play ball with their two
daughters on the roof of their New York
apartment.

2
Gerd Ludwig, photographer
David Griffin, designer
Susan Welchman, picture editor
Tom Kennedy, director of photography
National Geographic, client

A coal miner scrubs down after a day in the
pits outside Donetsk, Ukraine. "Broken
Empire."

3
Karen Kuehn, photographer
Lou DiLorenzo, art director
Bill Black, director of photography
Stephanie Syrop, picture editor
Margaret Staats Simmons, editor-in-chief
Travel Holiday, client

A kiva in New Mexico where Pueblo men
gathered for ceremonies, "American Moments."

4
Steve Payne, photographer
Gudrun Haraldsson, art director
The Globe and Mail, client

Profile of author Margaret Gibson and review
of *Sweet Poison*, her first book in fifteen years
after a misdiagnosis of mental illness.

1

2

Editorial

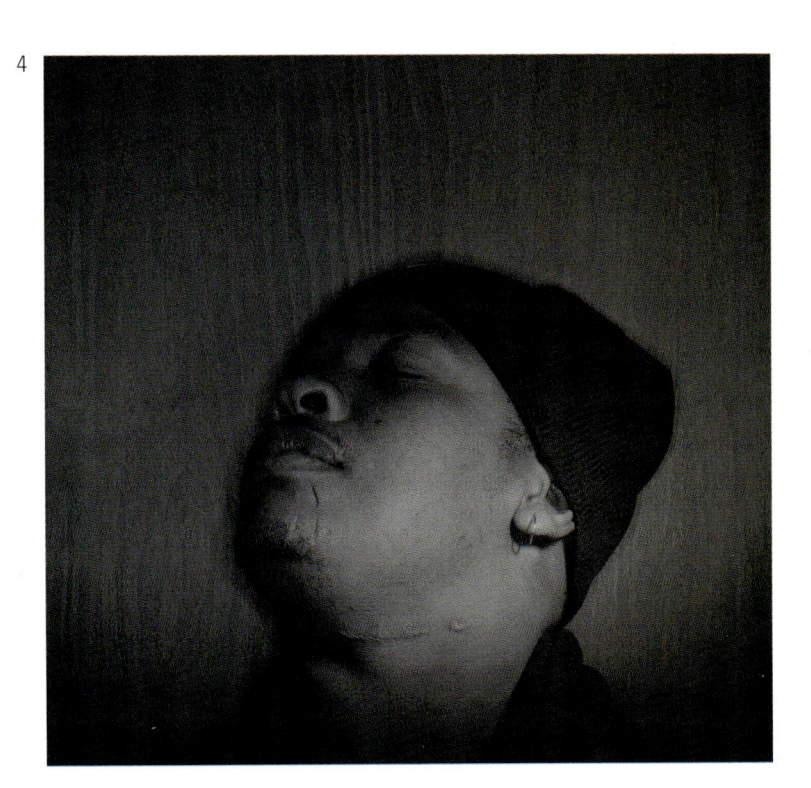

1
Antonin Kratochvil, photographer
Lou DiLorenzo, art director
Bill Black, director of photography
Stephanie Syrop, picture editor
Margaret Staats Simmons, editor-in-chief
Travel Holiday, client

The 13th century courtyard of the Imperial Palace in Vienna gets an overhaul.

2
Robb Kendrick, photographer
Tom Kennedy, director of photography
Dennis Dimick, picture editor
Bill Graves, editor
National Geographic, client

"Rice & Religion." An Indian girl is blessed by a temple elephant in Madras, India, for making an offering of rice to the temple.

3
Matuschka, photographer
Wolfgang Behnken, art director
Stern, client

"Classic Nude" is a self-portrait of the photographer.

4
Dan Winters, photographer
Mary Dunn, photography director
Mark Jacobson, assistant picture editor
Entertainment Weekly, client

Portrait of rapper Dr. Dre, "The Entertainers of the Year."

1

Editorial

1 (series)
André Panneton, photographer
Jean-Marc Martin, art director
Dick Walsh, style director
Christiane Valcourt, hand-coloring
Elle Québec, client

Fashion editorial, "Botero's Women."

2
Tim Page, Reportage Photos, photographer
David Friend, photo editor
Life, client

United Nations helicopters hover overhead in an effort to police elections in Cambodia, "In the Whirlwind."

Editorial

1
Geof Kern, photographer
David Armario, art director/designer
Discover, client

"The Vision Thing: Mainly in the Brain." The eye and brain work in partnership to interpret conflicting signals from the outside world.

2
Karen Kasmauski, photographer
David Arnold, illustration editor
Bill Marr, designer
National Geographic, client

Article titled "Viruses." This gay ex-Mormon, dying of AIDS, has not seen his daughter for eight years since he declared his homosexuality.

3 (series)
Håkan Ludwigson, photographer
Diana LaGuardia, design director
Condé Nast Traveler, client

Article about the best beaches in Mexico.

3

EDITORIAL

1 (series)
Scogin Mayo, photographer
D. J. Stout, art director
D. J. Stout/Nancy McMillen, designers
Texas Monthly, client

"Manhunt at Manard Creek." Surrounded by snarling dogs, a thief drowns in a muddy slough after a two-day chase through the big thicket.

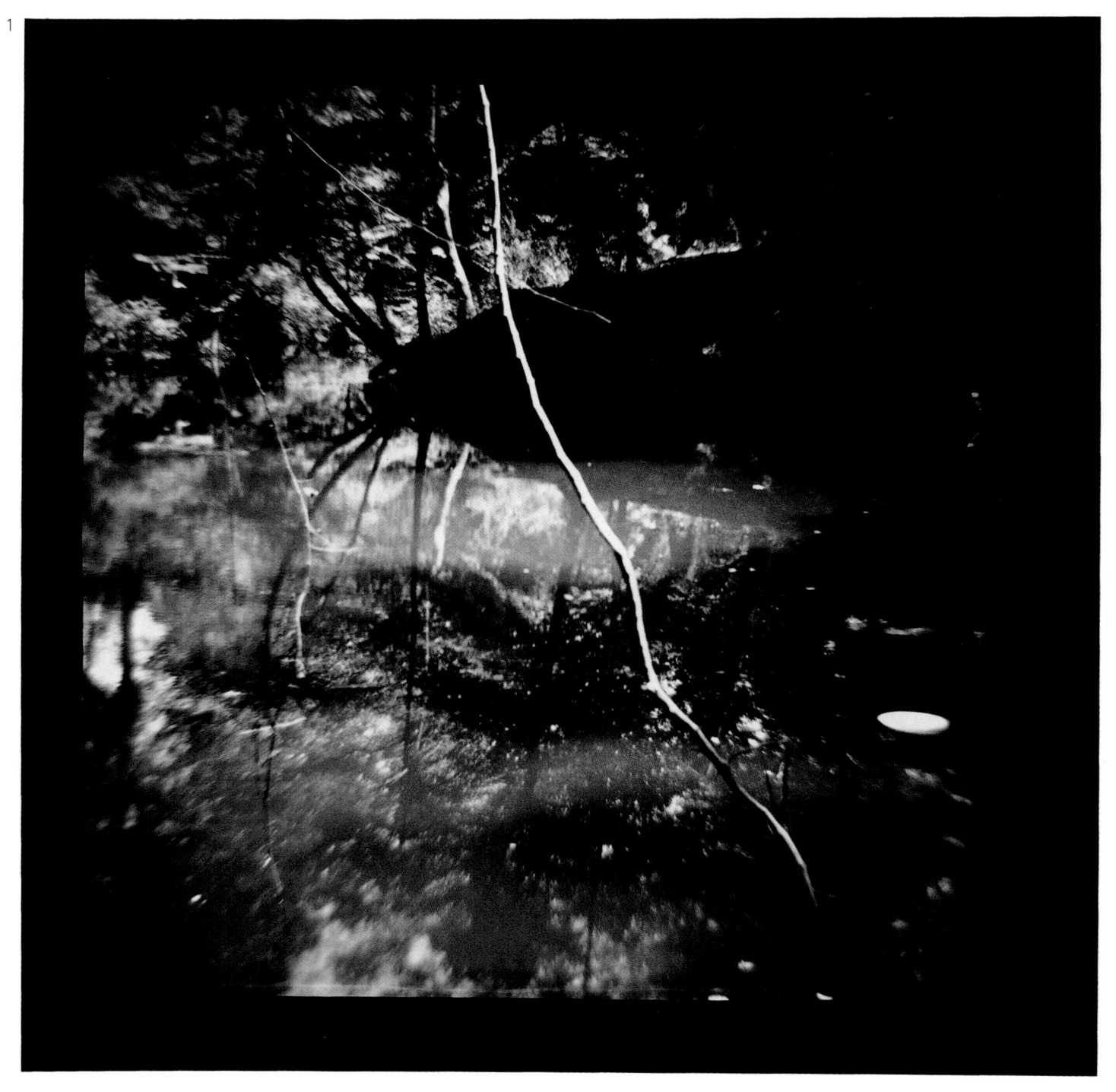

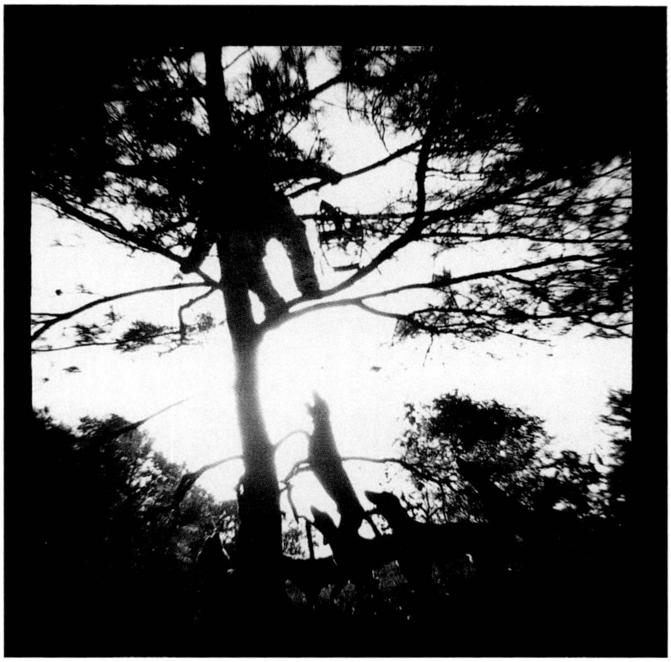

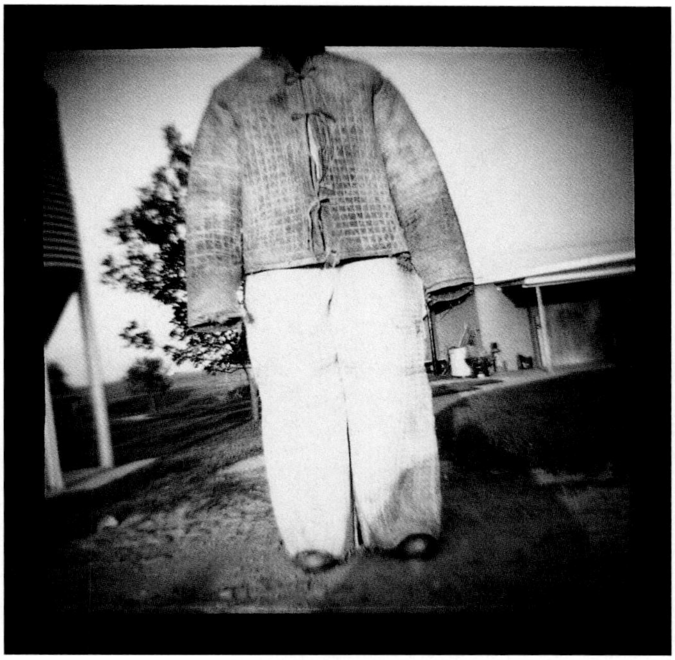

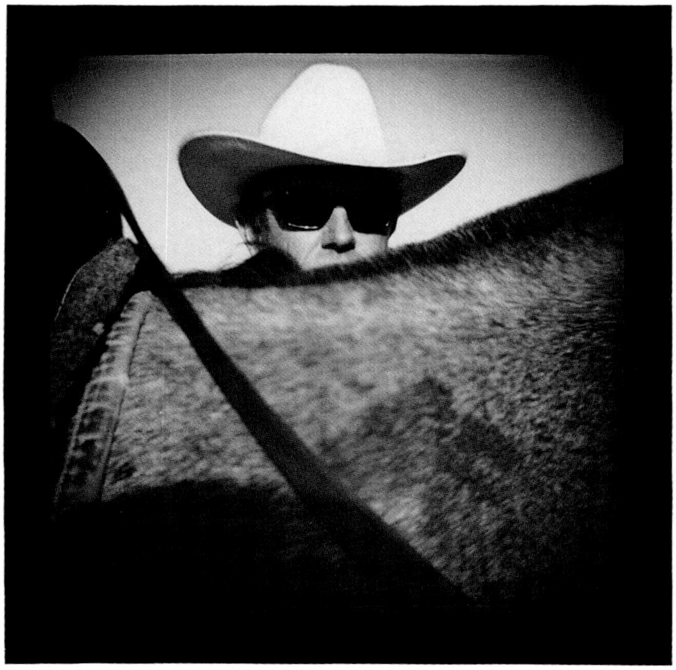

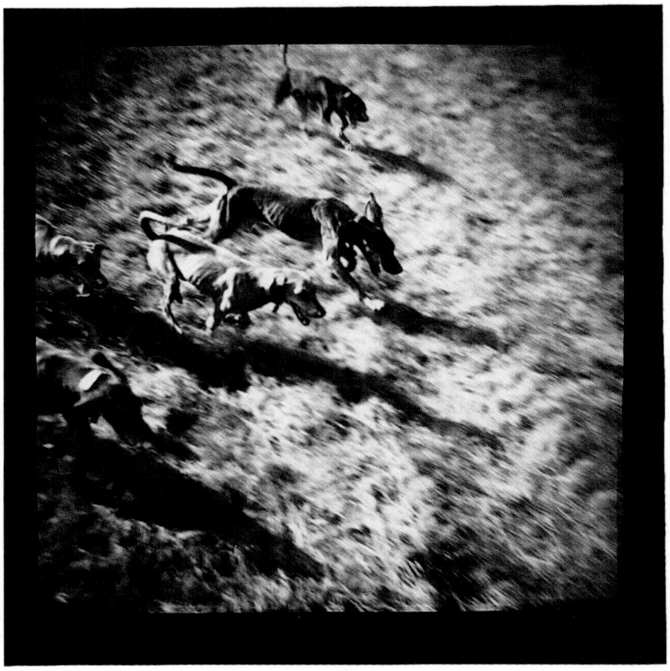

EDITORIAL

1
Matuschka, photographer
Janet Froelich, art director
Julie Skarratt, stylist
The New York Times Magazine, client

Cover, "Beauty Out of Damage."

2
Alistair Morrison, photographer
Mary Dunn, photography director
Doris Brautigan, picture editor
Entertainment Weekly, client

Portrait of actor Daniel Day-Lewis, "The Unbearable Politeness of Being."

3 (series)
Ernest H. Brooks, II, photographer
Charlene deJori, art director/designer
Charlene deJori/Cheryl Schorp, editors
Ocean Realm, client

Article teaching the techniques of black-and-white underwater photography, "Seeing the Light."

3

COMMUNICATION ARTS 67

EDITORIAL

1
R. Ian Lloyd, photographer
Marcello Biagioni, art director
Photo Life, client

2 (series)
Rodney Smith, photographer
Dennis Freedman, art director
Robert Bryan, fashion editor
W, Fairchild Publications, client

"Keep it Simple." Portfolio of men's fall clothes.

COMMUNICATION ARTS 69

EDITORIAL

1
Dan Winters, photographer
Mary Dunn, photography director
Mark Jacobson, assistant picture editor
Entertainment Weekly, client

Portrait of actor John Malkovich, "The Touch of Evil."

2
Michele McDonald, photographer
Joanne Rathe, photo editor
Boston Globe, client

"A Province's Parallel Societies." An Albanian child smokes a cigarette in Pristina, capital of Kosovo, where schools that taught children in Albanian have been closed.

3
Christian Belpaire, photographer
Lindsay Beadry, art director
Toronto Magazine, Globe and Mail, client

"The Agony & The Agony."

3

EDITORIAL

1 (series)
Raymond Meeks, photographer
Matthew Drace, art director/designer
Travel & Leisure, American Express Publishing, client

"East Germany Revisited," an American searches for the land of his youth.

72 PHOTOGRAPHY ANNUAL 1994

COMMUNICATION ARTS 73

1

Editorial

1 (series)
Matt Mahurin, photographer
Paul Lussier, associate art director
Michele Stephenson, picture editor
Mary Worrell, assistant picture editor
Time, client

"Is Freud Dead?"

2
Nita Winter, photographer
Paul Richer, art director
Rebecca Herman, editor
Children's Television Workshop, Sesame Street Magazine, client

Funnel cloud demonstration at the San Francisco Exploratorium, "Let's Explore."

3
Michael Melford, photographer
Lou DiLorenzo, art director
Bill Black, director of photography
Stephanie Syrop, picture editor
Margaret Staats Simmons, editor-in-chief
Travel Holiday, client

"Bermuda." It's 185 steps to the top of Gibbs Hill Lighthouse, built in 1846.

Editorial

1
Patrick Harbron, photographer
Carmen Dunjko, art director/designer
Saturday Night, client

Magazine portrait of comedian Jim Carrey, "Jim Carrey's Comic Twists."

2
John Dyer, photographer
Matthew Stockman, photography editor
John Meek, designer
Vince Aversano, editor
Inside Sports, client

"Dennis Rodman: A Worm of a Different Color." From his ever-changing hair to his deliberately one-sided game, this Spur never simply goes with the flow.

3
James Nachtwey, photographer
Paul Lussier, associate art director
Michele Stephenson, picture editor
Robert Steven, associate picture editor
Time, client

A famine victim in Sudan receives rehydration salts at a feeding center.

4
Karen Kuehn, photographer
Lou DiLorenzo, art director
Bill Black, director of photography
Stephanie Syrop, picture editor
Margaret Staats Simmons, editor-in-chief
Travel Holiday, client

"Redwood." View of unspoiled coastline from a redwood forest.

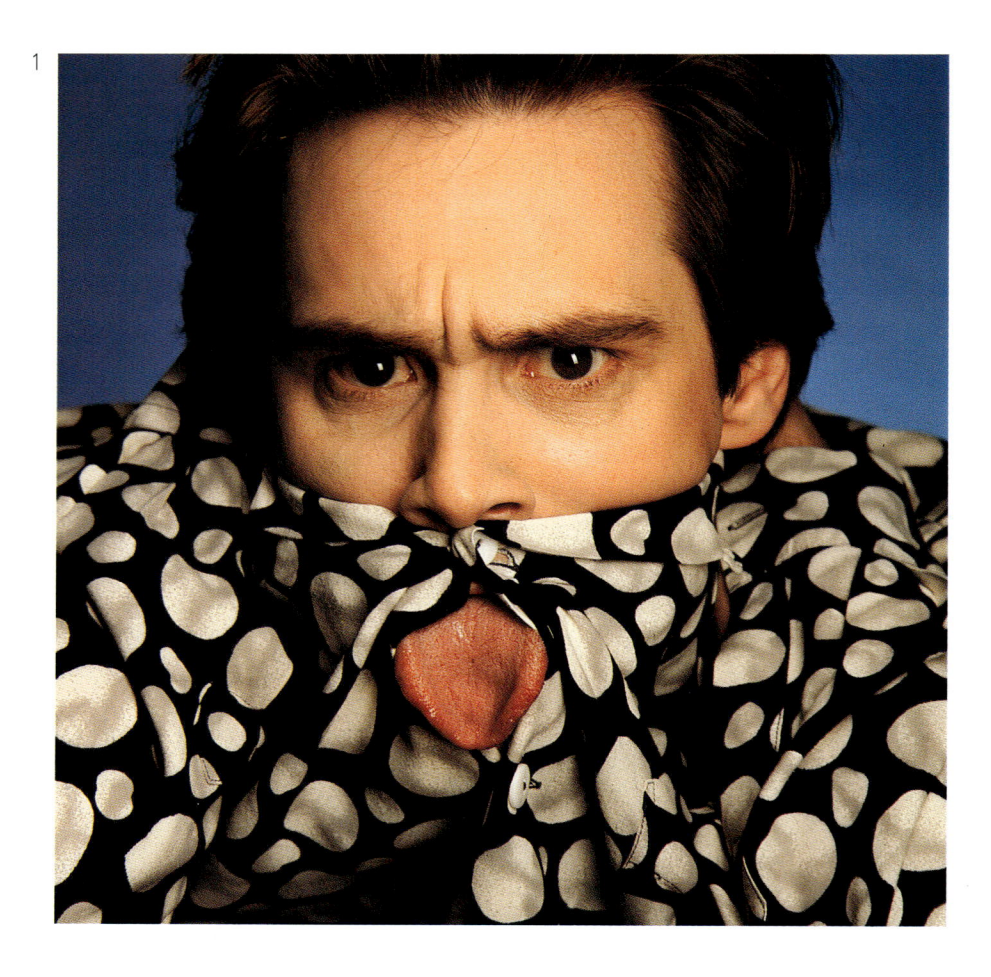

3

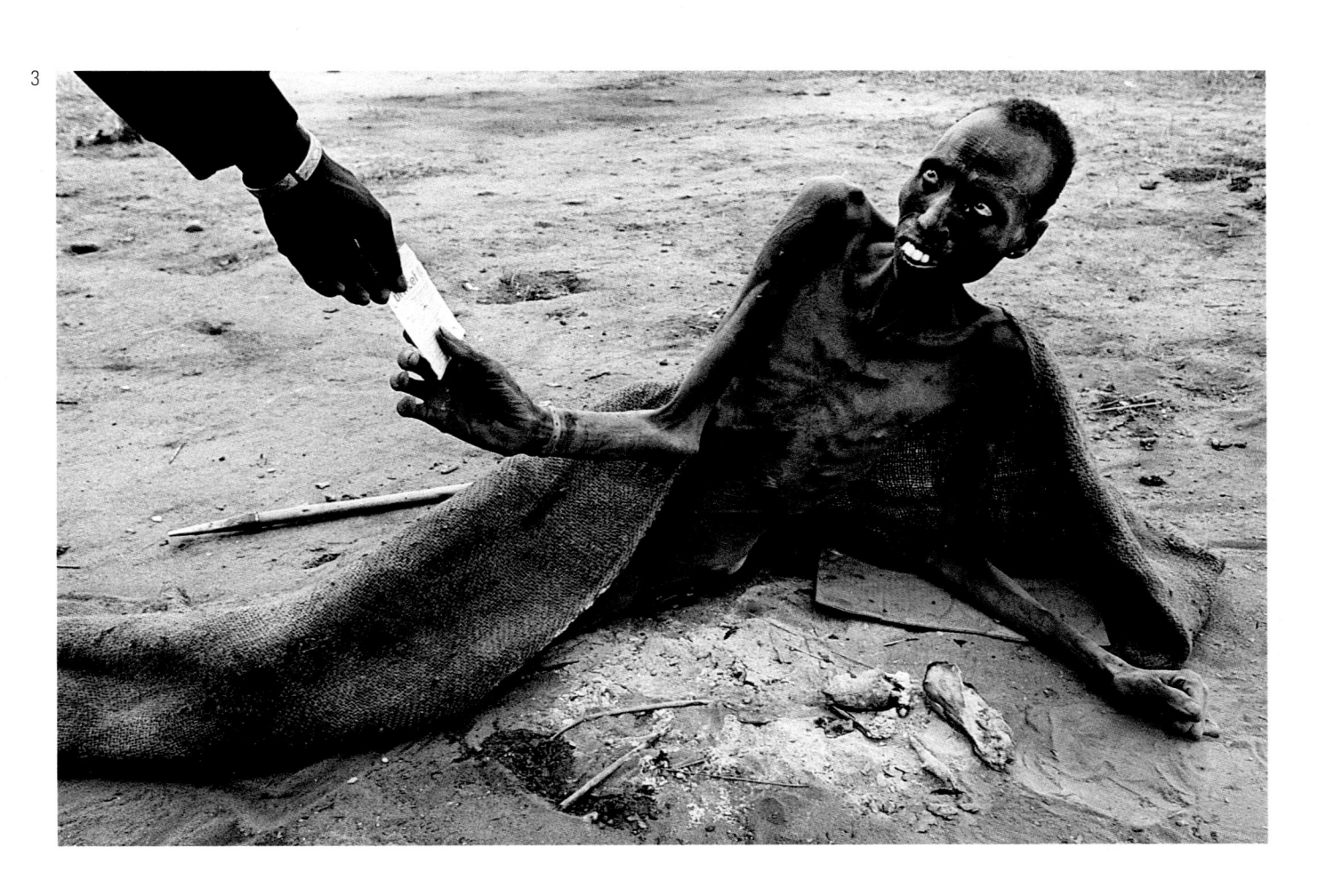

4

COMMUNICATION ARTS 77

1

Editorial

1
Cameron Davidson, photographer
Alan Carroll, art director
Connie Phelps, designer
Larry Nighswander, picture editor
Tom Kennedy, director of photography
National Geographic, client

"Andrew Aftermath," article on Hurricane Andrew.

2
Peggy Sirota, photographer
Mary Dunn, photography director
Mark Jacobson, assistant picture editor
Entertainment Weekly, client

Portrait of actor-director Jodie Foster, "Meet the New Boss."

3
Bob Krist, photographer
Lou DiLorenzo, art director
Bill Black, director of photography
Stephanie Syrop, picture editor
Margaret Staats Simmons, editor-in-chief
Travel Holiday, client

"I, the Camera" portrait of "de pipe man," a local character on the island of St. Croix.

1

2

Editorial

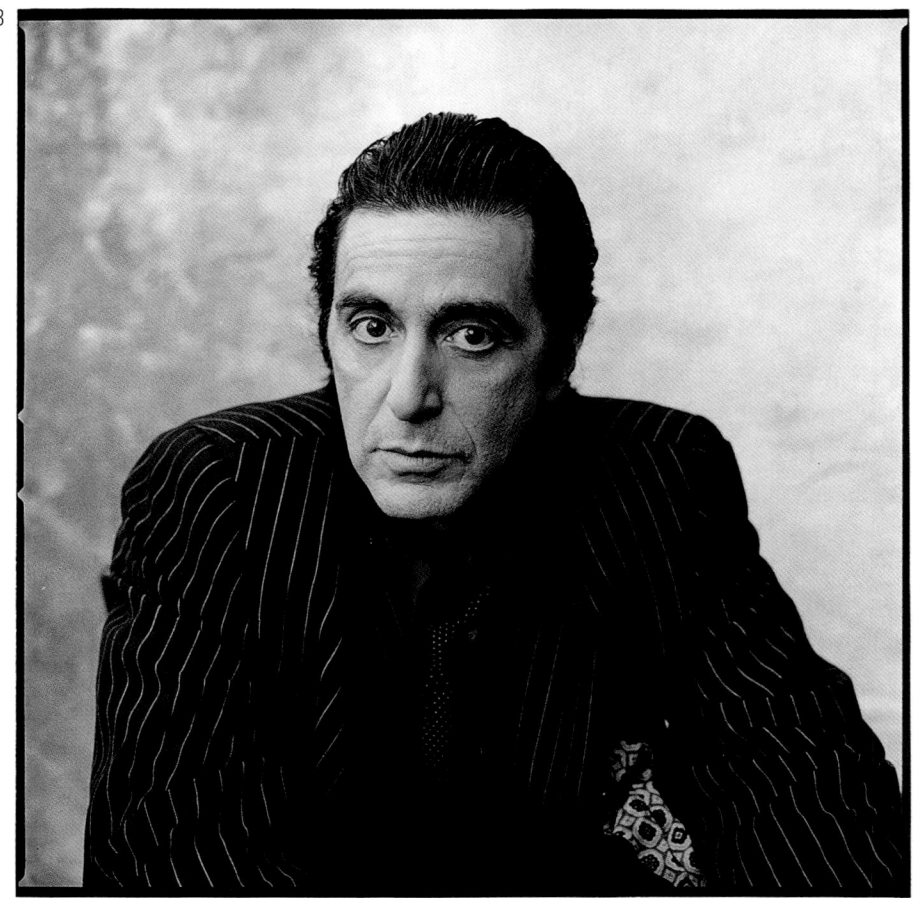

1
Jeff Mermelstein, photographer
Kathy Ryan, photography editor
The New York Times Magazine, client

"Into the Pit." Report on the latest dance craze, moshing.

2
Antonin Kratochvil, photographer
Lou DiLorenzo, art director
Bill Black, director of photography
Stephanie Syrop, picture editor
Margaret Staats Simmons, editor-in-chief
Travel Holiday, client

Boys on horseback at the Crow Indian Reservation in Montana, reenact Custer's defeat at Little Bighorn, "American Moments."

3
Ruven Afanador, photographer
Mary Dunn, photography director
Doris Brautigan, picture editor
Entertainment Weekly, client

Portrait of actor Al Pacino, "And Justice for Al."

4
Rino Noto, photographer
Gudrun Haraldsson, designer/editor
The Globe and Mail, client

"The Nature of Farley," a profile of Farley Mowat, author of over 30 books, appeared in the arts and books section. *Sea of Slaughter* was his 1984 chronicle of the environmental destruction in eastern North America.

EDITORIAL

1 (series)
Ed Kashi, photographer
John Echave, photography editor
Bill Marr, designer
National Geographic, client

Cover article, "Water in the Middle East."

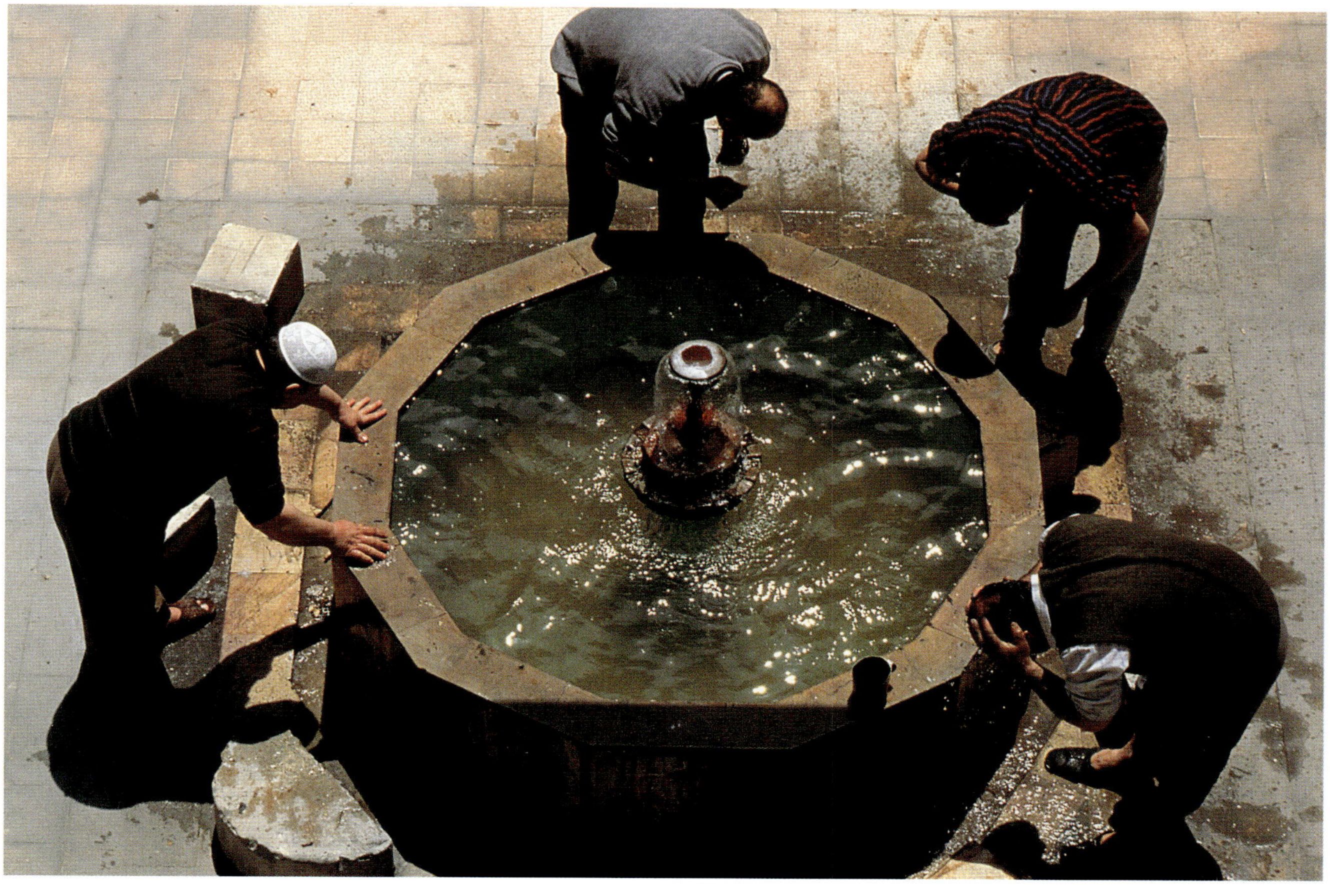

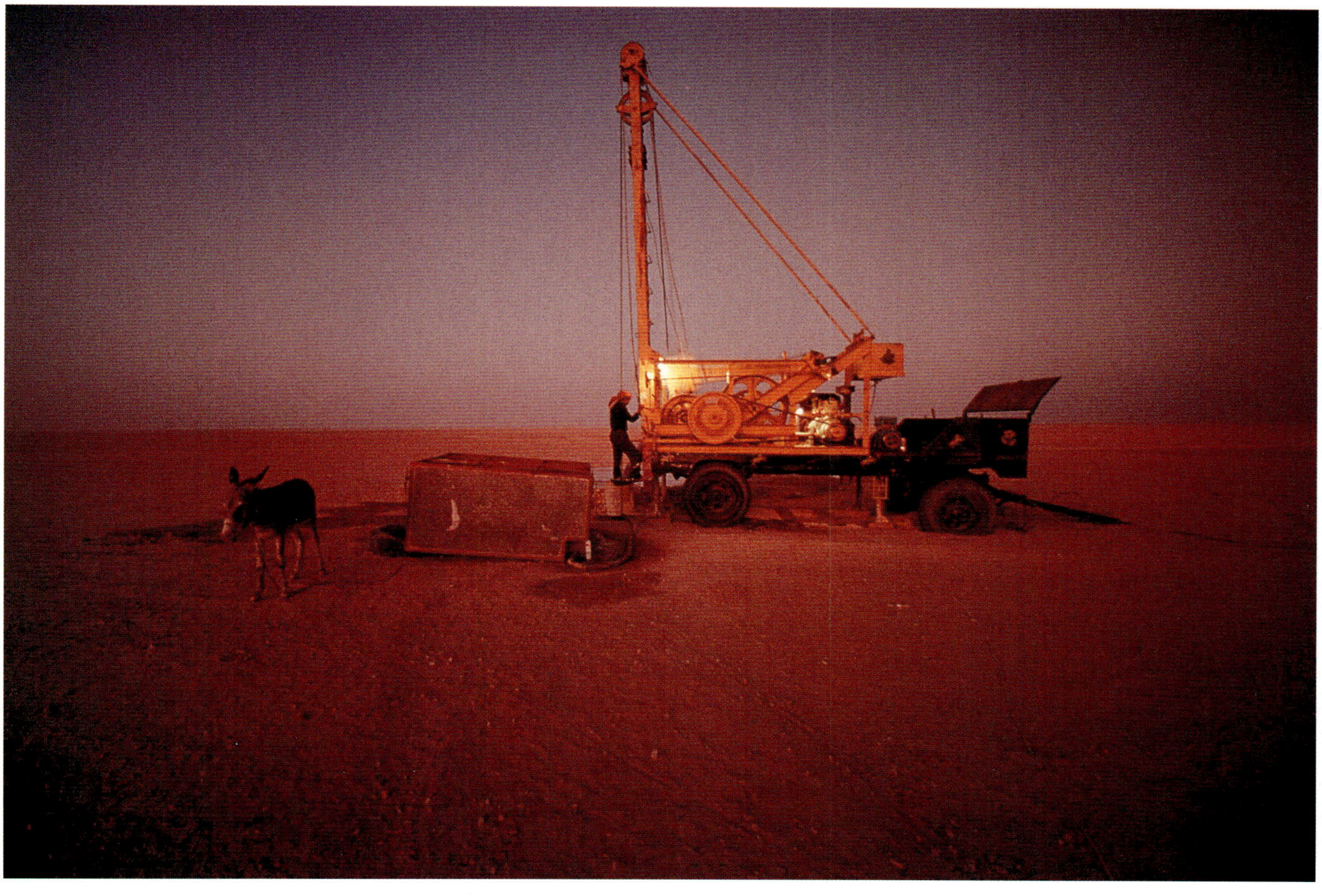

1

84 PHOTOGRAPHY ANNUAL 1994

Editorial

1 (series)
Tom Ryan, photographer
D. J. Stout, art director
D. J. Stout/Nancy McMillen, designers
Texas Monthly, client

"Cream of the Crops," a tribute to Texas's favorite growing places.

1

Editorial

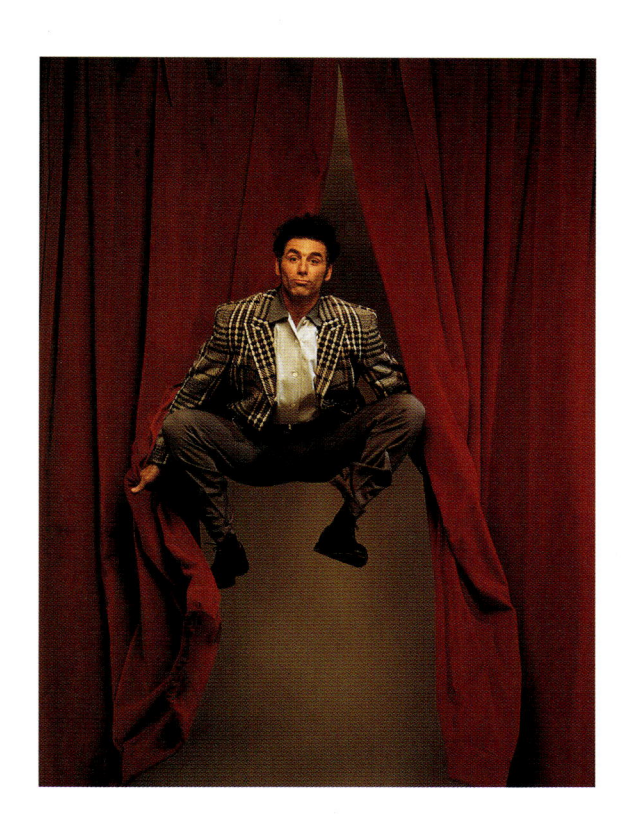

1 (series)
Edward Gajdel, photographer
Jill Armus, associate art director
Michael Grossman, design director
Mary Dunn, photography director
Alice Babcock, picture editor
Entertainment Weekly, client

Article on Michael Richards, "Kramer vs. Kramer."

For Sale

2
James Arrabito, photographer/client

Note card and poster.

INSTITUTIONAL

1
Michele Clement, photographer
Conrad Jorgensen, art director
Conrad Jorgensen/Larry Anderson, designers
Studio 2, design firm
Resound, client

Annual report image for Resound, maker of a new type of hearing aid.

2
Michael Kressley, photographer
Brianne Hurley, art director
Thermo Cardio, client/design

Commissioned for the 1993 annual report relating information about the innovative mechanical heart and its manufacture.

3 (series)
John Huet, photographer
Michele Mangiacotti, designer
Doyle Advertising and Design Group, ad agency
Saucony Athletic Shoes, client

Saucony fall catalog.

COMMUNICATION ARTS 89

1

Institutional

1 (series)
James Robinson, photographer
Benjamin Bailey, designer
Frankfurt Balkind Partners, design firm
The Seagram Company Ltd., client

1993 annual report. Budapest, Hungary, is restoring its architecture and revitalizing its tourist industry.

2 (series)
Fredrik Brodén, photographer
Tim Evans, art director
Evans and Associates, design firm
Voluntary Hospitals of America, client

Illustrations of people involved in the hospital.

INSTITUTIONAL

1 (series)
Eileen Hohmuth-Lemonick, photographer
Raju Chitraker, art director
Dale Davis/Kavre Community Based Rehabilitation
   Project Team, designers
Comex Communications Exponents, ad agency
Helen Keller International/Nepal Association for the
   Welfare of the Blind, clients

Calendar.

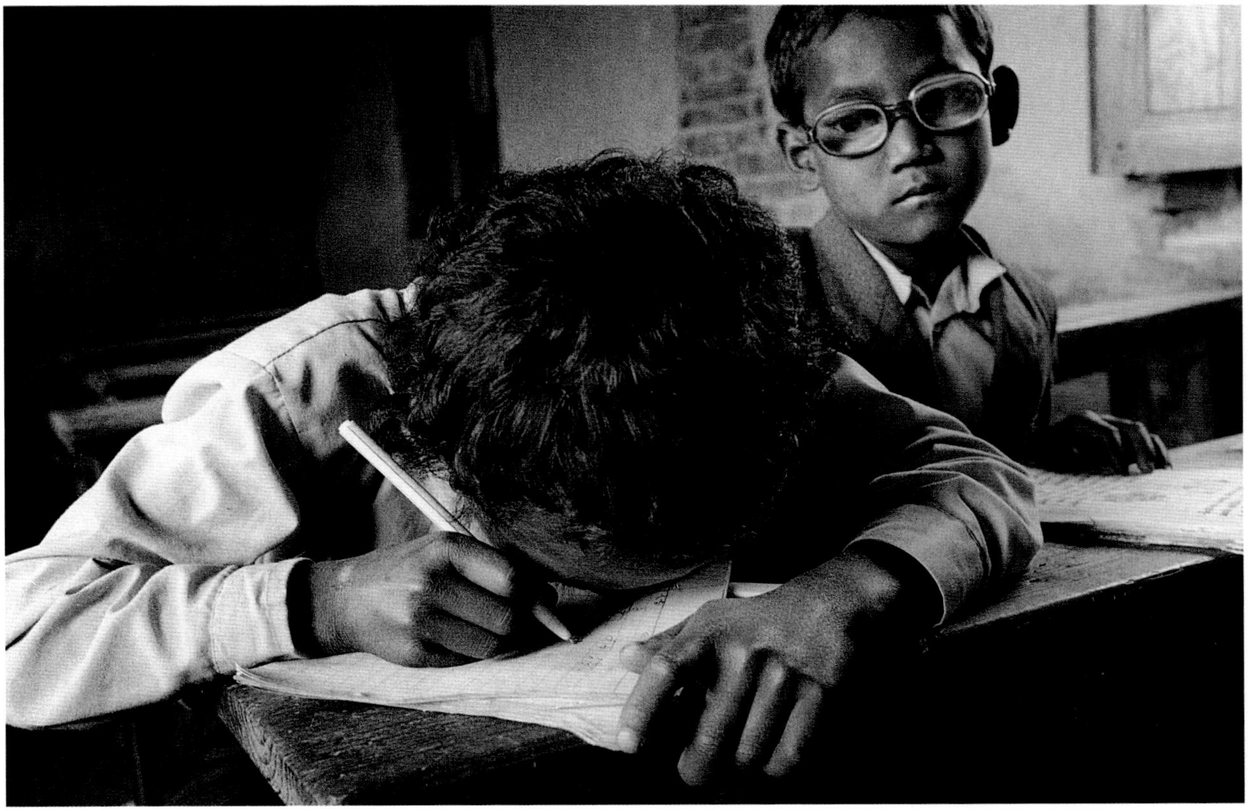

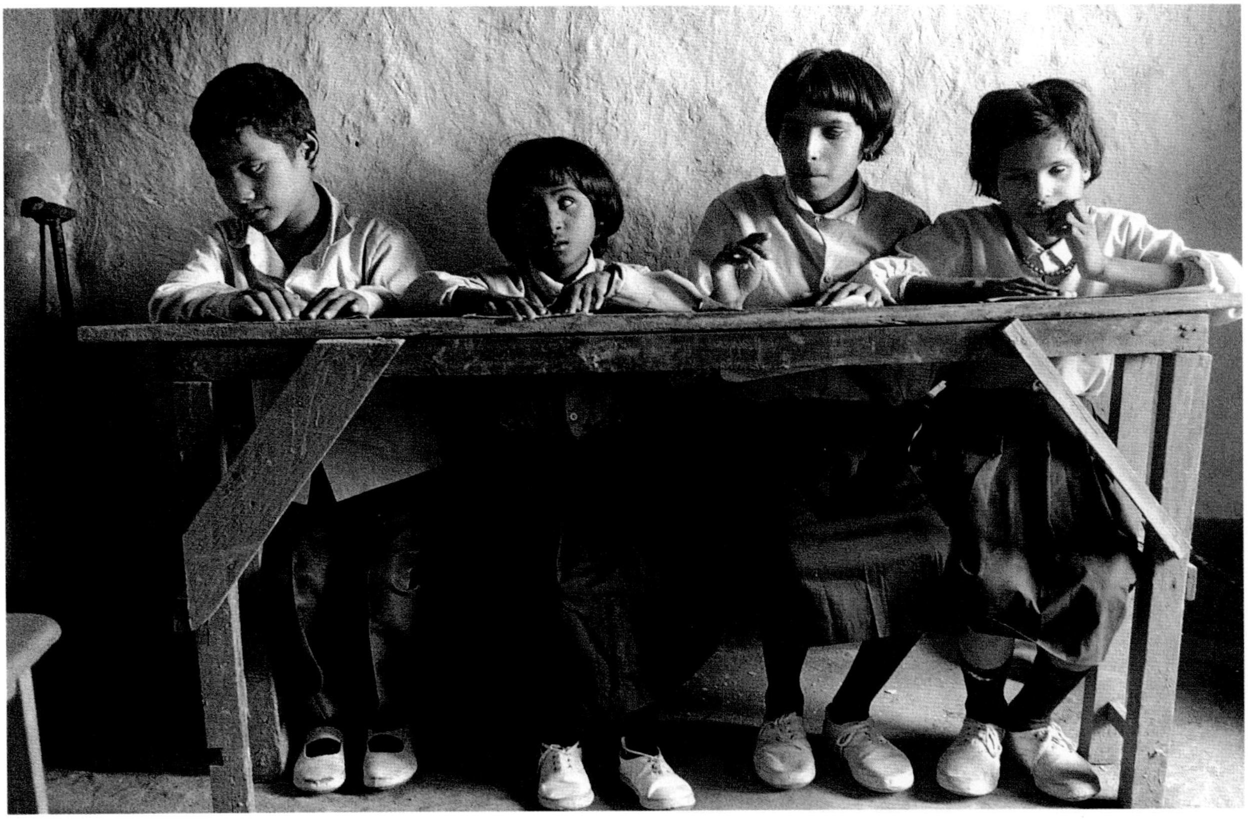

Institutional

1
David Mendelsohn, photographer/art director
Terry Hyland/Marie Hyland, designers
Cabletron Systems, client

Annual report photograph of rural Ireland, to illustrate the company's locations abroad.

2 (series)
Chris Shinn, photographer
Lana Rigsby, designer
Rigsby Design, design firm
Belmont Constructors, Inc., client

Capabilities brochure.

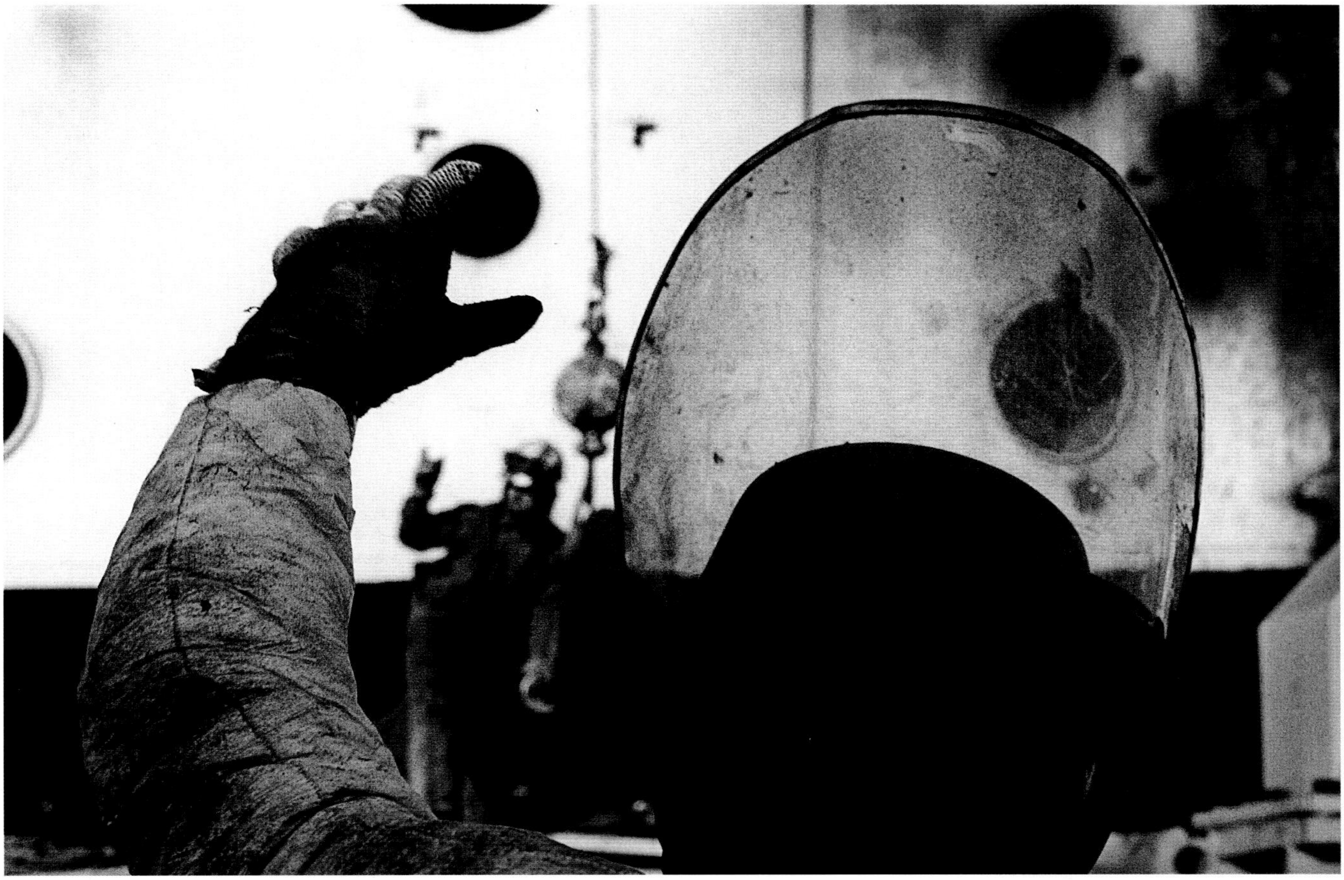

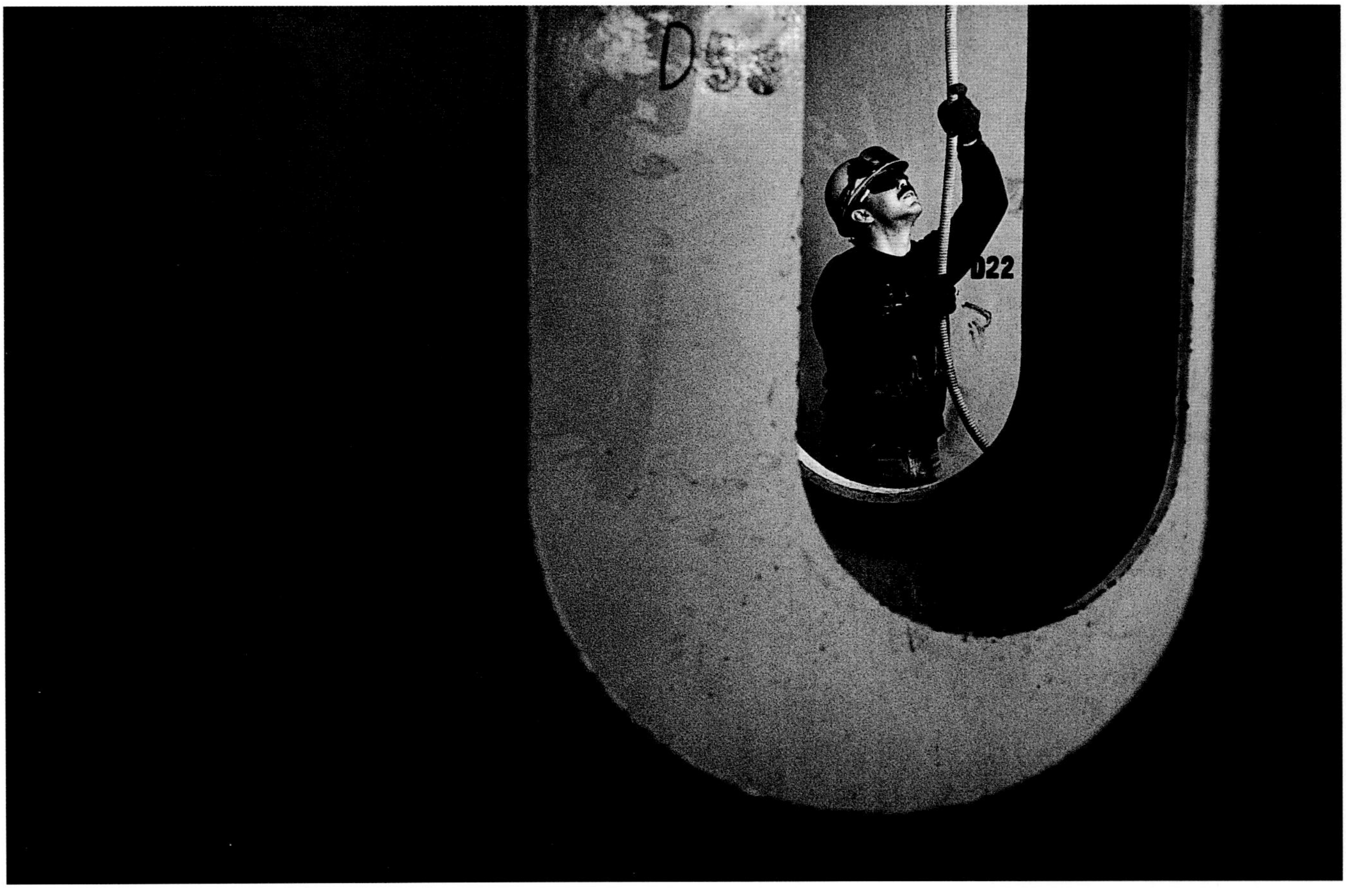
D22

1

2

INSTITUTIONAL

1 (series)
Michael Kressley, photographer
Michael Kressley/Eric Bornstein, art directors
Behind the Mask, client

Promotional images for a maskmaker used in a printed piece and a poster.

2
Yuri Dojc, photographer
Pro Passport, design
Eastman Kodak Company, client

"Steel Teeth." Back cover of company publication.

3
Randy Mayor, photographer
Jeff Gregory, art director
Alice Elliott, designer
Perry, Harper & Perry, ad agency
American Red Cross, Birmingham Chapter, client

Cover of the 1993 annual report.

4
Louie Palu, photographer
Hans Pellikaan, art director
Stratagem Marketing and Design, design firm
Aur Resources Inc., client

Annual report.

Institutional

1 (series)
Michael P. Morgan, photographer/designer
Jessica Xavier, art director
Outlook Eyewear Co./Bausch & Lomb Inc., clients

Catalog.

COMMUNICATION ARTS 99

INSTITUTIONAL

1
Key Sanders, photographer
Michael Clarke, designer
Michael Clarke Design, design firm
Covenant House, client

Annual report.

2
Russ Schleipman, photographer
Tom Morin, designer
Context, design firm
United Technologies, client

Annual report photograph depicts an important Asian market for the Pratt & Whitney subsidiary.

3 (series)
Anthony Arciero, photographer
Kevin Kuester/Bob Goebel, art directors
Bob Goebel, designer
The Kuester Group, design firm
Walden University, client

Promotional brochure.

3

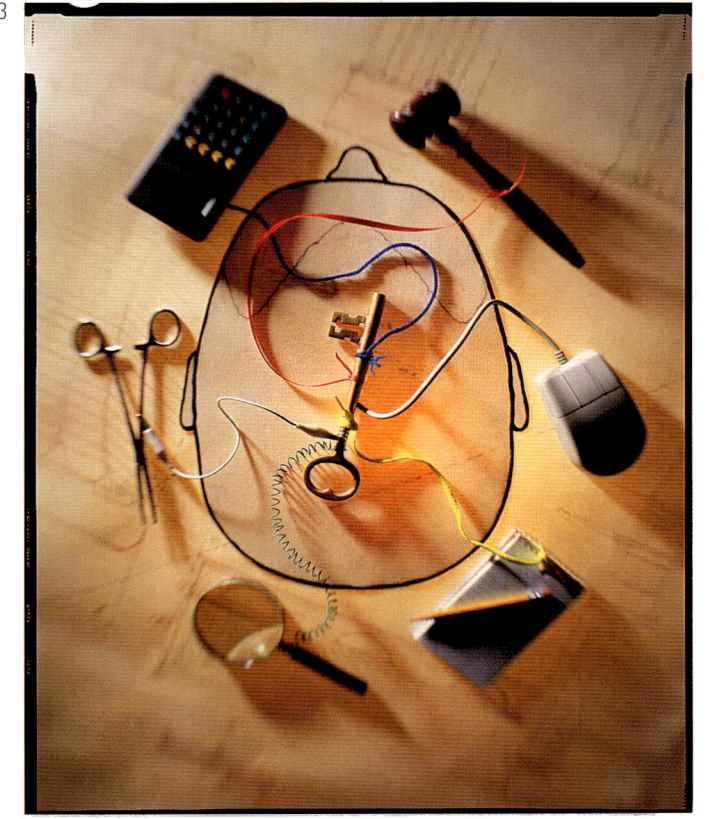

COMMUNICATION ARTS *101*

1

102   PHOTOGRAPHY ANNUAL 1994

Institutional

1 (series)
Arthur Meyerson, photographer
Arnold Saks, designer
Arnold Saks Associates, design firm
Overseas Shipholding Group, client

Annual report.

2
Robb Kendrick, photographer
Andy Dearwater, designer
Dearwater Design, design firm
Herman Hospital, client

Portrait of burn victim, Larry Sam, in a pressure suit for institutional magazine article, "Against All Odds."

Institutional

1
Adrian Ordeñana, photographer
Leslie Hanna, art director
San Francisco AIDS Foundation, client

Institutional newsletter, "Positive News." The article concerns housing discrimination for people afflicted with HIV/AIDS.

2
Mark Wiens, photographer
Shawn Money, designer
HG Design, design firm
Public Relations Society of America, client

Brochure photograph depicts a tool used in public relations.

Self-Promotion

3 (series)
Sari Makki, photographer

Mailers to art directors. 8 x 10 Polaroid, mix of color and sepia.

3

COMMUNICATION ARTS 105

1

2

SELF-PROMOTION

1
Daniel De Souza, photographer/art
 director/client

Leave-behind printed sample.

2
Dan Wilby, photographer

Promotional postcard.

3 (series)
James Salzano, photographer
Jon Parkinson, designer

Source book ads.

1

Self-Promotion

1 (series)
Craig Cutler, photographer
Tom Wood, designer
Wood Design, design firm

Mailer.

2
RJ Muna, photographer/art director/designer

Source book ad.

3
Hal Silverman, photographer
Bob Fucinato, art director
Tom Collins, designer
Hal Silverman Studio, Inc., client

Printed promotion.

Self-Promotion

1 (series)
Lynn Sugarman, photographer/client
Lynn Sugarman/Paula Scher, art directors
Paula Scher, designer
Pentagram, design firm

Promotional booklet, "After."

COMMUNICATION ARTS *111*

SELF-PROMOTION

1
Ed Nielsen, photographer
Chris Dean, Anderson & Lembke, art director
Michael Kerbow, Imagic, designer/illustrator
Imagic, client

Poster, "Spirit of Christmas."

2
George Simhoni, photographer/client
Partners III, art studio

Source book ad, "Nuclear Synchro Swimmers."

3 (series)
Oe/Ueda, photographer/client
John Clark/Oe/Ueda, designers
Looking, design firm

Booklet.

3

COMMUNICATION ARTS   *113*

Self-Promotion

1
Don Glentzer, photographer
Jay Loucks, art director
Chuck Thurman, designer
Loucks Atelier, design firm
Art Directors Club of Houston, client

Mailer to solicit donations for the club's art auction.

2
Parish Kohanim, photographer/designer
Parish Kohanim Studio, client

Direct mail and source book ad.

3
Tim Bieber, photographer/client
Steve Liska, designer
Liska & Associates, design firm

Calendar page, Harlem, New York.

4
Mark Clifford, photographer/art director
Mark Clifford Photography, client

Studio Christmas card.

3

4

COMMUNICATION ARTS *115*

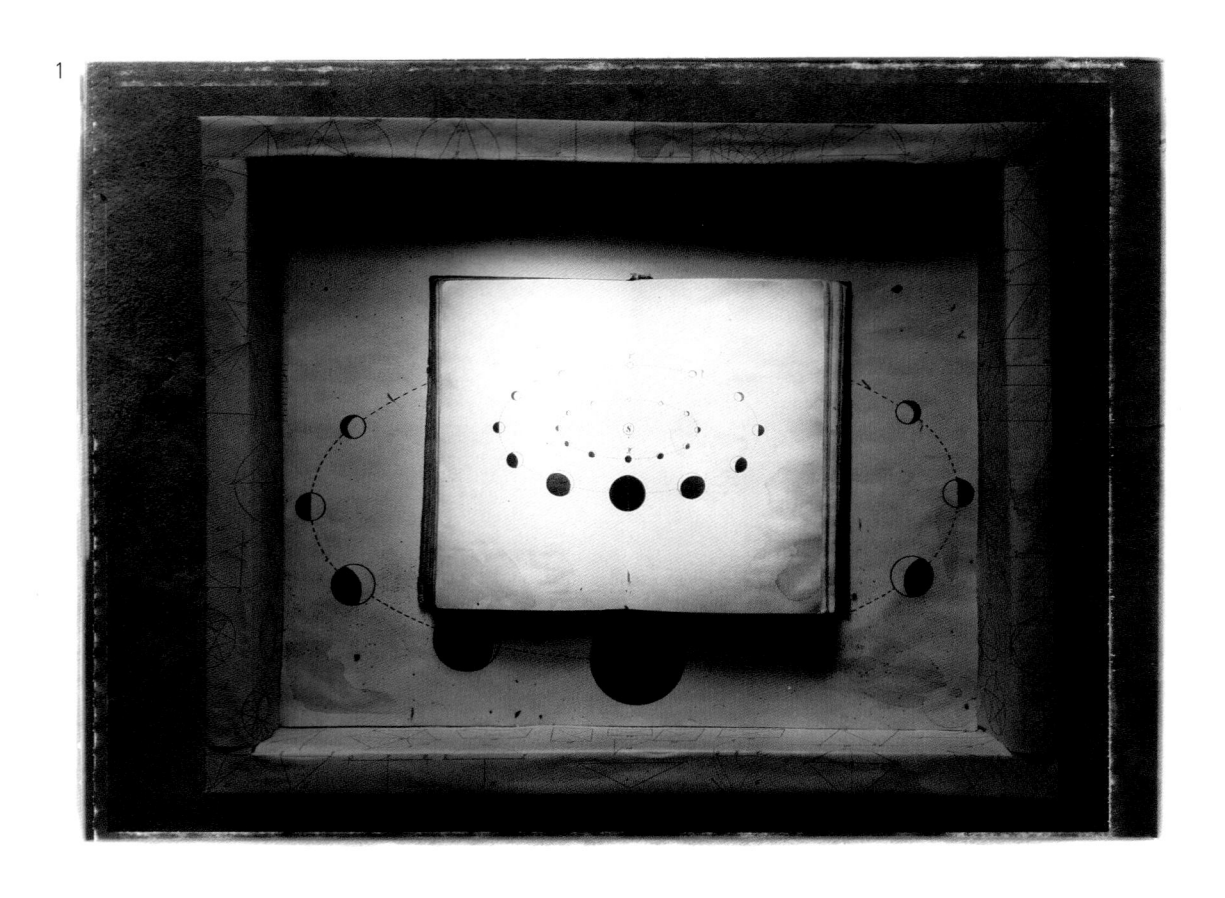

1

SELF-PROMOTION

1 (series)
Sean Kernan, photographer/designer
Sean Kernan, Inc., client

Calendar.

SELF-PROMOTION

1
Susan Ashukian, photographer/art director/client

Studio Christmas card, "Peace on Earth."

2
Heimo, photographer
Kara Wetherby, art director
Heimo Inc., client

Mailer and leave-behind.

3 (series)
Hans Neleman, photographer
Hans Wolf, art director
Bas Van Der Paardt, designer
Art Directors Club of the Netherlands, client

Award program booklet.

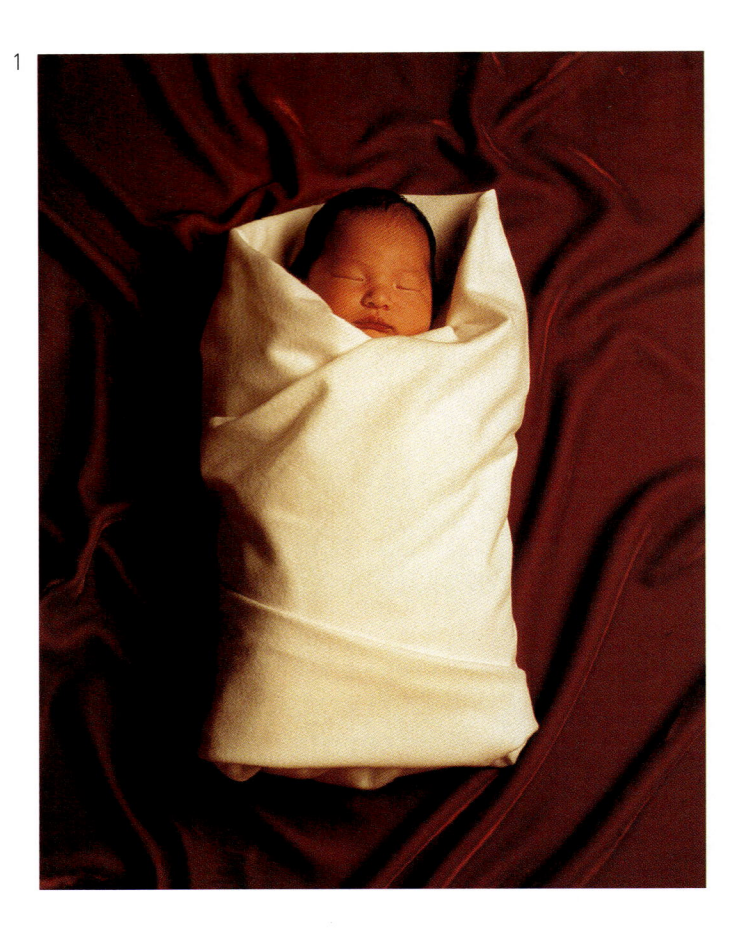

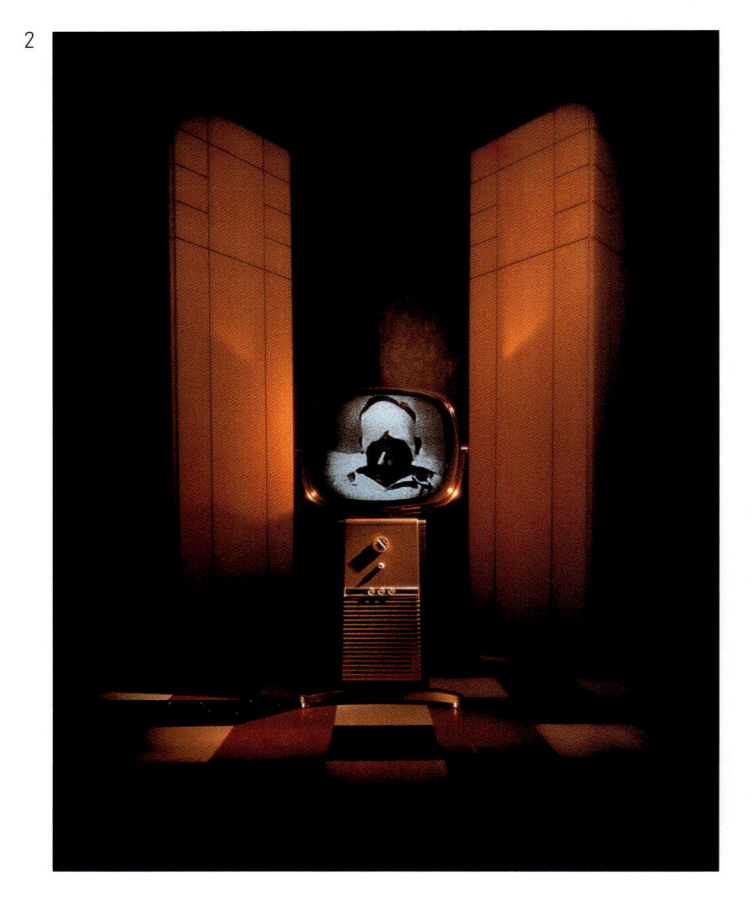

3

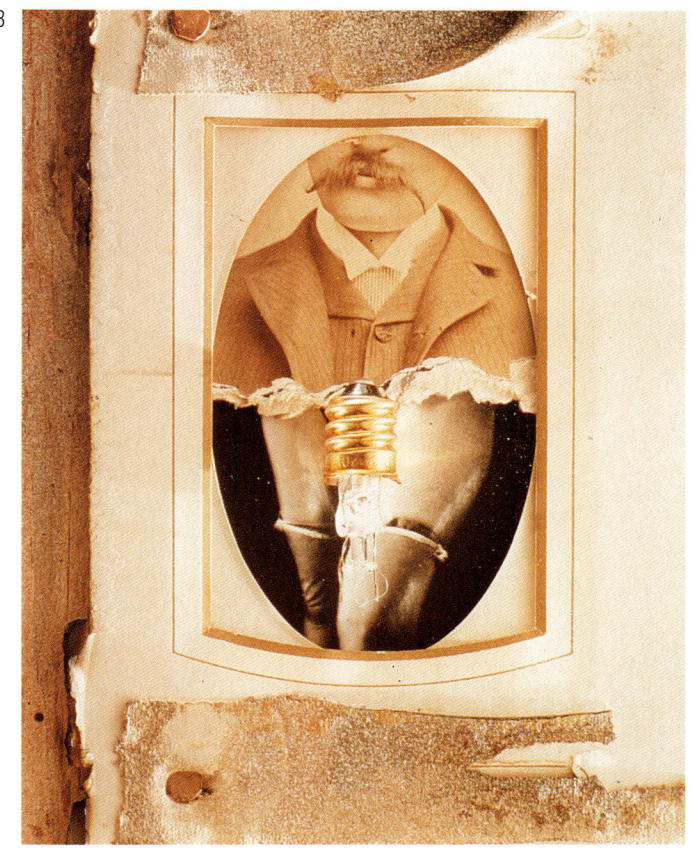

SELF-PROMOTION

1 (series)
Jay Corbett, photographer
Mark Von Ulrich, designer
Design Thing, design firm

Source book ads.

2
Curtis Johnson, Jim Arndt Photography, photographer/client
Curtis Johnson, art director

Mailer.

3
RJ Muna, photographer/art director/designer

Source book ad.

120 PHOTOGRAPHY ANNUAL 1994

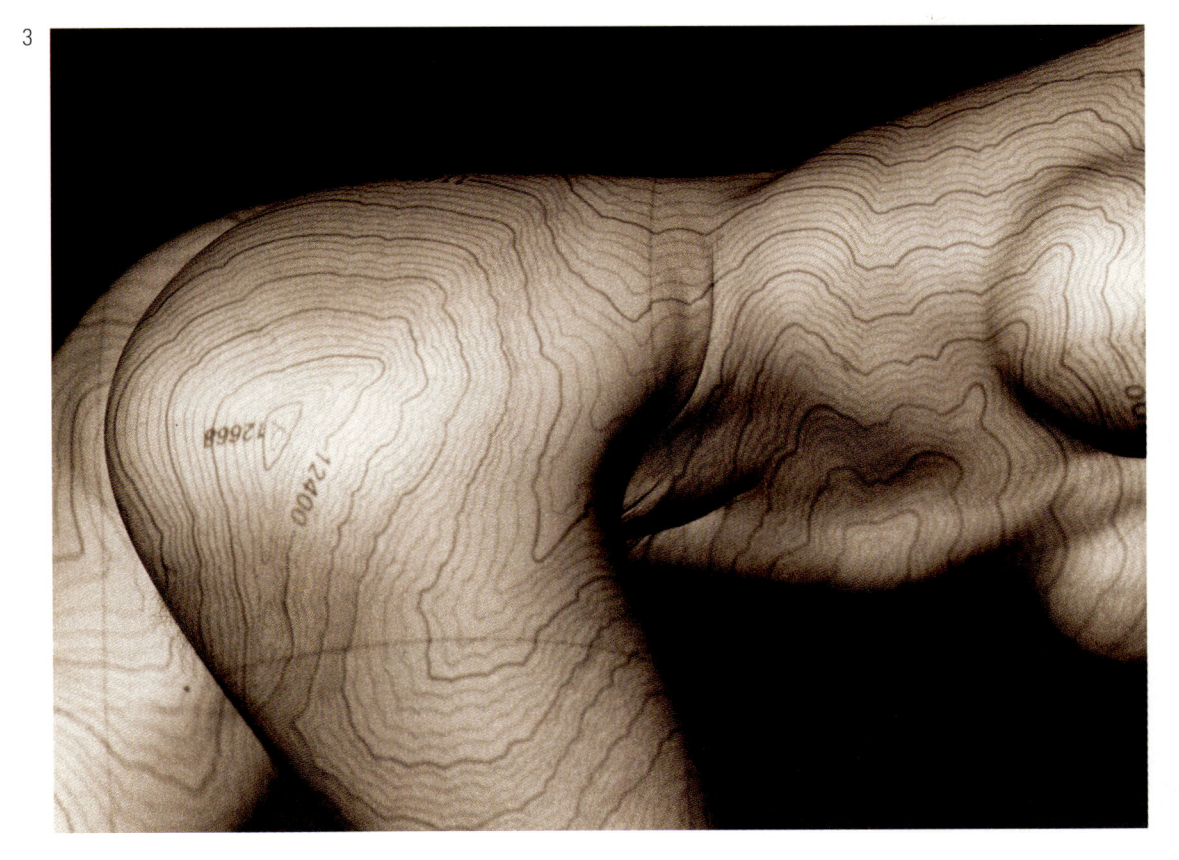

2

3

1

2

122 PHOTOGRAPHY ANNUAL 1994

SELF-PROMOTION

1
Stewart Tilger, photographer
Luane Bice, designer
Bice Design, design firm
Stewart Tilger Photography, client

Directory image.

2
Scott Barrow, photographer
Karen Beckwith, art director
Theresa Kraft, designer
Beckwith Barrow, Ltd., design firm
Scott Barrow, Inc., client

Source book ad.

3
Daniel De Souza, photographer/art director/client

Leave-behind.

4
Dominique Malaterre, Tilt Inc., photographer/art director
Tilt Inc., client

"Who said you could be blinded by love?" Promotion hand-delivered on St. Valentine's Day.

1

Self-Promotion

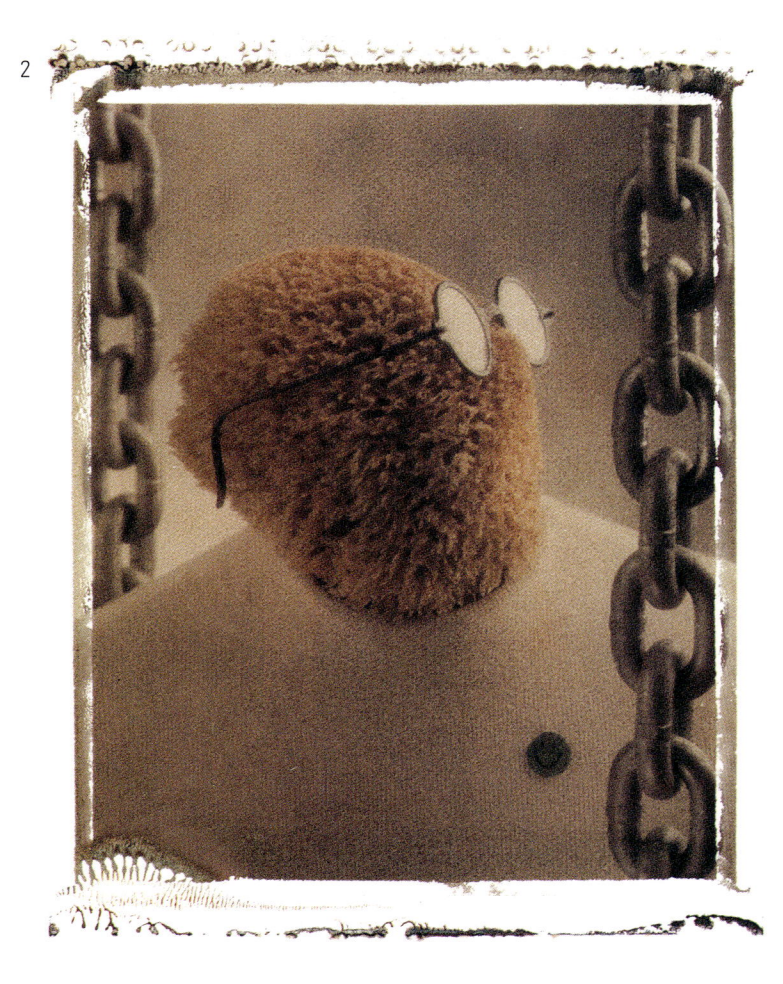

1 (series)
Scott Ferguson/Mark Katzman, Ferguson & Katzman
   Photography, photographers/art directors
Reneé Walsh, designer
Pfeiffer + Company, design firm
Reprox Printing of St. Louis, client

Brochure to promote waterless press.

2
Paul Mutino, photographer/art director

Leave-behind.

Unpublished

3
Kay Canavino, photographer

"Night-blooming Cereus/Double Dead."

© 1994 Kay Canavino

UNPUBLISHED

1
J. W. Burkey, photographer

Demonstration of the studio's digital capabilities.

© 1994 J. W. Burkey

2 (series)
Chip Forelli, photographer/art director/client

© 1994 Chip Forelli

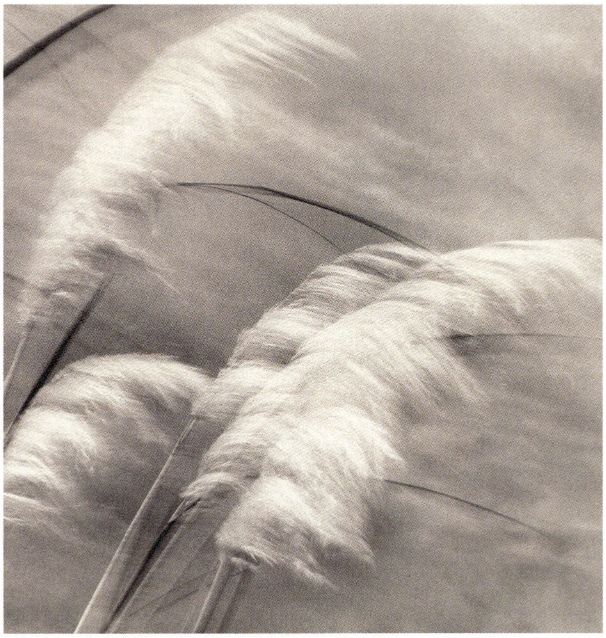

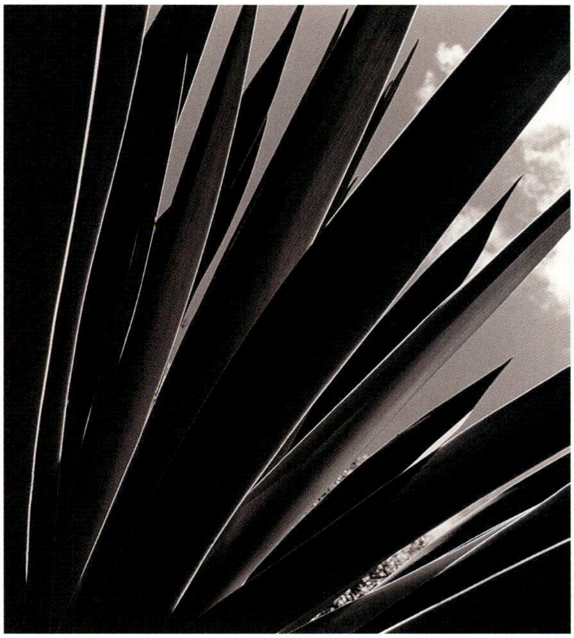

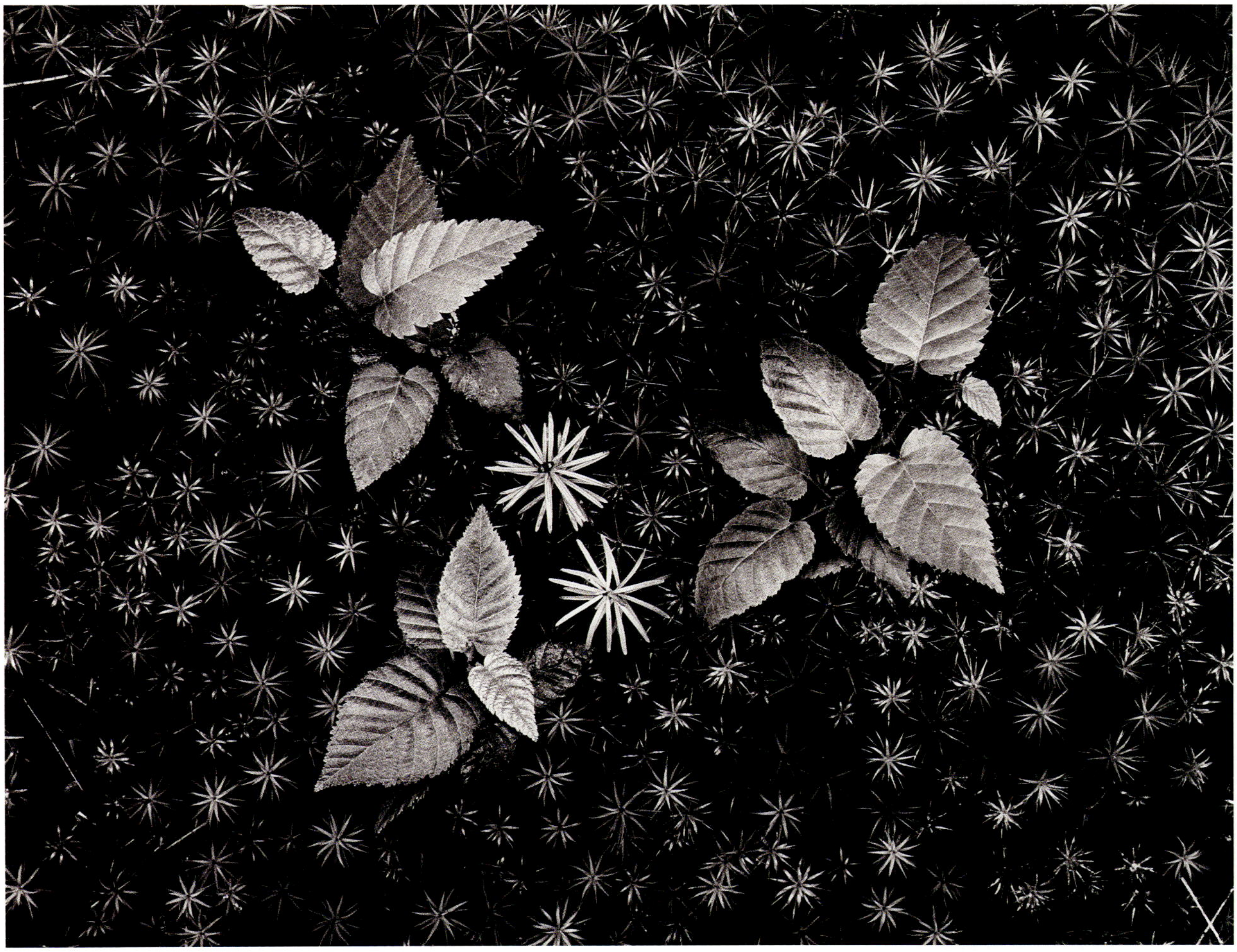

Unpublished

1
Les Ward, photographer

Portfolio sample.

© 1994 Les Ward

2 (series)
Raymond Meeks, photographer
Matthew Drace, art director

Outtakes from *Men's Journal* article on Romania.

© 1994 Raymond Meeks

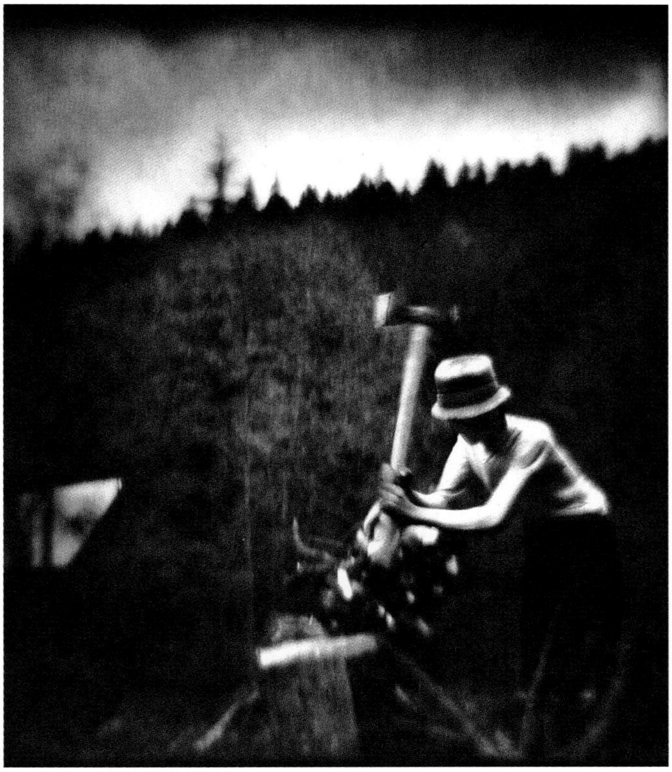

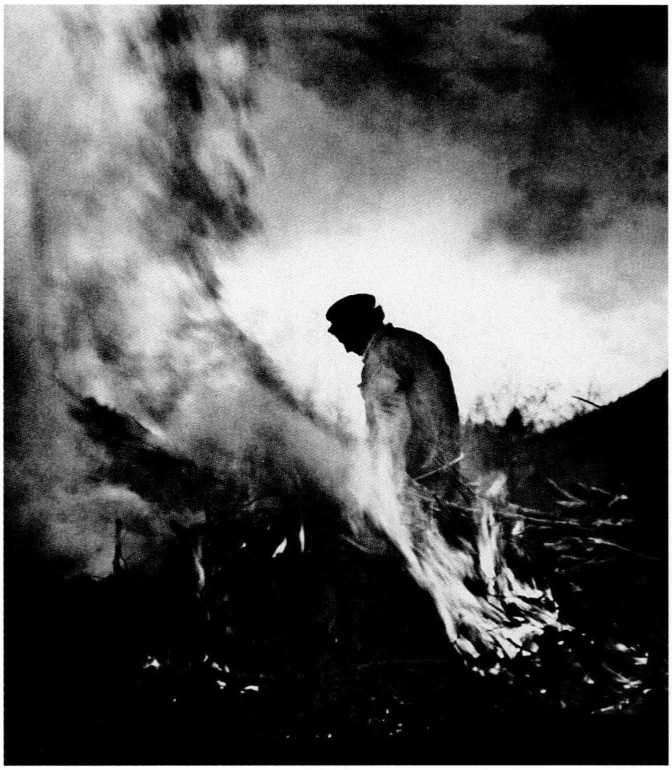

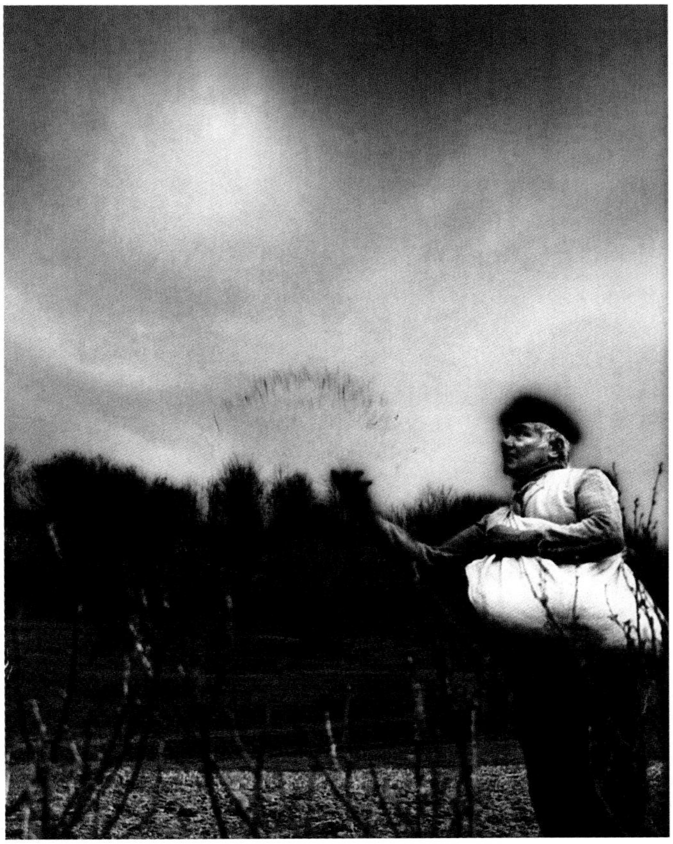

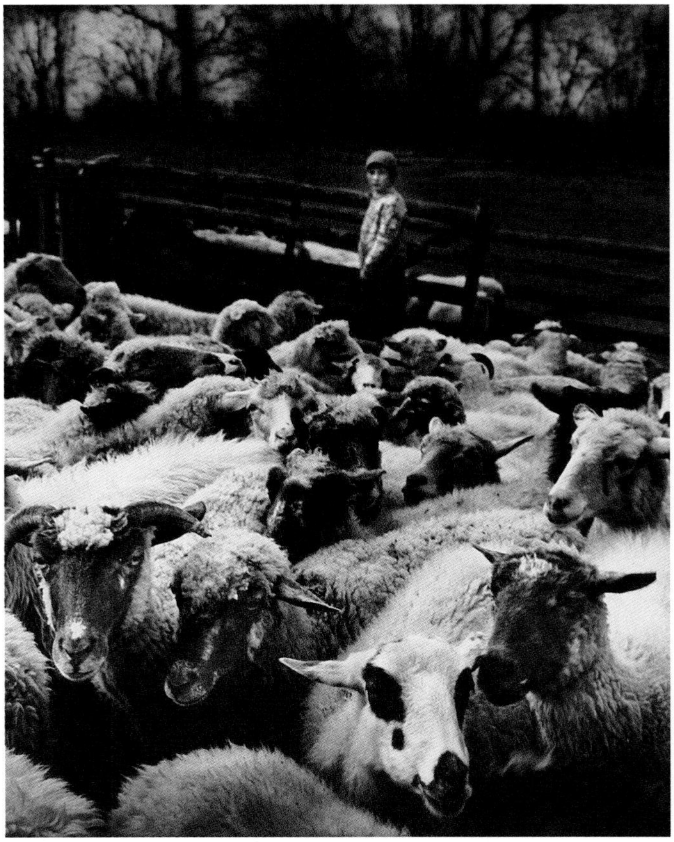

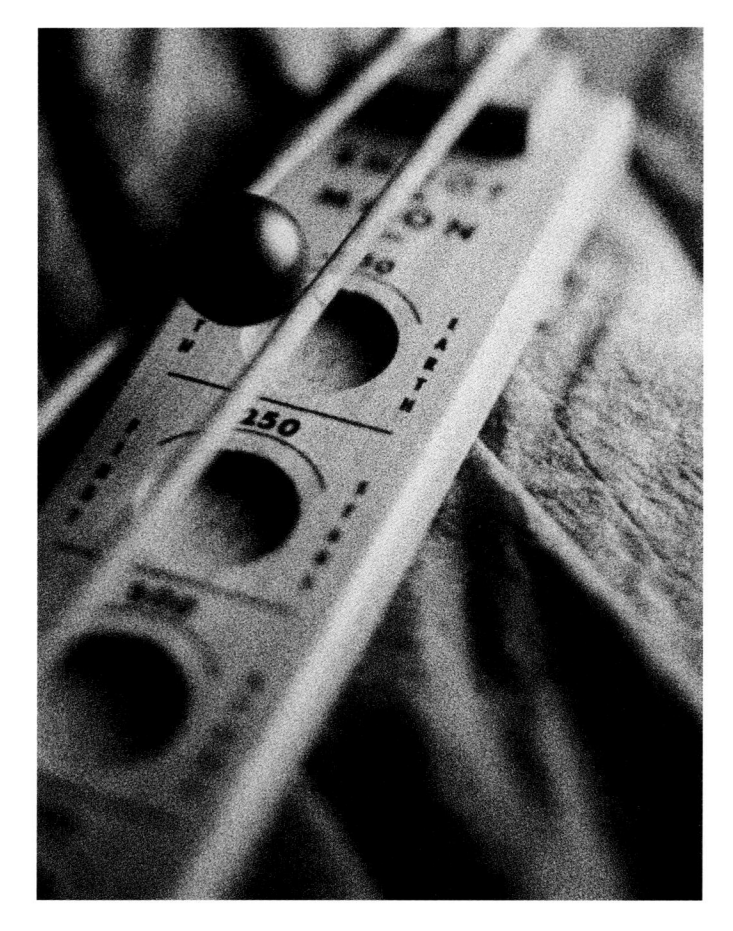

1

Unpublished

1 (series)
Pete Lacker, photographer
Ken Phillips, art director

Personal photographs of old games.

© 1994 Pete Lacker

2
Peter Dazeley, photographer

"Sunflower." Polaroid emulsion transfer manipulated on cartridge paper.

© 1994 Peter Dazeley

3
Robert David Atkinson, photographer

Portfolio piece.

© 1994 Robert David Atkinson

UNPUBLISHED

1 (series)
Jennifer Krogh, photographer/art director

Eastern State Penitentiary in Philadelphia.

© 1994 Jennifer Krogh

2
John Cleveland Garofalo, photographer

© 1994 John Cleveland Garofalo

3
Ed Kashi, photographer

A living community in Cairo's cemetery, "The City of the Dead."

© 1994 Ed Kashi

2

3

COMMUNICATION ARTS *133*

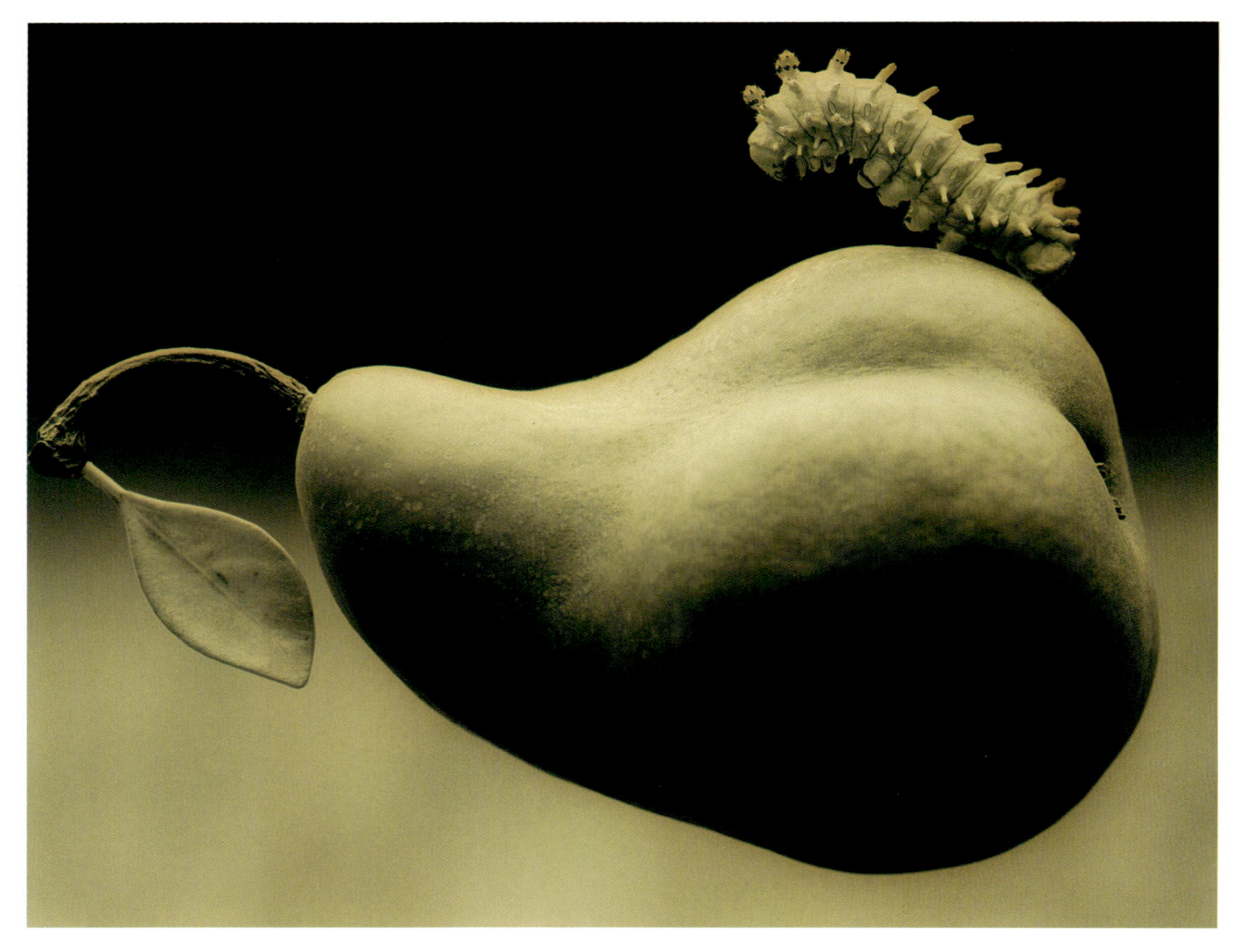

1

134 PHOTOGRAPHY ANNUAL 1994

Unpublished

1 (series)
Mark Laita, photographer/art director

Three of a series of toned black-and-white prints.

© 1994 Mark Laita

2
Dale Higgins, photographer

"I Got Milk."

© 1994 Dale Higgins

3
Eric Mencher, photographer

One from a series based on the premise that life imitates art.

© 1994 Eric Mencher

UNPUBLISHED

1
Bob Blankenship,
   photographer/art director

Study of the Schloss Furnaces in Birmingham, Alabama.

© 1994 Bob Blankenship

2
Jamie Tanaka, photographer

© 1994 Jamie Tanaka

3 (series)
Fredrik Bröden, photographer

"Beach People."

© 1994 Fredrik Bröden

3

1

Unpublished

1 (series)
Jim Erickson, photographer

India portfolio.

© 1994 Jim Erickson

2
David Humphreys, photographer/art director

Portfolio/show piece, "One Religion."

© 1994 David Humphreys

1

UNPUBLISHED

1 (series)
Marcy J. Appelbaum, photographer

"Family Series."

© 1994 Marcy J. Appelbaum

140 PHOTOGRAPHY ANNUAL 1994

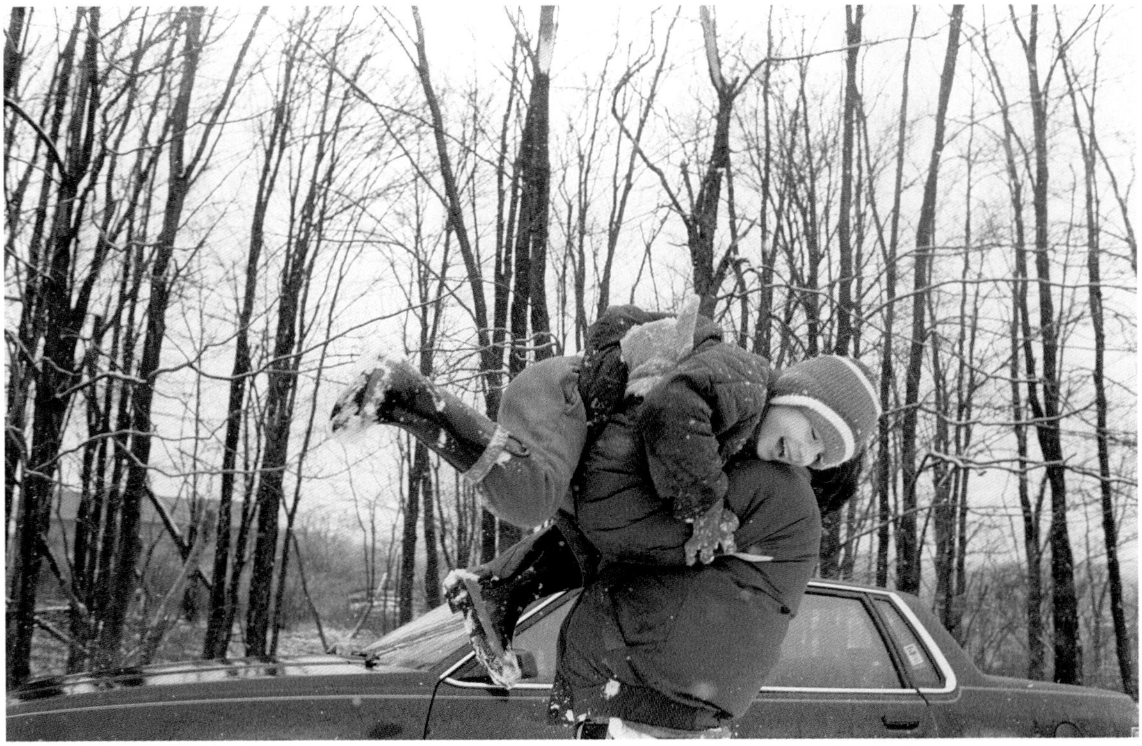

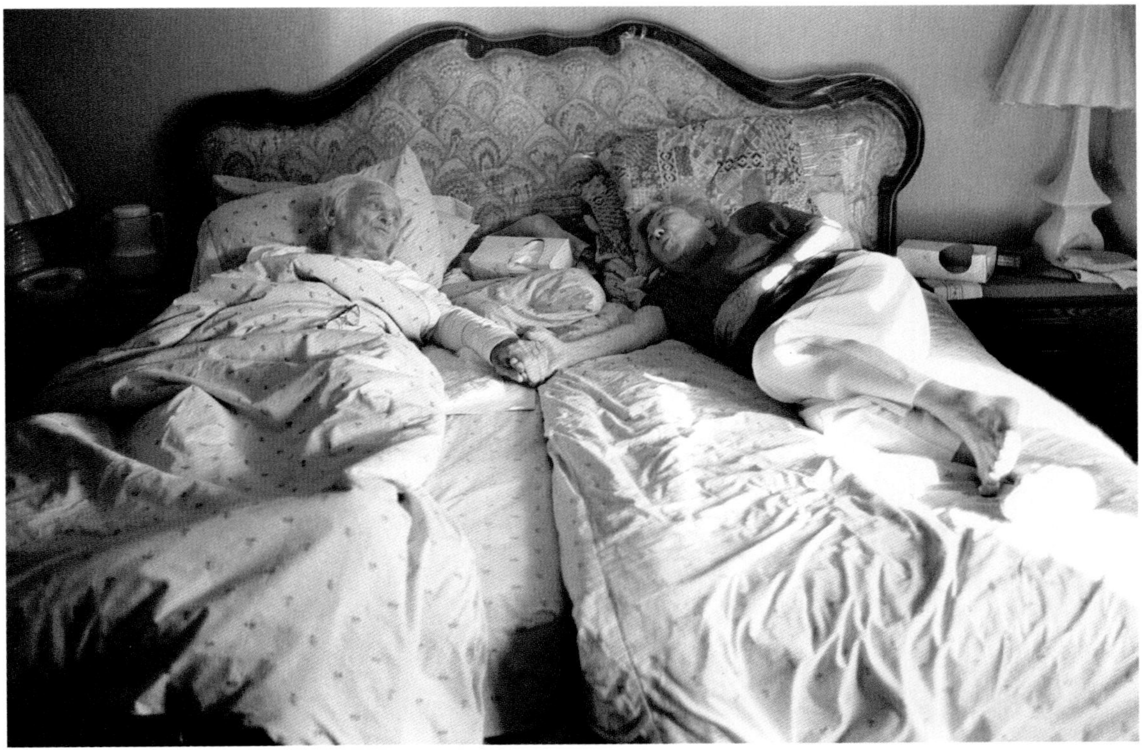

142 PHOTOGRAPHY ANNUAL 1994

Unpublished

1 (series)
Hector E. Prida, photographer

Personal project.

© 1994 Hector E. Prida

2
Jim Erickson, photographer

Self-assignment in Mexico, "Bullpen."

© 1994 Jim Erickson

1

144 PHOTOGRAPHY ANNUAL 1994

Unpublished

1 (series)
Duncan McNicol, photographer

Reed cutter in Norfolk, England.

© 1994 Duncan McNicol

2
Greg Slater, photographer/art director

© 1994 Greg Slater

UNPUBLISHED

1 (series)
Sarah Fawcett, photographer

Photographs from ongoing personal project, "Memorial Day, San Francisco, Remembering War."

© 1994 Sarah Fawcett

1

PART TWO

35

ILLUSTRATION ANNUAL

CATEGORIES

6
ADVERTISING

30
BOOKS

53
EDITORIAL

84
FOR SALE

94
INSTITUTIONAL

114
SELF-PROMOTION

128
UNPUBLISHED

T H E   J U R Y

CHRISTINE CURRY
has been the illustration editor at the *New Yorker* since March 1989.
She introduced color illustrations to the magazine and created a department to facilitate this change,
working directly with editor Tina Brown and the contributing writers. Prior to this position,
Curry was a free-lance production coordinator at Condé Nast Publications and an assistant to Rochelle
Udell at *Gentlemen's Quarterly*. Chris graduated from the Rhode Island School of Design in 1983
with a BFA in painting and a minor in art history.

MICHAEL FARMER
is the art director of children's books at Harcourt Brace Trade Division, in San Diego, California,
and consulting art director to the School Books Division in Orlando, Florida. He is directly responsible
for the art direction and design of approximately 125 children's books each year.
After undergraduate study in art and design at California College of Arts and Crafts, Farmer continued
his education at California Polytechnic University, where he graduated with honors and a Bachelor
of Science degree in graphic communications in 1982.

DITI KATONA
is a partner and principal with her husband, designer John Pylypczak, of Concrete Design
Communications Inc., based in Toronto, Canada. The firm has received international recognition for its
work in various publications such as *Communication Arts*, *Graphis*, *Print* and *Applied Arts*
as well as from the Art Directors Club of New York. In addition to lecturing and jurying for various
organizations, Katona has taught graphic design at York University and the
Ontario College of Art in Toronto.

GARY KELLEY
is a free-lance illustrator based in Cedar Falls, Iowa. Kelley has a degree in art from the University of
Northern Iowa, with an emphasis in drawing, painting and design and began his career as a graphic
designer and art director before turning to illustration in the mid '70s. Awards include the Hamilton
King Award from the Society of Illustrators in 1992; seventeen gold and silver medals from the Society
of Illustrators and the Ben Franklin Award from the National Booksellers Association, as well as
numerous citations from CA's Illustration Annuals; *Print*'s Regional Design Annuals; American
Illustration; Art Directors Club of New York and the Bologna, Italy, Book Fair.

JERRY SULLIVAN
a native of Montana, has been a principal of Sullivan Haas Coyle Advertising and Public Relations in
Atlanta, Georgia, for twelve years serving as co-creative director. Sullivan graduated from the Ringling
School of Art and Design in 1962. His career has included three years as vice president and creative
director with Cecil West & Associates, three years as creative group supervisor with McDonald and
Little and four years as an art director with Cole Henderson Drake.

ADVERTISING

1
Shane W. Evans, illustrator/art director/designer
Odds & Ends, client

Promotional flyer and poster for jeans designer. 24 x 36, oil on denim.

2
Gerald Bustamante, illustrator
José Serrano, art director
Mires Design, design firm
Peninsula YMCA, client

Poster for the bay to bay rowing and paddling regatta. 19½ x 12¼, acrylic on chipboard.

3
Jerry Lofaro, illustrator
Woody Litwhiler, art director
Bozell, Inc., ad agency
Minolta, client

Ad for copy machines sold with a no-risk guarantee. Headline: Maybe the best way to handle risk is to avoid it altogether. 22 x 28, acrylic airbrush and paint.

3

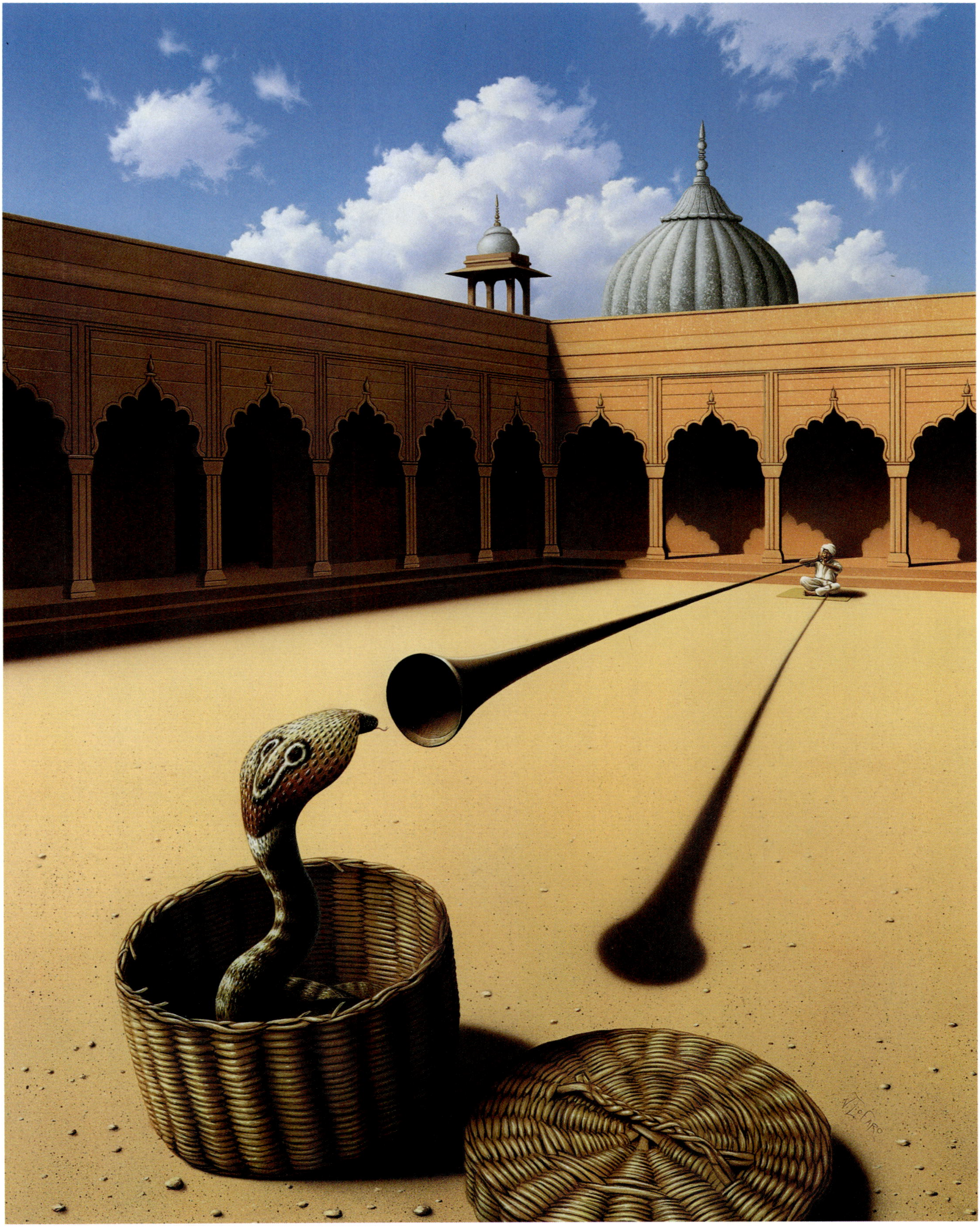

1

Advertising

1
Rick Sealock, illustrator
Andy Anema, art director/designer
Ogilvy & Mather, ad agency
Sears, Roebuck & Company, client

Ad for video games and adapters. 11 x 14, mixed media.

2
Rich Borge, illustrator/designer
Rich Borge/John Murphy, art directors
Gravity Workshop, design firm
Black Vinyl Records, client

CD cover "Propeller" for Shoes. 12 x 12, mixed media.

3
Mark Ryden, illustrator
Jeri Heiden, art director/designer
Warner Bros. Records/Third Matinee, clients

CD packaging. 10 x 10, oil.

Advertising

1
Braldt Bralds, illustrator
David Bartels, art director
Bartels & Company, ad agency
Saint Louis Zoo, client

Poster "Above and Beyond." 14 x 28, oil on Masonite.

2
Gary Baseman, illustrator/designer
David Carson, art director
David Carson Design/Gary Baseman, design firms
Ray Gun, client

Subscription page. 16 x 20, mixed media.

3
Cathleen Toelke, illustrator
Nelson Kane, art director
Art Spikol, Inc., ad agency
Promotrak Software, IMS America, client

Brochure cover promoting the speed and maneuverability of the software. 7½ x 9, gouache.

4
Brad Holland, illustrator
Guy Marino, art director/designer
Merkley, Newman, Harty, ad agency
Banker's Trust, client

Double page ad. Headline: Risks hardly ever travel alone. 22 x 20, acrylic on Masonite.

COMMUNICATION ARTS 11

1

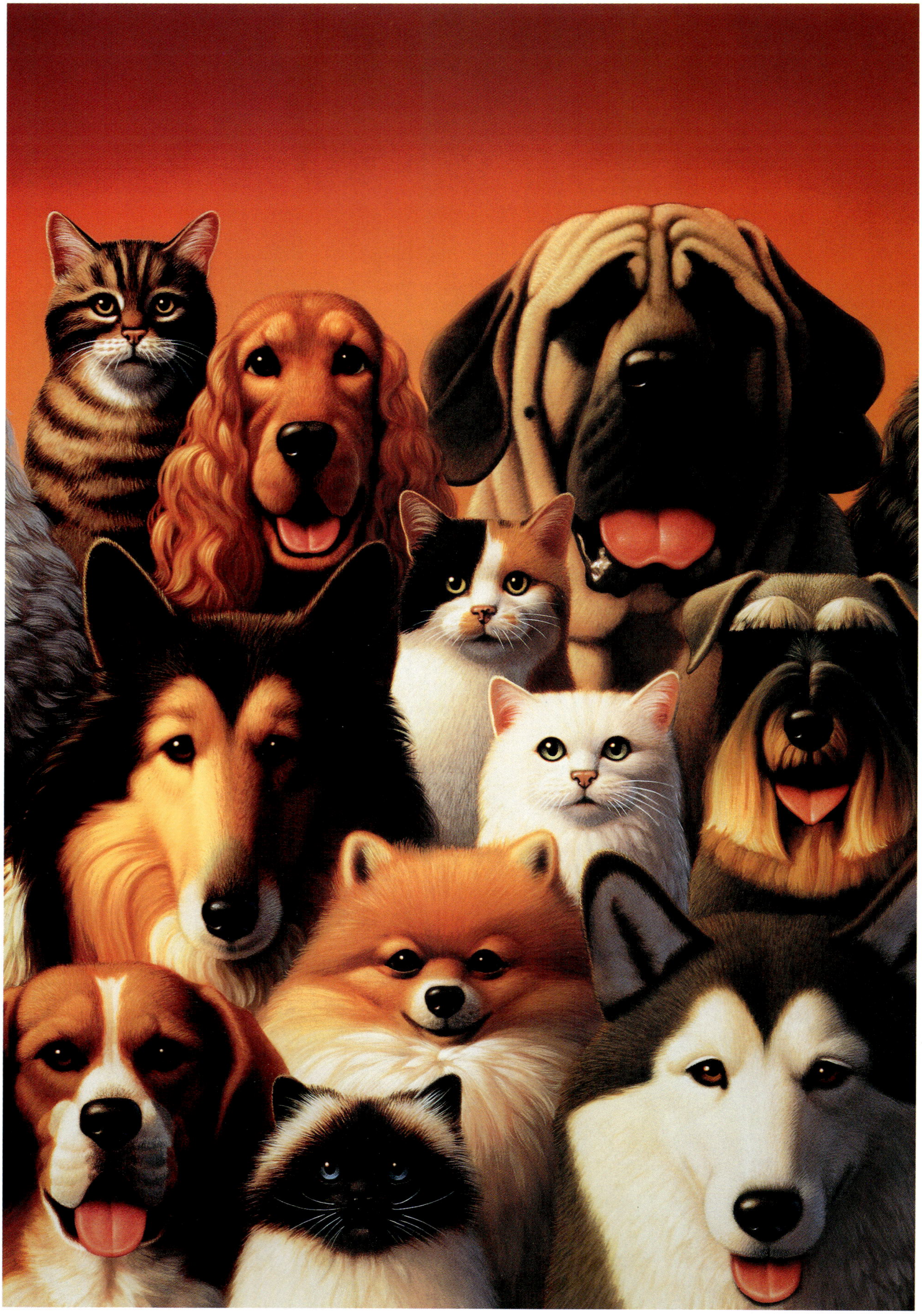

Advertising

1
Leland Klanderman, illustrator
Michael Cory, art director
The Zipatoni Company, ad agency
Ralston Purina, client

Poster. 26 x 38, acrylic.

2
Mark Braught, illustrator
Bill Carson, art director
Hal Riney & Partners, ad agency
Saturn Corp., client

Ad depicting the fuel economy of the car. 10 x 10, pastel.

3
Joel Nakamura, illustrator
Linda Cobb, art director/designer
Warner Bros. Records/Not Drowning,Waving, clients

CD cover of "Follow the Geography." 20 x 20, acrylic.

Advertising

1
Michael Schwab, illustrator
Michael Schwab Design, design firm
Lord Fletcher's Restaurant, client

Poster. 22½ x 30, silk screen.

2 (series)
Bill Mayer, illustrator
Bill Haffner, art director
Scripto-Tokai, Inc., client

Back to school packaging. Approximately 10 x 15, airbrush, gouache and dye.

COMMUNICATION ARTS 15

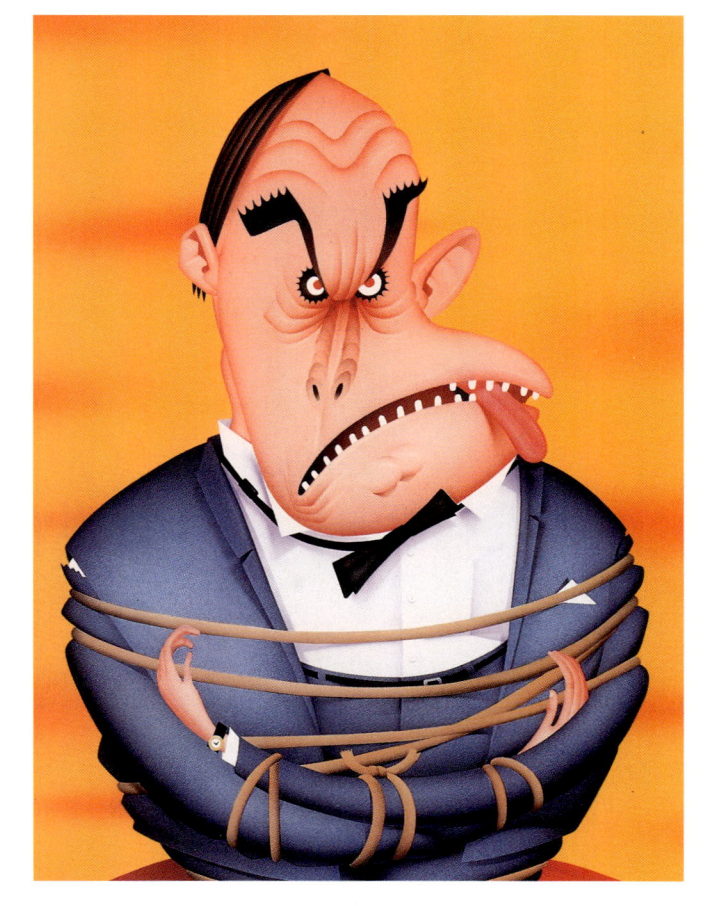

ADVERTISING

1
Joseph Daniel Fiedler, illustrator
Howard Fritzson, art director
Sony Music, design/client

CD cover of "Billie Holiday, 16 Most Requested Songs." 11 x 11, alkyd on paper.

2
Michael Bartalos, illustrator
Jim De Barros, art director/designer
Sony Music, design/client

LP and CD cover art for a compilation titled "Hey, Mr. D.J." 7½ x 7½, gouache.

3 (series)
Daniele Melani, illustrator
Agostino Reggio, art director/designer
Reggio Del Bravo Pubblicita, ad agency
Eugenio Fabozzi Onoranze Funebri, client

Billboards advertising an undertaking firm. Headline: Why get there before you have to? 23 x 12, mixed media on paper.

PERCHE' ARRIVARE PRIMA?

QUANTO SFUMI AL GIORNO?

SCHIANTI CLASSICO

1

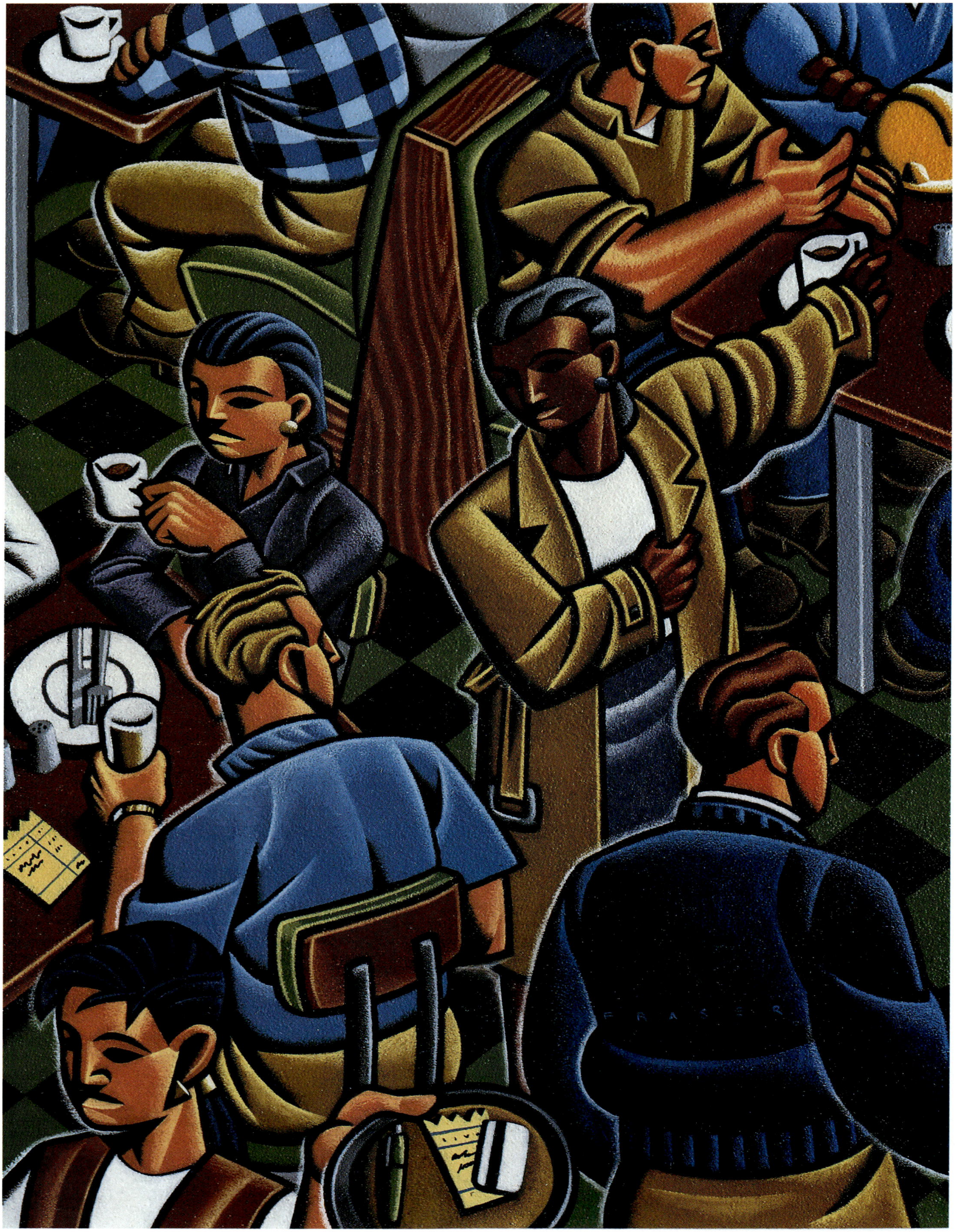

Advertising

1
Douglas Fraser, illustrator
Greg Roditski, art director/designer
McCaffrey & Company, ad agency
Merck Group, Astra, client

Ad image to promote a drug for high blood pressure. Headline: Who's a candidate? 10 x 15, alkyd on paper.

2
Waldemar Swierzy, illustrator/art director
Galeria Sztuki, client

Poster for the gallery featuring Duda Gracz. 9 x 11, gouache.

3
Gary Kelley, illustrator
Connie Soteropulos, art director
Matt Eller, designer
Dayton Hudson, Department Store Division, client

Poster to promote an animated Christmas display. 20 x 28, pastel on paper.

ADVERTISING

1
Marco J. Ventura, illustrator
David Hadley, art director
KSK Communications, Ltd., ad agency
Lucas Management Systems, client

Trade magazine ad and brochure cover.
Headline: What would happen if you chose the wrong project management software?
4½ x 8½, oil on paper.

2
Rafal Olbinski, illustrator
Lisa Leleu-Gingras, art director/designer
Full Moon Creations, Inc., design firm
Eberhard Faber, client

Poster headline: The art of recycling. 20 x 30, acrylic on canvas.

3
James Marsh, illustrator
Keith Terry, art director
Saatchi & Saatchi, ad agency
Burger King Corp., client

Poster headline: But you can change your burger to a Burger King Burger. 13¾ x 15¾, acrylic on canvas board.

4
Stasys Eidrigevicius, illustrator
Jimmy Seacat, art director
Actors Theater of Louisville, client

Poster. 21 x 16, pastel.

COMMUNICATION ARTS 21

ADVERTISING

1
Paul Davis, illustrator/designer
Fran Michelman, art director
Paul Davis Studio, design firm
Mobil, client

Poster for "The Inspector Alleyn Mysteries." 30 x 45, acrylic.

2 (series)
Ann Field, illustrator
Aubyn Gwinn, art director/designer
Foote Cone & Belding, ad agency
Levi Strauss & Company, client

In-store banners and panels. Approximately 12 x 15, pastel chalk.

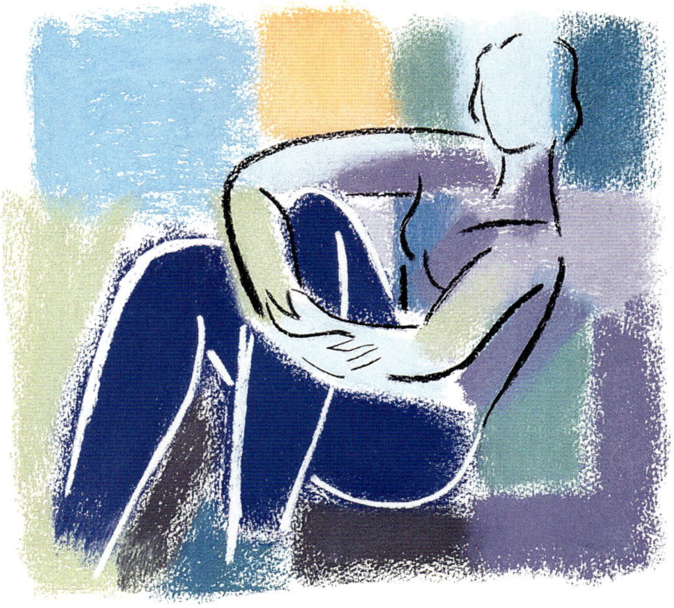

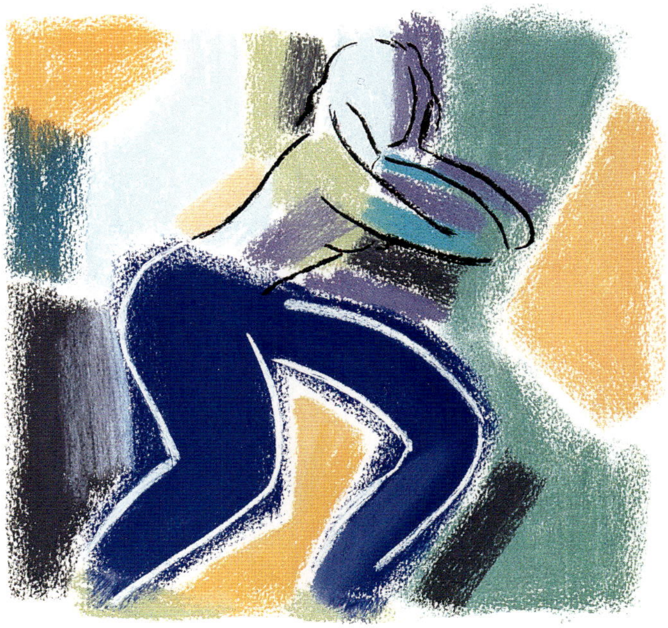

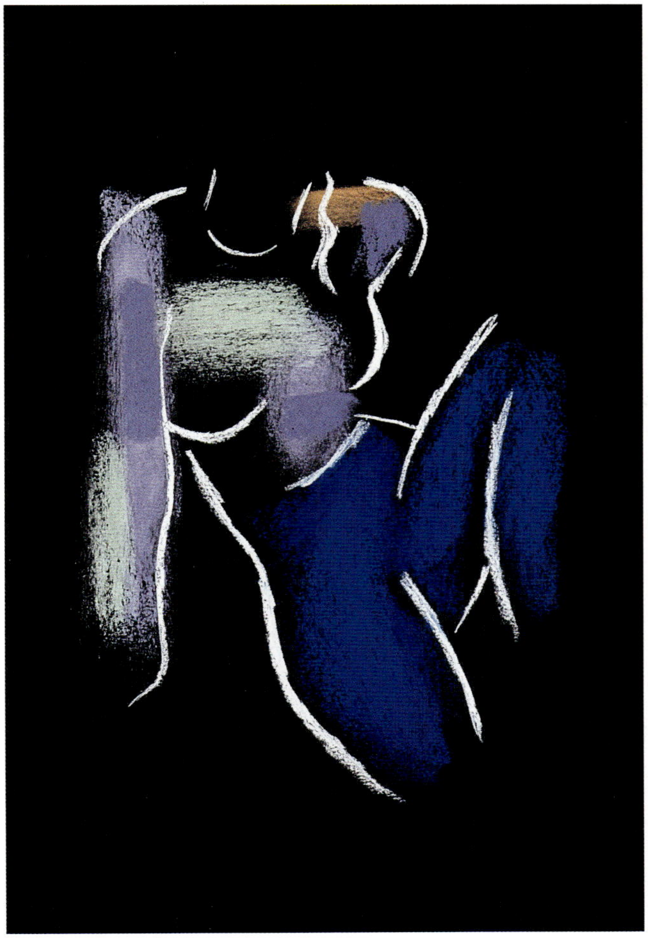

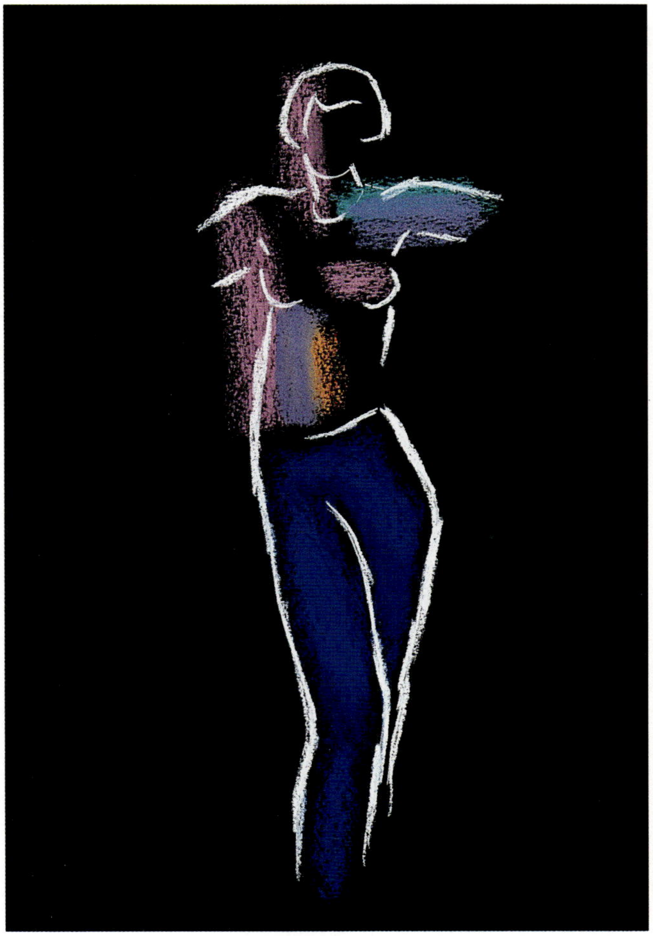

1

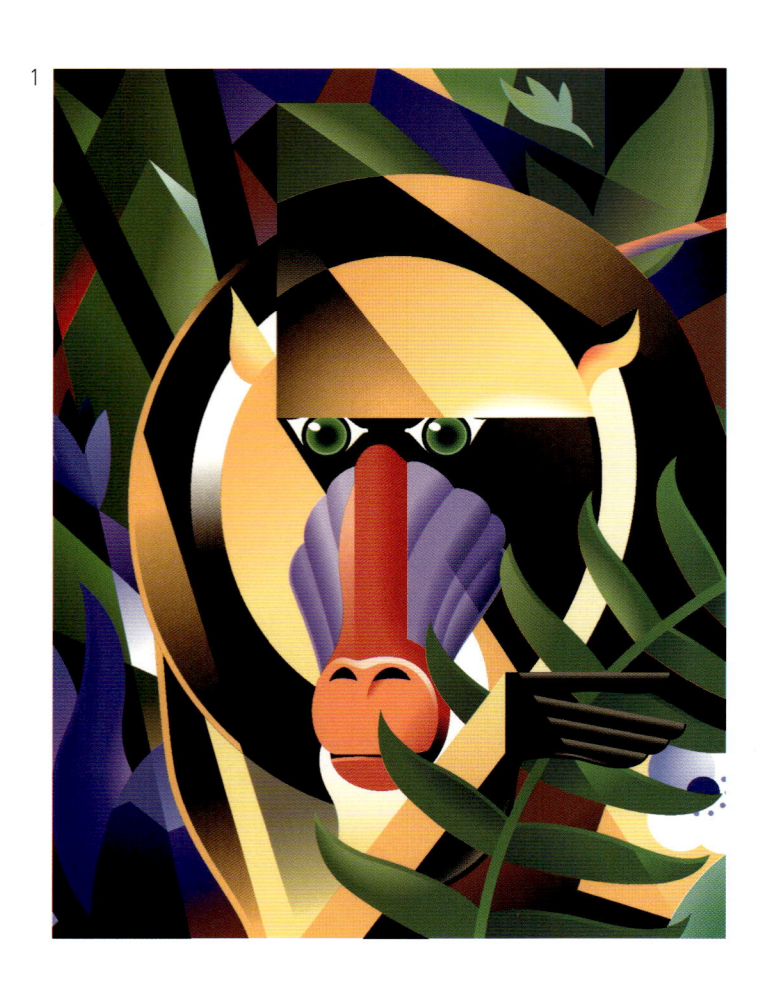

2

3

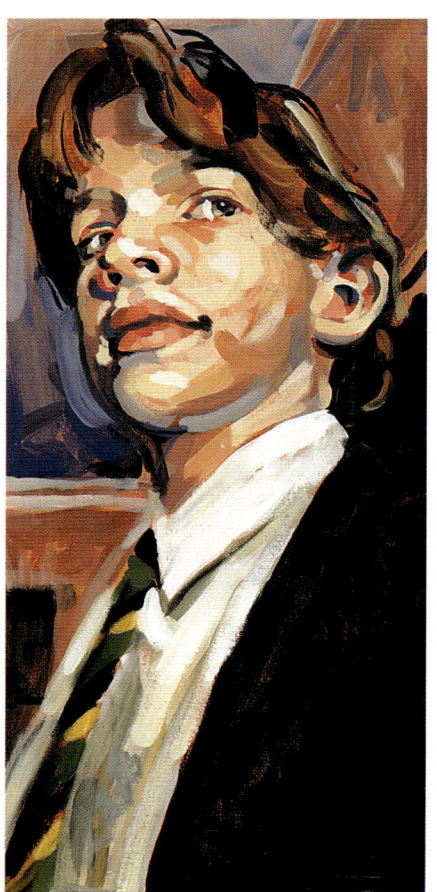

24 ILLUSTRATION ANNUAL 1994

Advertising

1
Ron Chan, illustrator
David Hunter, art director
Foote Cone & Belding/Technology, ad agency
Adobe Systems, Inc., client

"Wild Thing" used for posters, buttons and various collateral material for the introduction of Adobe Illustrator 5.0. Digital.

2
James Gallagher, illustrator/designer
Sasha Frere-Jones, art director
Hemiola Records/UI, clients

Concert poster. 18 x 24, mixed media.

3 (series)
Colin Davidson, illustrator
Alison Gault, art director
Rodney Miller Associates, design firm
The Lyric Players Theatre, Belfast, client

Posters: *Volunteers*; *The Hidden Curriculum*; *Taming of the Shrew*; *Pictures of Tomorrow*. 11¾ x 24, acrylic and oil on canvas.

Advertising

1
John Mattos, illustrator
Jill Savini, art director/designer
CKS Partners, ad agency
S.S. Norway, client

Poster for cruise ship. 15 x 20, airbrush ink.

2
C.F. Payne, illustrator
Gary Greenberg, art director/designer
Rossin Greenberg Seronick, ad agency
Stratus Computer, Inc., client

Ad headline: Before you commit to high availability computing, maybe you should take a closer look. 12 x 16½, mixed media.

3
Gregory Manchess, illustrator
Matt Reinhard, art director
Foote Cone & Belding, ad agency
Coors Brewing Company, Killian's Red Beer, client

Ad headline: We spent Friday night at the fights at the Green Garden Arena. 33 x 24, oil on gesso board.

4
Braldt Bralds, illustrator
Arnold Arlow, art director
TBWA Advertising, ad agency
Carillon Importers, Ltd., client

Ad. 18 x 24, oil on Masonite.

5
Hayes Henderson, illustrator/art director/designer
Henderson Tyner Art Co., design firm
Piedmont Guitar Society, client

Poster. 16¼ x 22¾, oil.

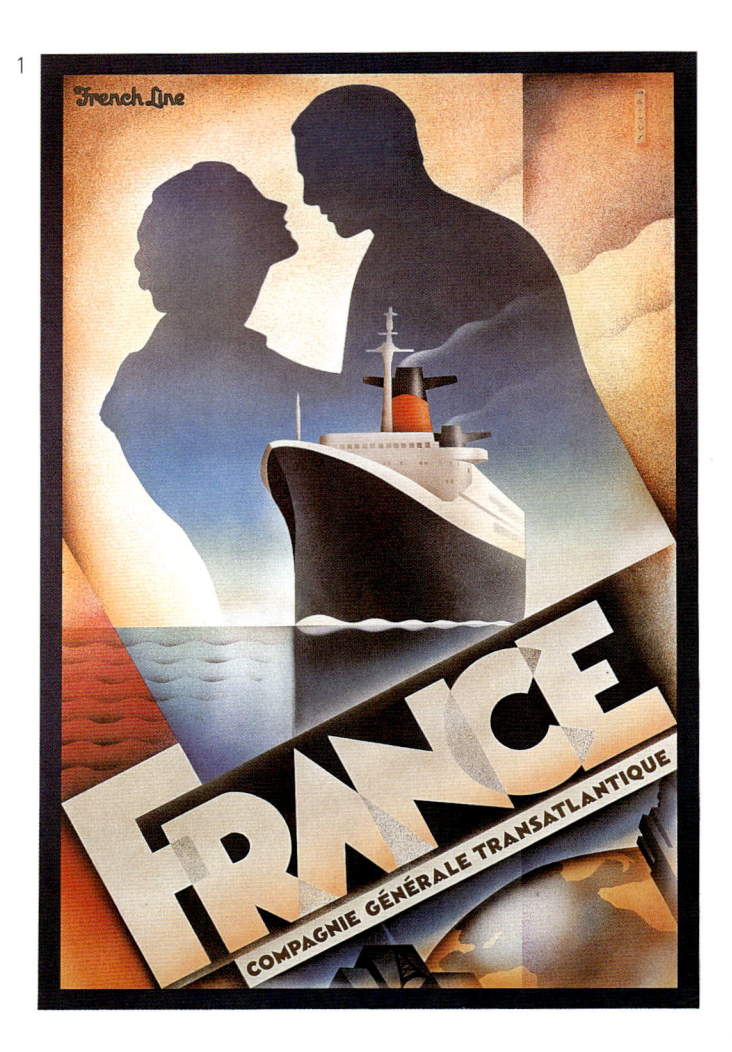

3

4

5

COMMUNICATION ARTS 27

ADVERTISING

1
Bryan Leister, illustrator
David Schiedt/Herb Allison, art directors
Thomas & Perkins, ad agency
Central City Opera, client

Poster. 9 x 22, oil.

2
Chris A. Gall, illustrator
Ted Nuttal, art director
Young & Associates, ad agency
Software Marketing Association, client

Cover of a software package for UFO enthusiasts. 8 x 12, scratchboard and dyes.

3
Allen Garns, illustrator
Mike Pacelli, art director
Kaizer Communications, design firm
Spelling Films International, client

Poster for the Robert Altman film, *Short Cuts*. 30 x 40, oil.

4
Jerry Lofaro, illustrator
Kristine Pallas, art director
Pallas Advertising, ad agency
Brown & Caldwell, client

Ad for a company that has developed a technique to blow-dry strawberries and other produce in the field to limit pesticide runoff into the water table. 24 x 18, acrylic, airbrushed and painted.

2

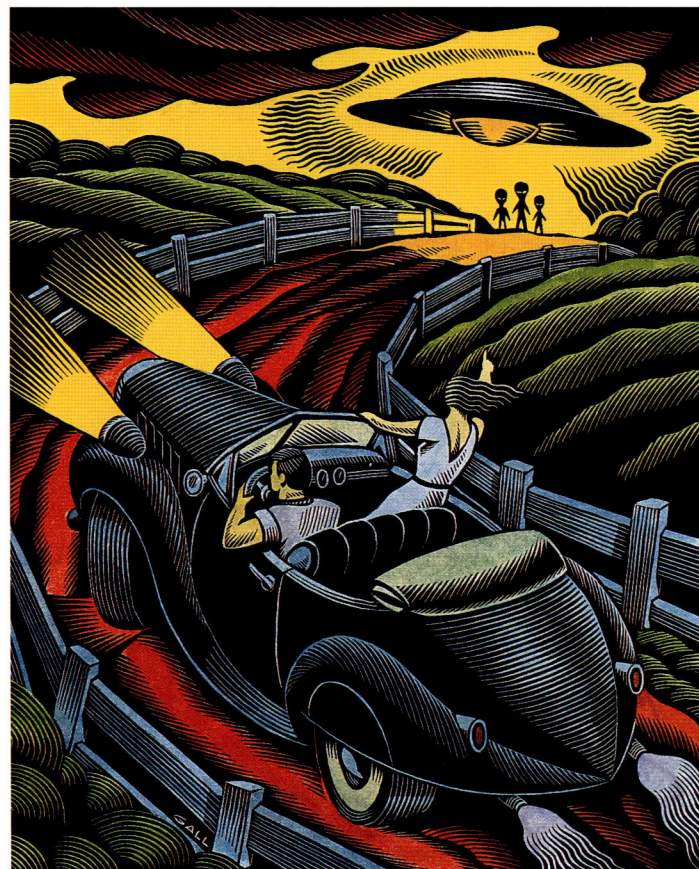

3

4

COMMUNICATION ARTS 29

Advertising

1
Glenn Harrington, illustrator
Glenn Harrington/Rick Fehrs, art directors
Artefact, client

Poster advertising the store. 8 x 12, oil.

2
Guy Porfirio, illustrator
David Bartels, art director/designer
Bartels & Company, design firm
Anheuser-Busch, client

Point-of-purchase poster, "Keep Florida Clean." 9 x 11¼, acrylic and colored pencils.

3
Gregory Manchess, illustrator
Alfredo Paredes, art director
Polo, Ralph Lauren, client

Original art for the interior of the New York store. 24 x 36, oil on canvas.

Books

4
Earl Keleny, illustrator
Michael Accordino, art director/designer
St. Martin's Press, design/client

Cover of *Footsteps in the Blood*, a Charmian Daniels mystery, 12 x 17½, acrylic.

5
Rebecca J. Leer, illustrator
Lucille Chomowicz, art director
David Neuhaus, designer
Simon & Schuster, client

A page from *The Girl Who Listened to Sinks*, a children's book about a girl who betters her life and her mother's by listening to inanimate objects. 14 x 19, pastel.

6
Adam Niklewicz, illustrator
Michael Accordino/Doris Borowsky, art directors
St. Martin's Press, client

Cover for *Third Man Out*, a gay mystery novel concerning conspiracy. 10 x 15, acrylic.

COMMUNICATION ARTS *31*

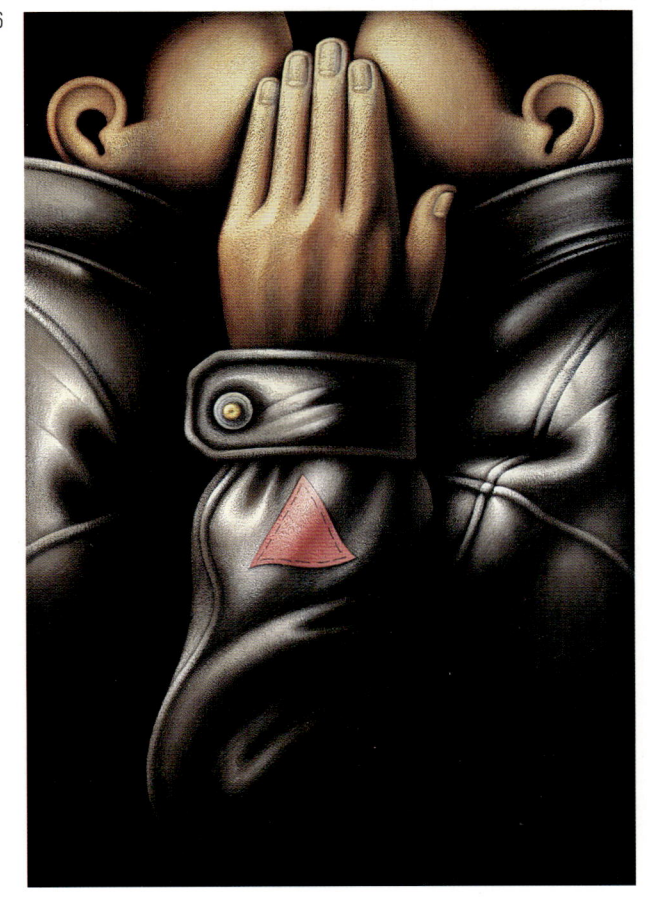

1

Books

1 (series)
Paul Cox, illustrator
Howard Klein, art director
Clarkson N. Potter, Inc. Publishers, client

Illustrations from *The Russian Tea Room, A Tasting*. Various sizes, watercolor.

2
Joanna Yardley, illustrator/designer
Nanette Stevenson, art director
Philomel Books, client

Jacket for *The Bracelet*, a children's book describing one child's experience in the Japanese internment camps. 11 x 13, watercolor and colored pencil.

3
Mary GrandPré, illustrator
Terry Czeczko, art director
Dell Publishing, client

Stories That Go Hiss in the Night, a collection of ghost stories. 16 x 20, pastel.

1

Books

1 (series)
Rocco Baviera, illustrator
Gunta Alexander, art director/designer
Philomel Books, client

Cover and interior illustrations for a children's book, *A Boy Called Slow*, the true story of Sitting Bull. Various sizes, alkyds and construction.

Books

1 (series)
Christopher Denise, illustrator
Nanette Stevenson, art director
Philomel Books, client

Interior illustrations from *The Fool of the World and the Flying Ship*, a Russian folktale. Approximately 12 x 9¾, acrylic on gessoed watercolor paper.

COMMUNICATION ARTS 37

1

Books

1 (series)
John Thompson, illustrator
Claire B. Counihan, art director
Scholastic Inc., client

Interior illustrations from *Christmas in the Big House, Christmas in the Quarters*. Various sizes, acrylic on Strathmore 5-ply kid finish Bristol board.

2
Wiktor Sadowski, illustrator
Joan Sommers, art director/designer
Joan Sommers Design, design firm
University of Chicago Press, client

Cover of *The Bridge on the Drina* by Ivo Andric, winner of the 1961 Nobel Prize for Literature. 12 x 14, acrylic.

1

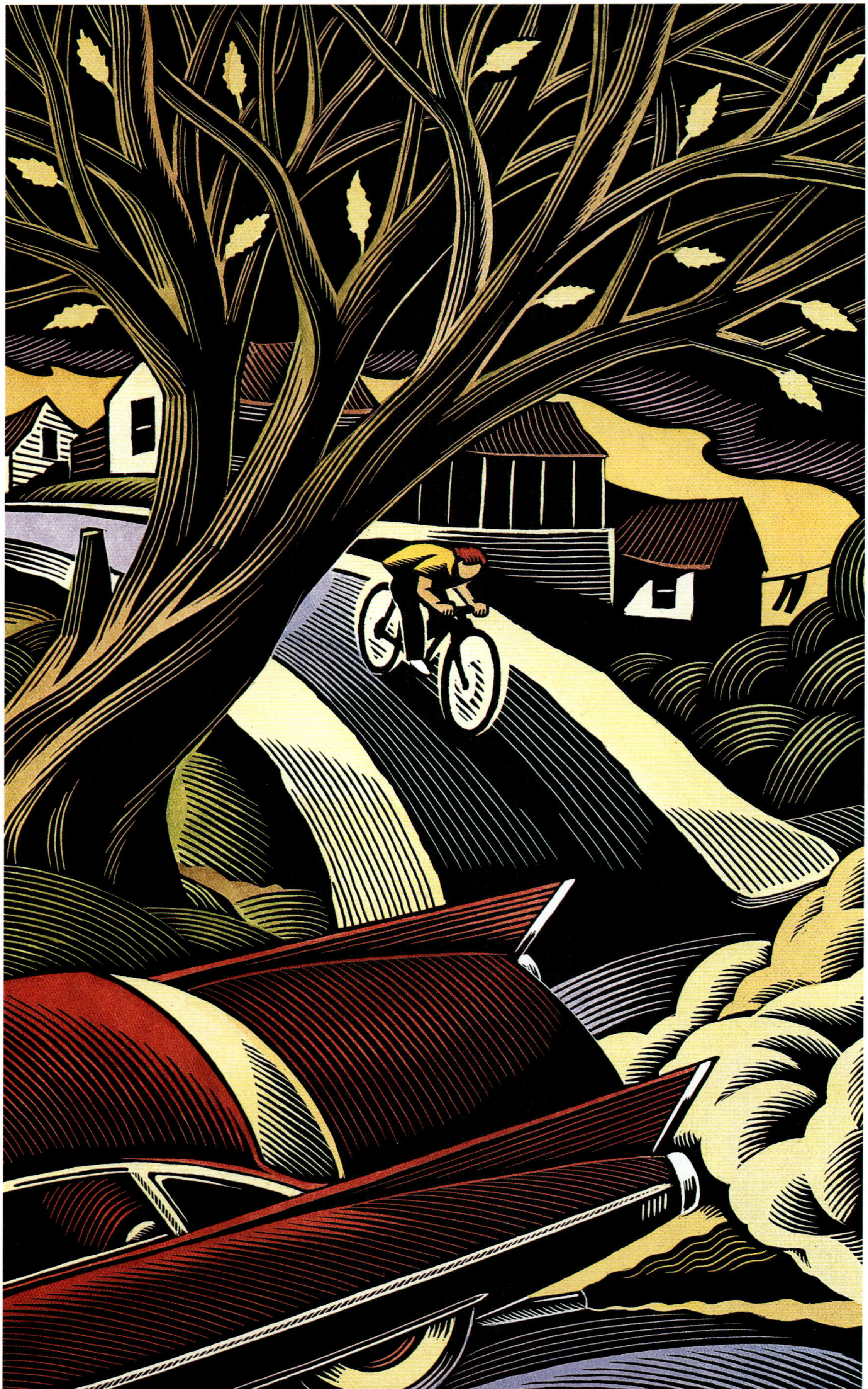

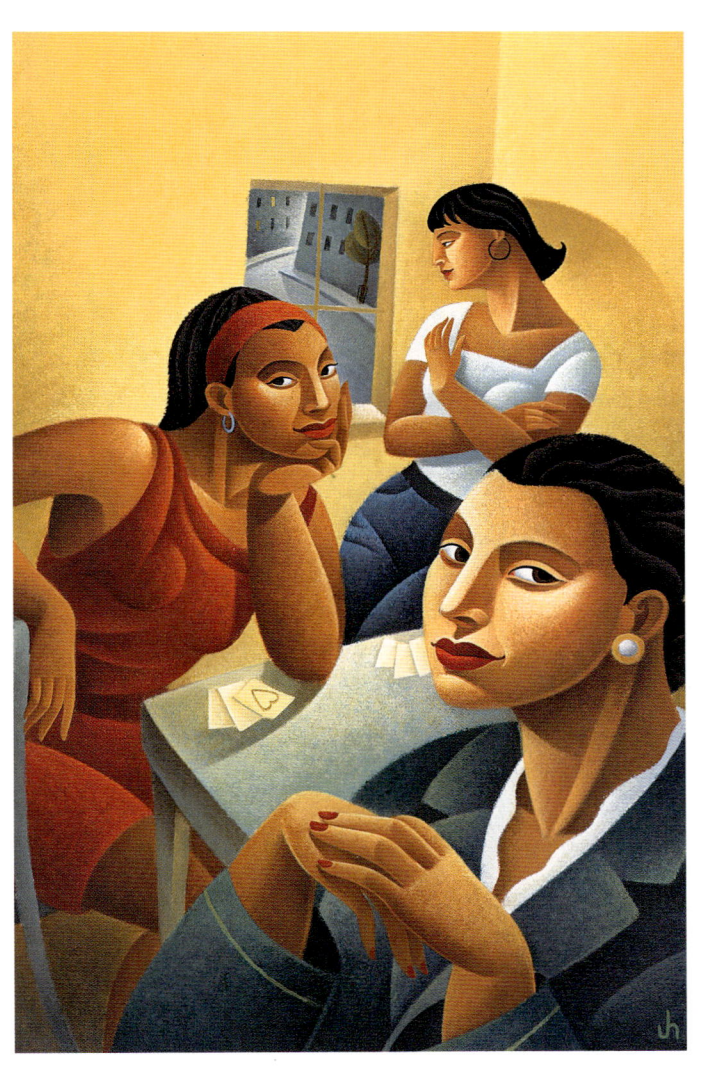

Books

1
Chris A. Gall, illustrator
Nick Krenitsky, art director
HarperCollins Publishers, client

Cover of *Gypsy Davey*, a novel about a poor retarded boy who gains freedom on his bicycle. 7 x 12, scratchboard, dyes.

2
Jody Hewgill, illustrator
Suzanne Noli, art director
HarperCollins Publishers, client

Cover of *Sisters & Lovers*, a novel that follows the loves, lives, choices and rivalries of three sisters. 9½ x 13½, acrylic.

3
Ashley Wolff, illustrator/designer
Sara Reynolds, art director
Dutton Children's Books, publisher

Interior illustration for *Stella & Roy*. Even though Stella's bike is much faster than Roy's, he manages to win their race around the park because she keeps stopping to enjoy its natural beauty. 7½ x 8⅜, linoleum block and watercolor.

Books

1
Ward Schumaker, illustrator
Sharon Smith, designer
Sharon Smith Design, design firm
Mercury House, client

Reading Jazz cover illustrates a collection of historical pieces on the subject of jazz by famous authors. 6 x 9, ink on tissue on acetate.

2 (series)
Tatsuro Kiuchi, illustrator
Yumiko Sakuma, art director
Masuro Tsujimura, designer
Fuzanbo, client

Children's book, cover and interior illustrations from *Hyouga Nezumi No Kegawa* (The Hunter and Fur). A man going hunting is stopped by polar bears. 20 x 18, oil on panel.

COMMUNICATION ARTS 43

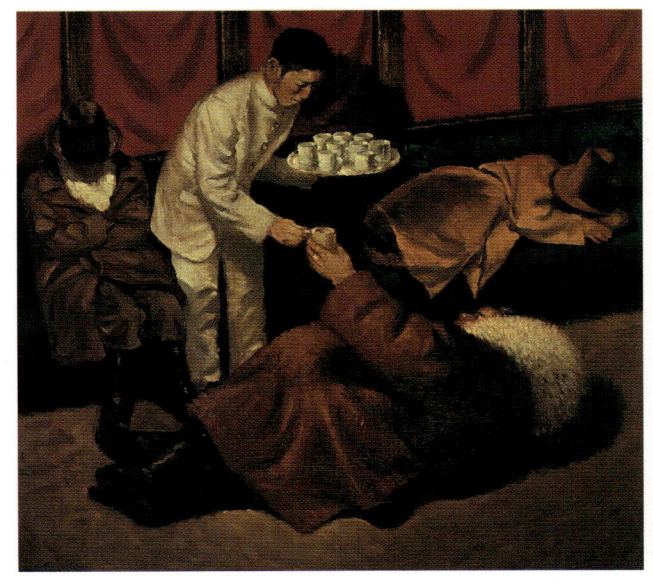

BOOKS

1 (series)
Gary Kelley, illustrator
Rita Marshall, art director
Louise Fili, designer
Louise Fili Ltd., design firm
Creative Editions, client

Rip Van Winkle. Various sizes, pastel on paper.

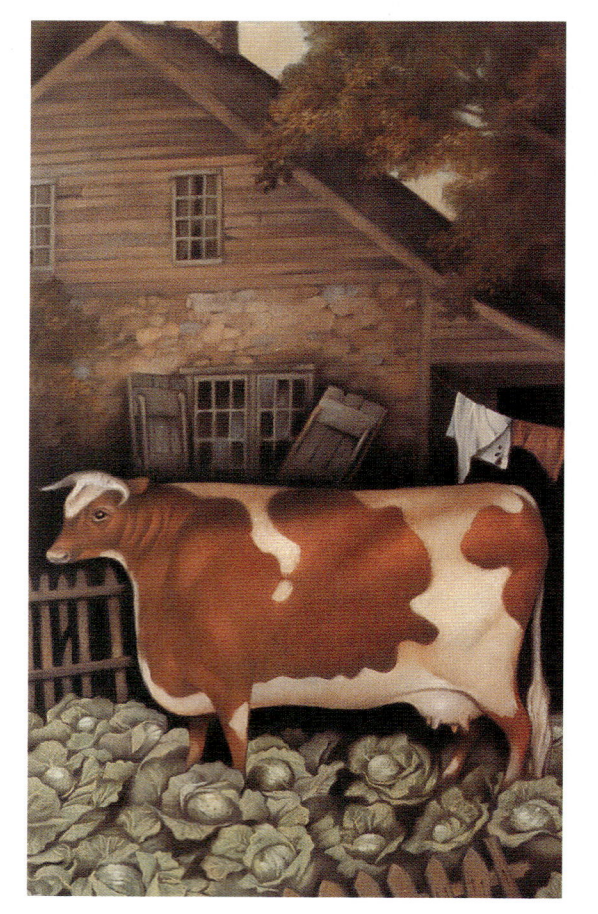

COMMUNICATION ARTS 45

BOOKS

1
Pol Turgeon, illustrator
Michael Accordino, art director/designer
St. Martin's Press, client

Cover of *Unsolicited*, a detective story set in the London literary milieu. 10¾ x 16, ink, gouache, pastel, colored pencils, oil, varnish and collage.

2 (series)
Edward S. Gazsi, illustrator
Laura Geringer, editor
HarperCollins Publishers, client

Children's book, *Kimbo's Marble*. At birth, Princess Kimbo, a girl of great spirit and independence, is given a magic marble and with it the gift of understanding the language of animals. 7 x 7, acrylic.

COMMUNICATION ARTS 47

1

Books

1
Eric Dinyer, illustrator
David Tran, art director
Oxford University Press, client

Book jacket. *Goddess* is a rich and respectful introduction to the archetypal figure, Goddess, as she has emerged in myth and belief from prehistory to the present. 8½ x 11½, mixed media, digital.

2
Chris A. Gall, illustrator
Julia Kushnirsky, art director
Warner Books, client

Cover of *Borderlines*, one from the series of Joe Gunther detective mysteries set in Vermont. Arson ignites tension between cultists and townspeople. 7 x 12, scratchboard and dyes.

3
Scott Menchin, illustrator/designer
Steve Brower, art director
Carol Publishing, client

History of Witchcraft cover. 5 x 8, pen and ink and photography.

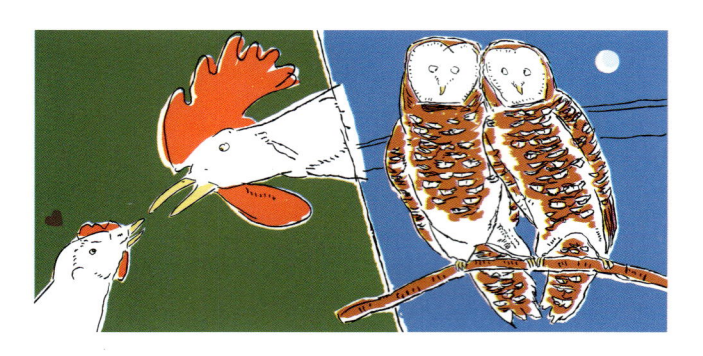

1

Books

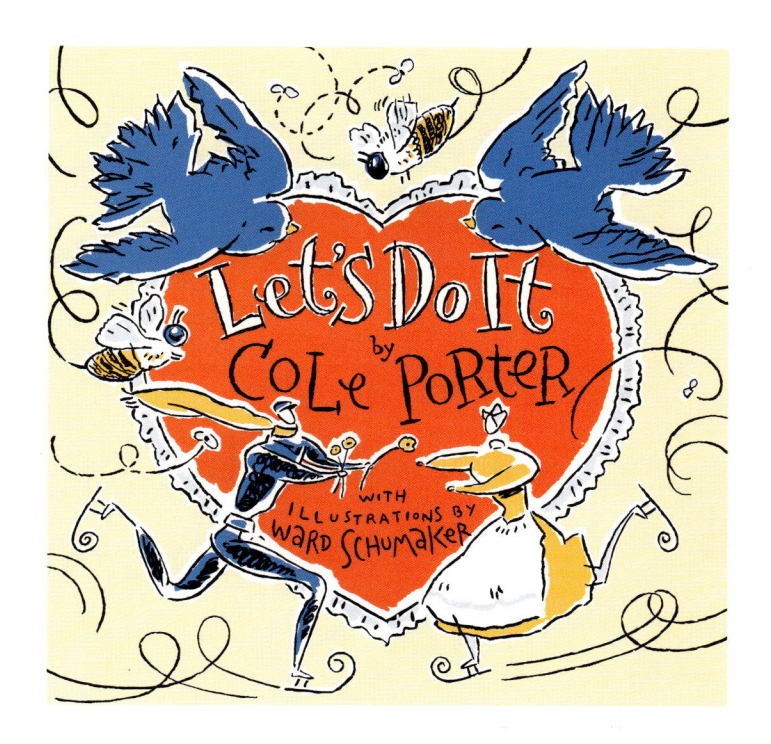

1 (series)
Ward Schumaker, illustrator
Michael Carabetta, art director
Gretchen Scoble, designer
Chronicle Books, client

Cover and spreads from *Let's Do It*, a book based on the Cole Porter song. Various sizes, ink on tissue on acetate.

2
Cathleen Toelke, illustrator
Georgia Morrissey, art director
Ballantine Books, Random House, client

Cover of *Daughters of the House*. In rural India, three self-sustaining women struggle with love and loyalties when a man enters their lives. 7½ x 11, gouache.

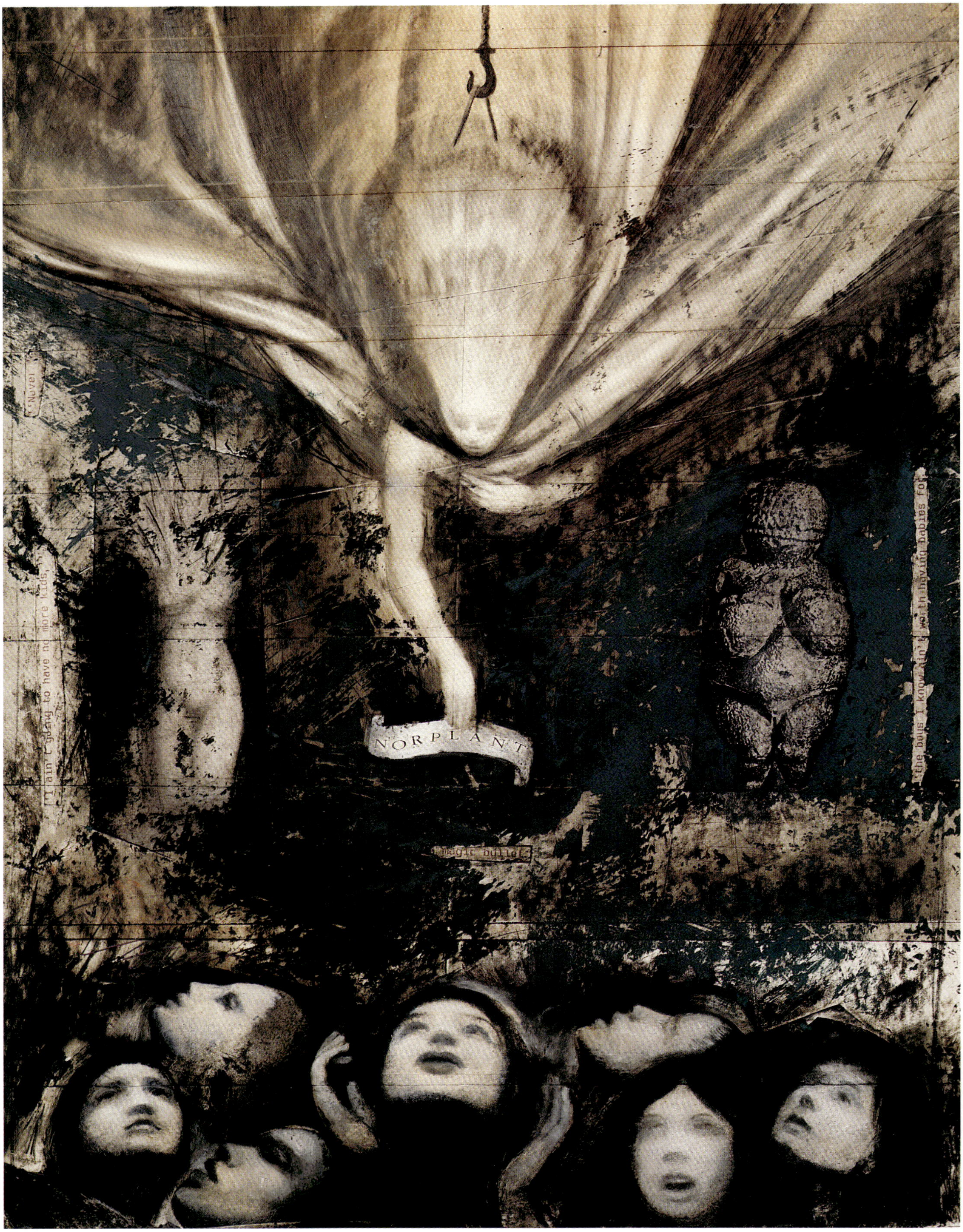

Editorial

1
Greg Spalenka, illustrator
Nancy Duckworth, art director
Los Angeles Times Magazine, client

Article on Norplant, a controversial contraceptive drug. 12 x 18, mixed media.

2
Glynis Sweeny, illustrator
Fred Woodward, art director
Debra Bishop, designer
Rolling Stone, client

"Jackson's Dangerous Game," the self-crowned King of Pop ruled on prime time, but did we get the truth? 9 x 12, Prismacolor pencil.

3
John Craig, illustrator
John Lyle Sanford, art director
Destination Discovery, client

Article on artificial intelligence, "It Thinks, Therefore It Is." 12 x 11, collage to film with overlays.

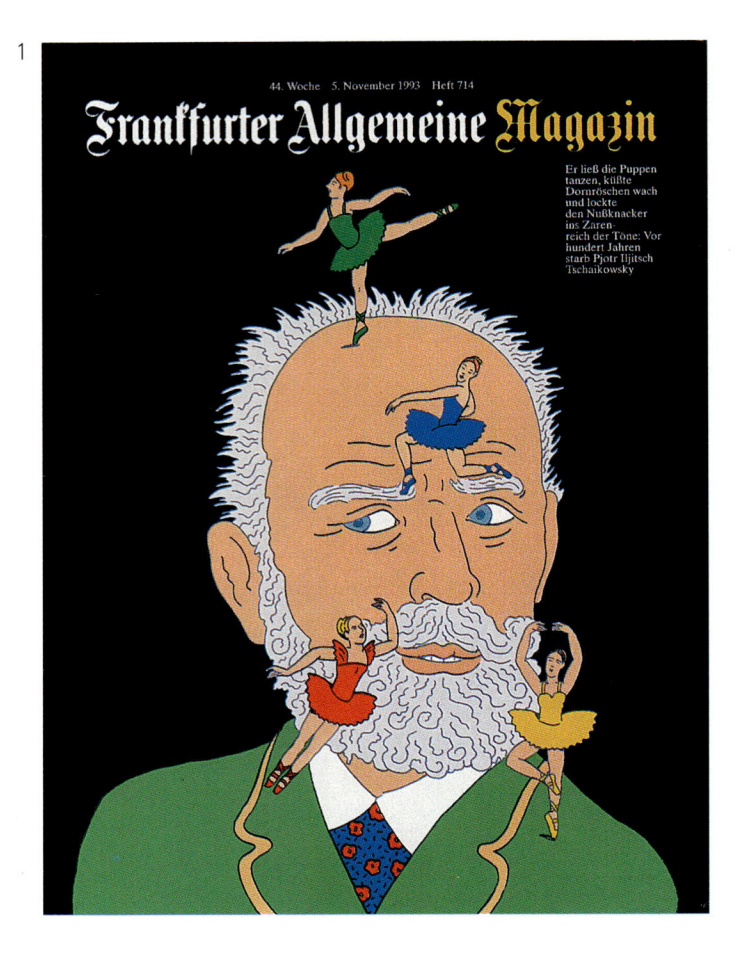

EDITORIAL

1 (series)
Seymour Chwast, illustrator
Hans-Georg Pospischil, art director
Frankfurter Allgemeine Magazin, client

Article on the anniversary of Peter Tchaikovsky's death. Various sizes, Celotak.

2
Courtney Granner, illustrator
Richard Leeds, art director
Keyboard, client

Magazine article on coming to terms with the critic within oneself, "Slings & Arrows." 7 x 11, gouache.

3
Carter Goodrich, illustrator
Richard Steadham, art director
Governing, client

Cover of a magazine for states and localities, "Can the Press Be Tamed?" 13¼ x 16¼, colored pencil and watercolor.

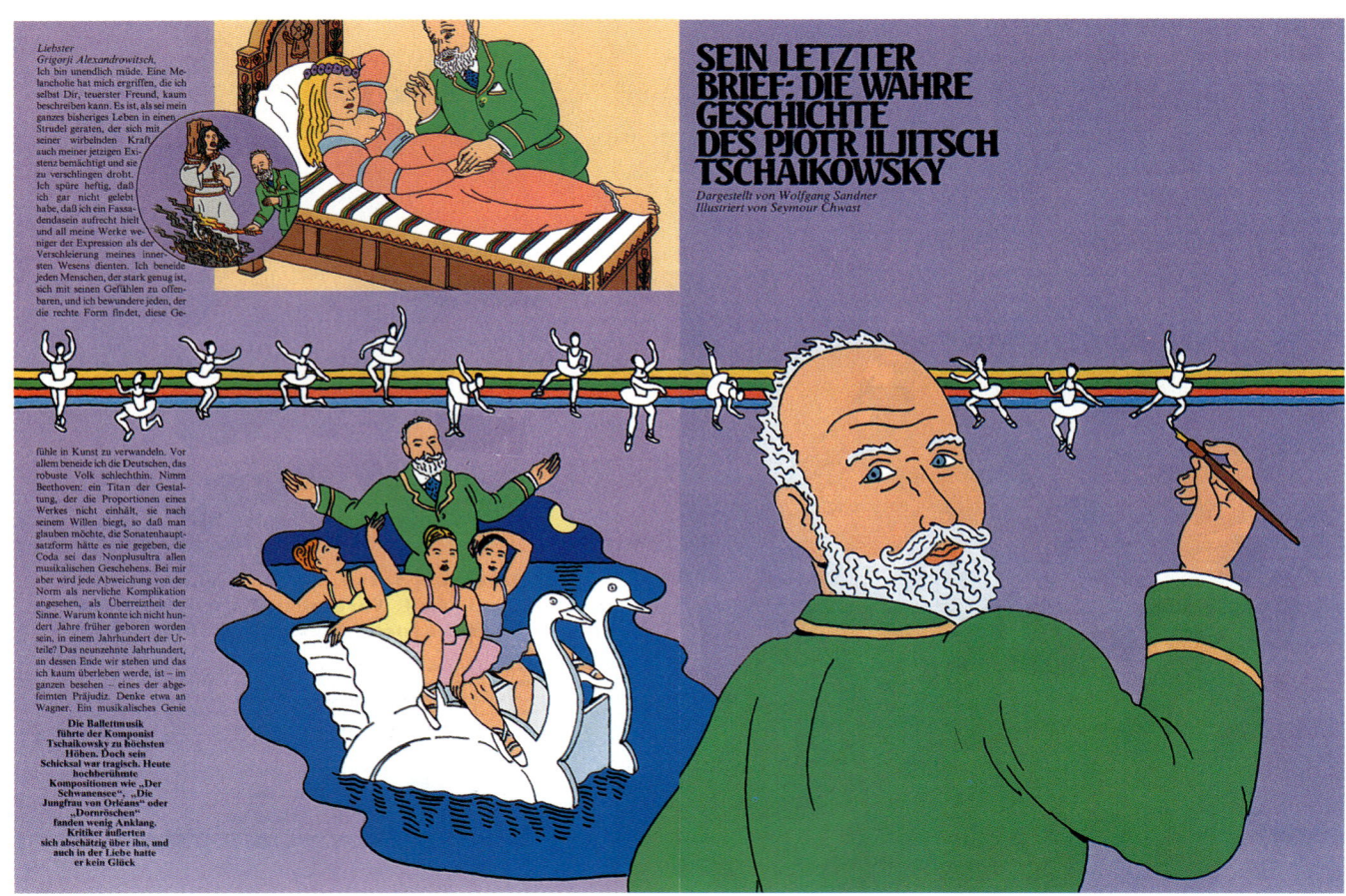

2

3

COMMUNICATION ARTS 55

1

Editorial

1
Rob Day, illustrator
John Plunkett, art director
Wired, client

Portrait of Jaron Lanier, pioneer of virtual reality. 11 x 13, oil on paper.

2
Philippe Lardy, illustrator
Patricia Bradbury, art director
Doris Jewett, designer
Newsweek, client

The latest research from physicists may reveal where the smallest particles in the universe came from. 4 x 7, watercolor and ink.

3
Jack Unruh, illustrator
Joseph Connolly, art director/designer
Boy's Life, Boy Scouts of America, client

First in a series of magazine articles on the American Indian. 25 x 18, mixed media.

EDITORIAL

1 (series)
Skip Liepke, illustrator
David Cuccurito, art director/designer
Penthouse, client

Paintings for an ongoing series of articles on erotica. Various sizes, oil.

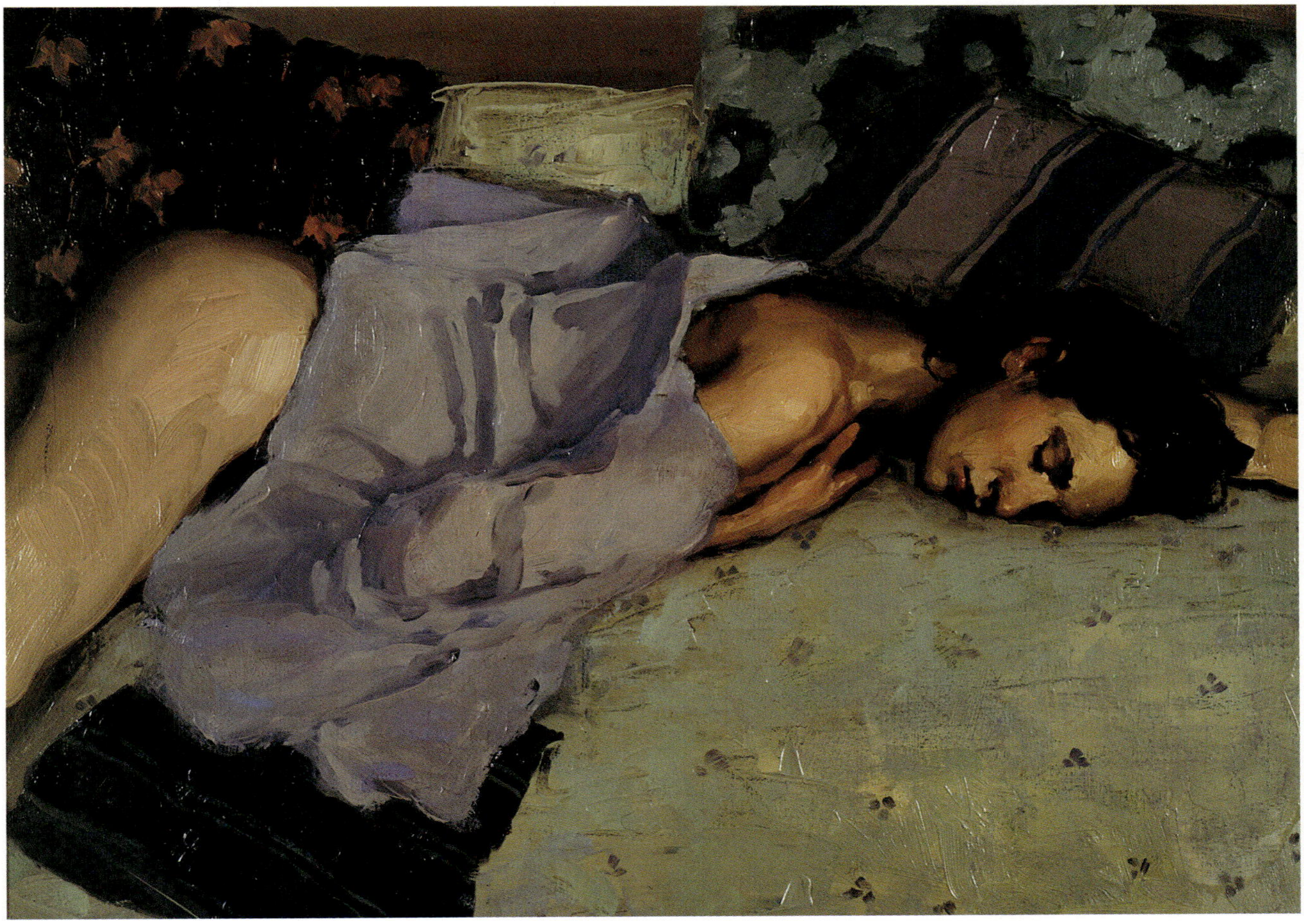

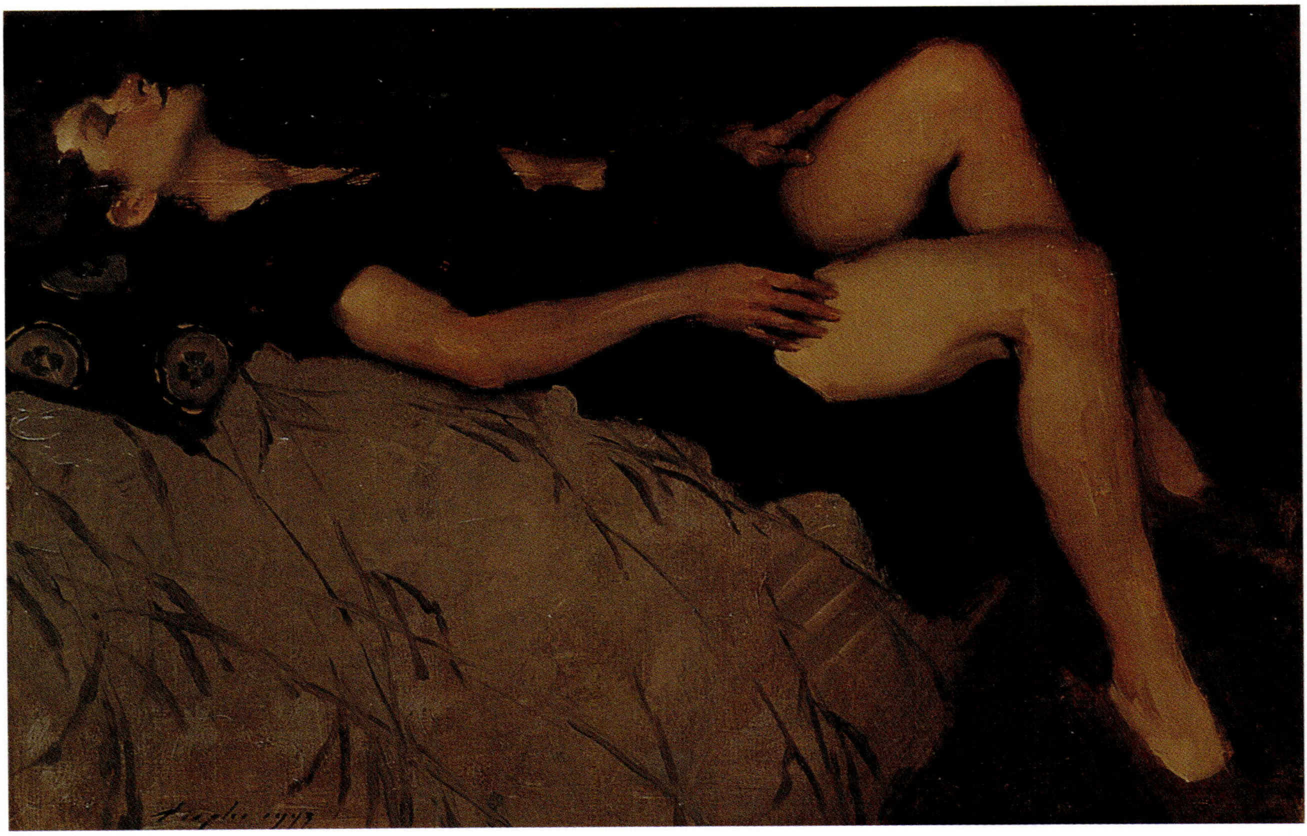

EDITORIAL

1
Richard Thompson, illustrator
Marty Barrick, art director
The Washington Post, client

Cover for national weekly section, titled "That Pesky Perot."

2
Marshall Arisman, illustrator
Tom Staebler, art director
Playboy, client

Magazine article about Catholic priests being arrested for pedophilia, "Sins of the Fathers." 28 x 23, oil on ragboard.

3
Alan E. Cober, illustrator
Fred Woodward, art director
Rolling Stone, client

Movie review of *Carlito's Way* starring Al Pacino.

3

1
2
3

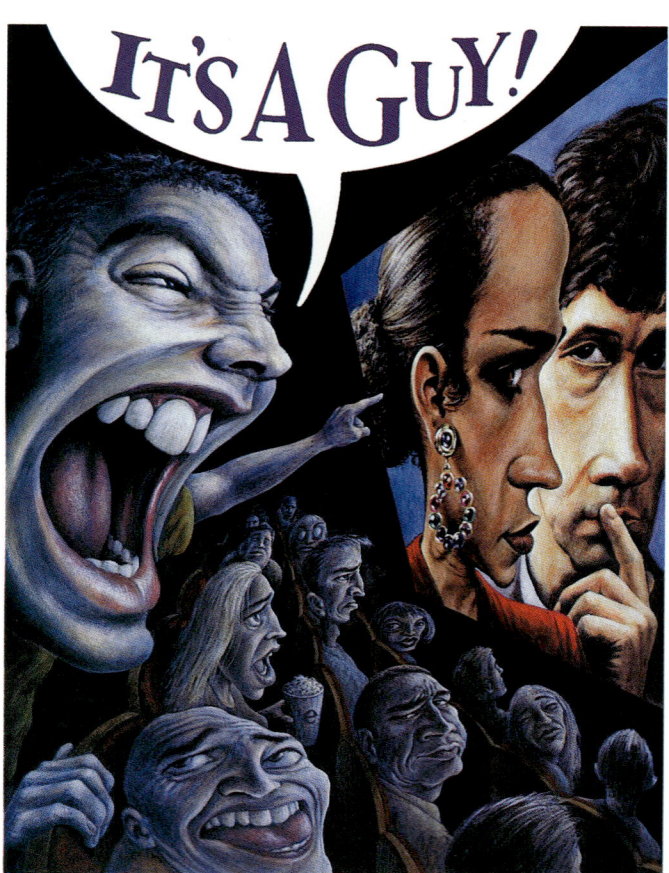

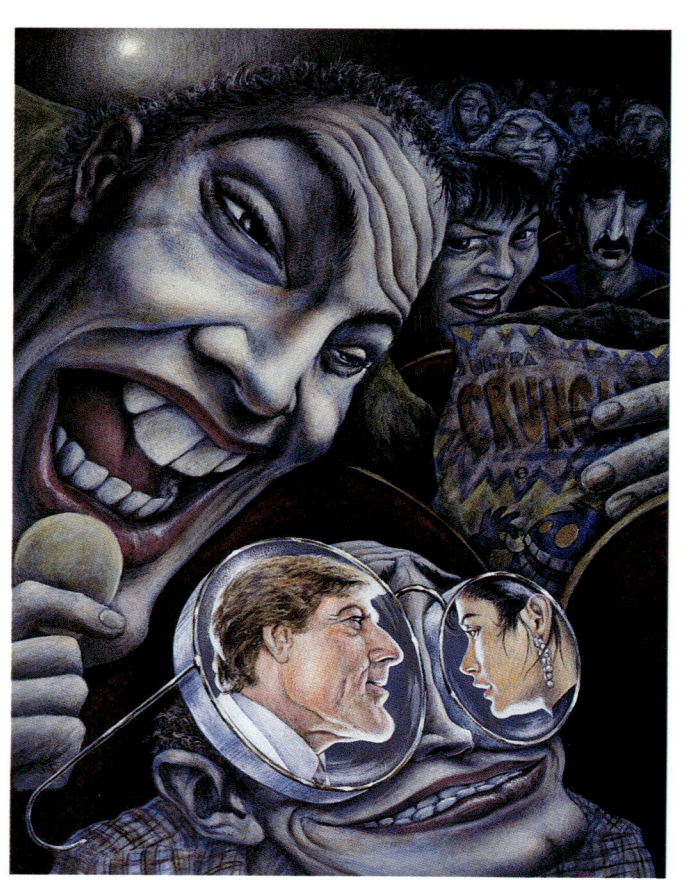

EDITORIAL

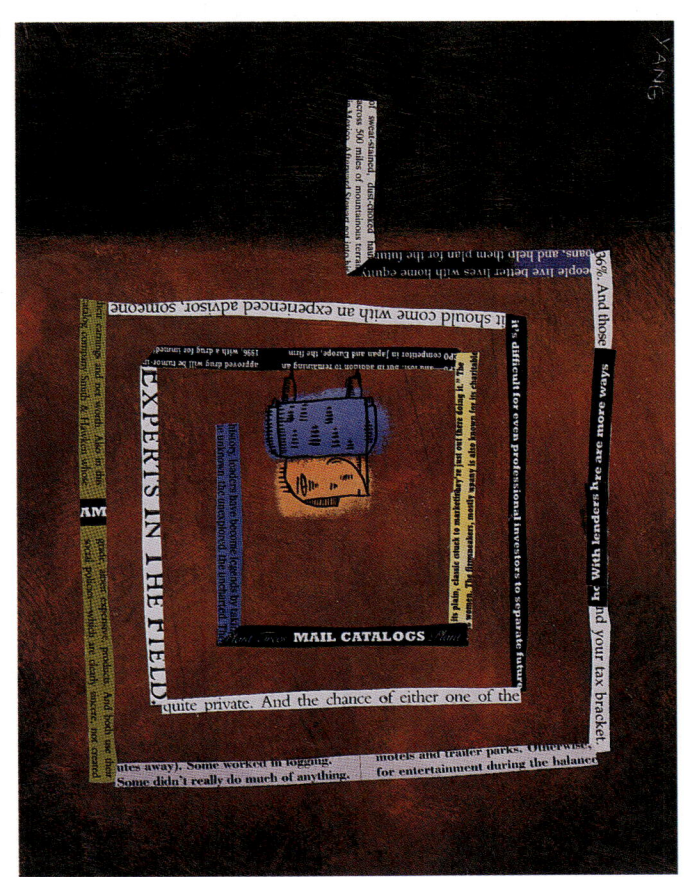

1
Robert Andrew Parker, illustrator
Laura Frank/Allison Martin, art directors
World Monitor, client

Magazine illustration. 18 x 20, monoprint and watercolor.

2
Mirko Ilíc, illustrator
Wayne N. Fitzpatrick, art director
Emerge, client

"The First Amendment: Friend and Sometimes Foe," magazine editorial about freedom of speech and racism. 12 x 15, colored scratchboard.

3 (series)
Eric White, illustrator
Alex Alexander/Kevin Robie, art directors
Movieline, client

Magazine article, "Confessions of a Cineplex Heckler." 9 x 12, acrylic on board.

4
Andrea Ventura, illustrator
Chris Curry, art director
The New Yorker, client

Magazine article on writer Nathan McCall. 10 x 14, charcoal and acrylic on paper.

5
James Yang, illustrator
Ron Stucki, art director
Wordperfect Publishing, client

Magazine illustration, "Terrific Text Borders." 8½ x 11, acrylic, collage and ink.

1

Editorial

1
Gary Kelley, illustrator
Ron McClellen, art director/designer
Iowa City Magazine, client

Story about a woman playing jazz in a man's world, "Mama Played First Chair." 14 x 19, pastel on paper.

2
Richard Downs, illustrator
David Armario, art director
David Armario Design, design firm
Stanford Medicine, client

Office of Communications magazine article, "Gene Jocks & Docs." 13½ x 13½, mixed media.

3
Joe Sorren, illustrator
Scott Clum, art director/designer
ride design, design firm
Bikini, client

Magazine portrait of The Velvet Underground for an article about their brief reunion, "The Velvets—What Happened?" 30 x 30, acrylic on canvas.

1

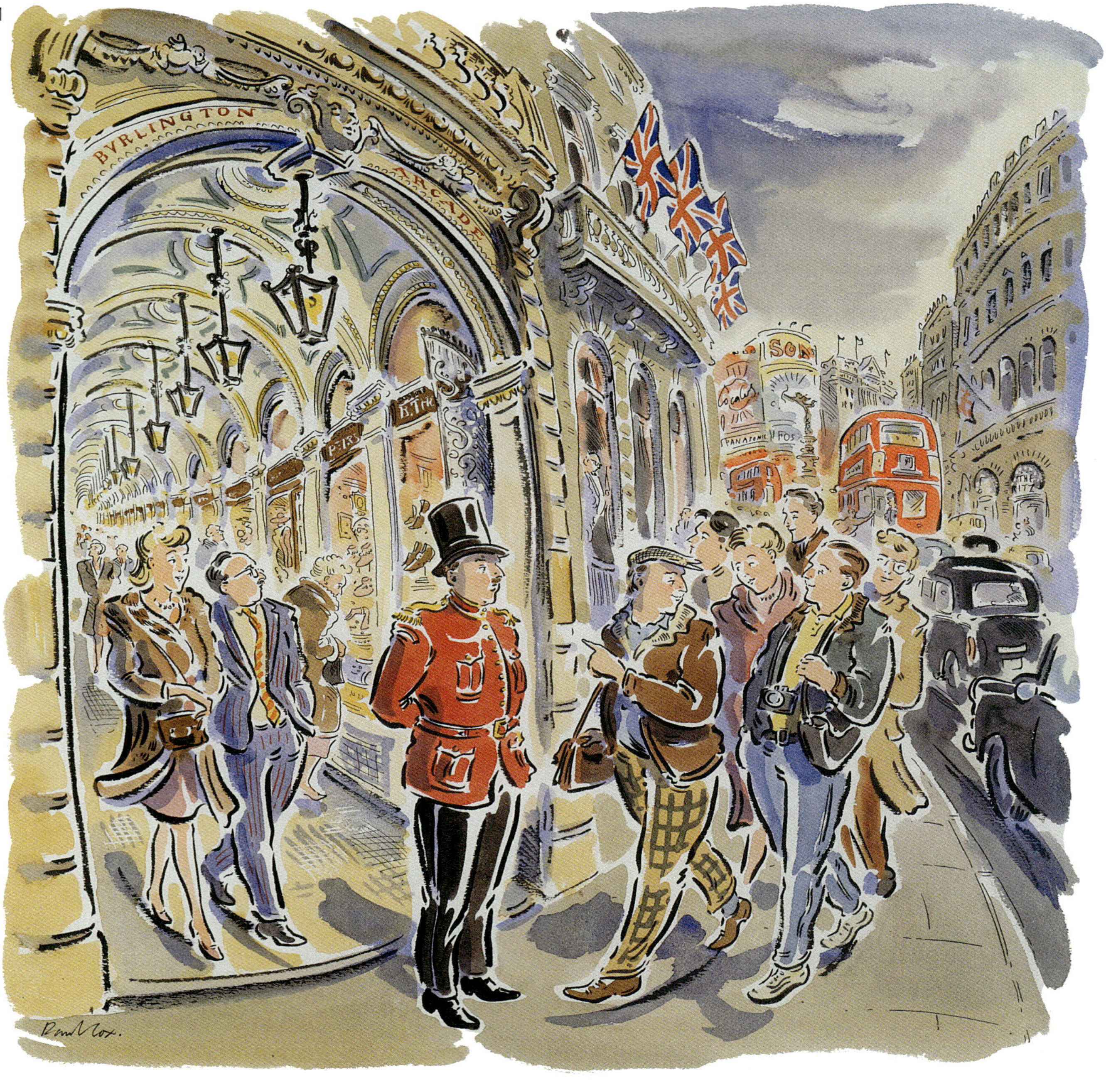

Editorial

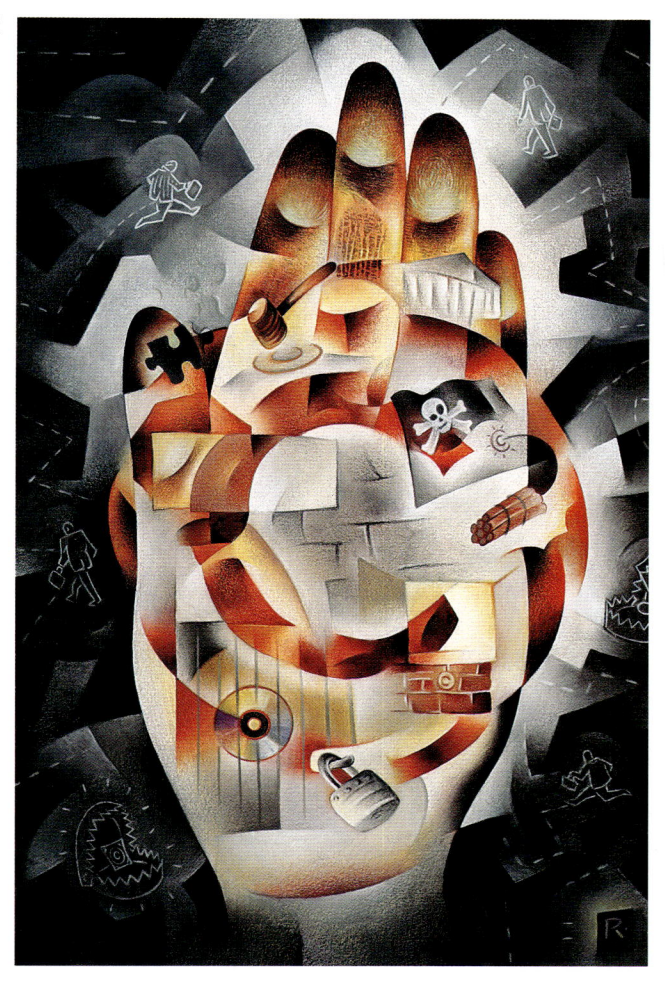

1
Paul Cox, illustrator
Mike Grinley, art director
Walking Magazine, client

Article, "The Changing of the Guides." It's royalty today, the Ripper tomorrow. The best way to see London is through the eyes of its walking tour guides. 23 x 22, watercolor.

2
Robert M. Pastrana, illustrator
Nancy Cutler, art director
NewMedia, client

Magazine article, "Rights of Passage," about the complexity and confusion of multimedia copyright law and the caution software developers must take to avoid getting into legal trouble.
10½ x 15¾, watercolor and colored pencil.

3
Jeffrey Fisher, illustrator
Joe Dizney, art director
SmartMoney, client

Magazine article, "Confused About Insurance." 8 x 10, watercolor.

1

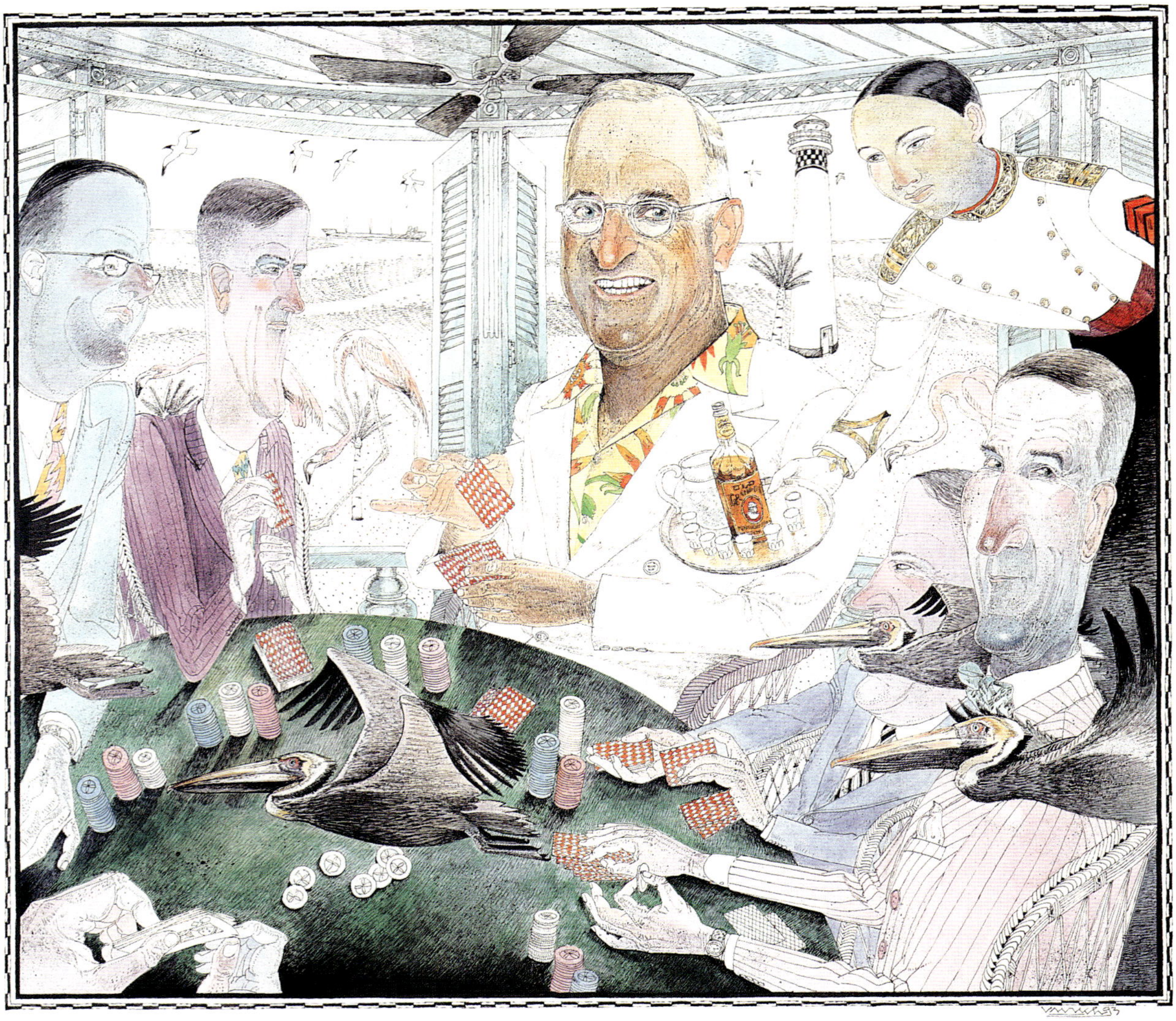

2

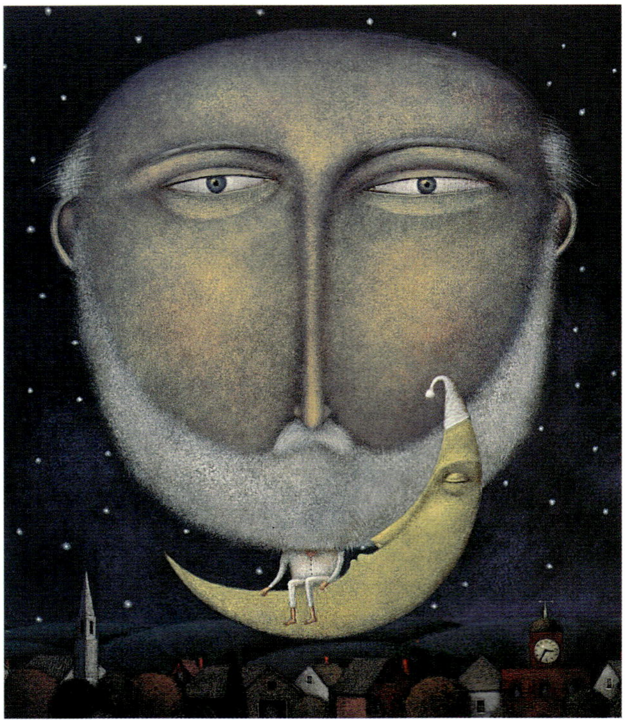

3

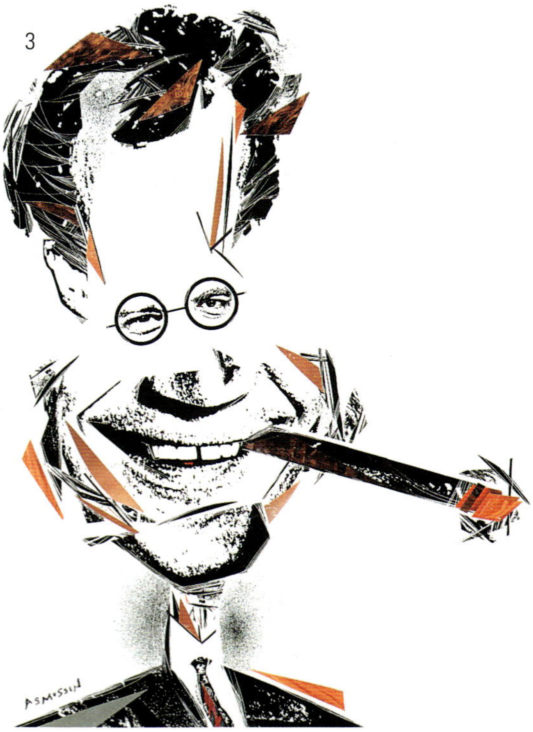

EDITORIAL

1
Jack Unruh, illustrator
Albert Chiang, art director
Islands, client

Magazine excerpt of *Key West Tales* by John Hersey, a collection of historical and contemporary stories set on that Florida island. "A Little Paperwork" concerns President Harry Truman. 16 x 14½, ink and watercolor.

2
Tom Curry, illustrator
J. Porter, art director/designer
Yankee Magazine, client

Article, "The Man Who Never Slept." 12½ x 13½, acrylic on hardboard.

3
Don Asmussen, illustrator
Dolores Motichka, art director/designer
The Washington Times, client

Portrait of David Letterman, "The King of Late Night." 14 x 20, pen, ink and collage.

4
Randy Lyhus, illustrator
John Anderson, Jr., art director/designer
The Washington Post, client

Business section grades lending practices, "Good Bank, Bad Bank." 6⅝ x 6⅝, scratchboard.

5
Peter de Sève, illustrator
Françoise Mouly, art director
The New Yorker, client

Cover. 14 x 17, watercolor and ink.

Editorial

1
Nigel Buchanan, illustrator
Tim Donnellan, art director
Australian Penthouse, client

Article about the lack of funding for male health issues in Australia, "Men's Health." 7 x 9, gouache.

2 (series)
Normand Cousineau, illustrator
Tony Chambers, art director
The Sunday Times Magazine, client

Each week the magazine runs "Bookwise," a literary quiz with a different theme. This question was: Can you name these female impersonators? In which books do they appear? *The Shadow*; *My Time With Rosie*; *Hugh MacDiarmid, The Complete Poems*; *How I Became a Holy Mother*; *Sir Lancelot, Morte d'Arthur*. 5½ x 6, ink and gouache.

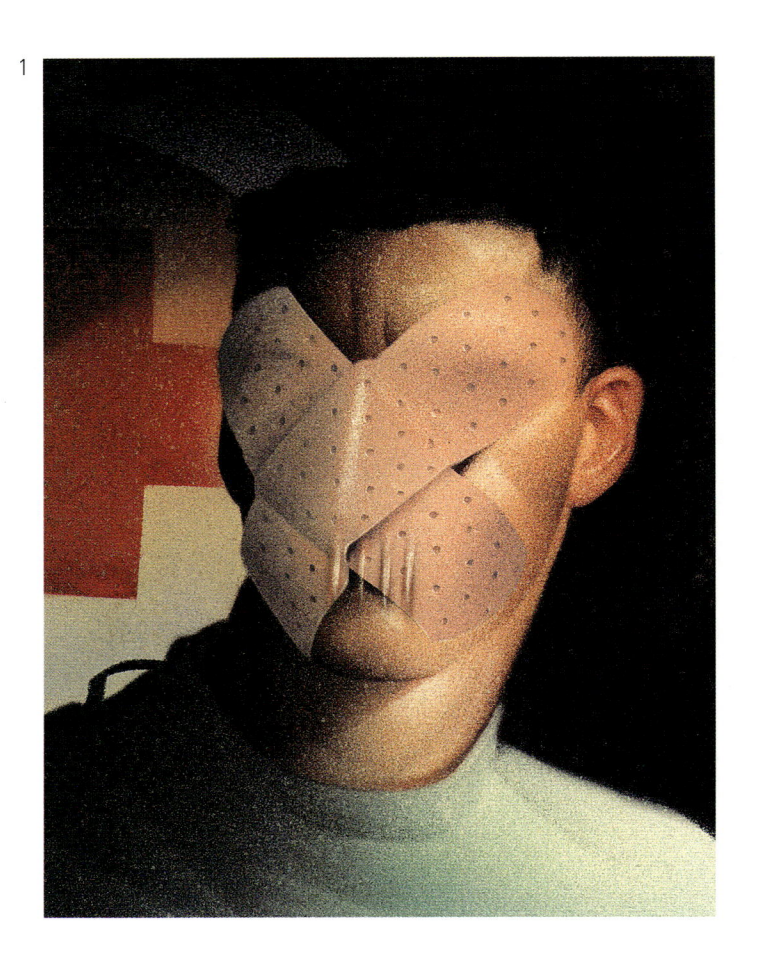

COMMUNICATION ARTS 71

EDITORIAL

1
Philip Burke, illustrator
Fred Woodward, art director
Rolling Stone, client

Portrait of Run of Run-D.M.C. on table of contents page. 40 x 72, acrylic.

2
William Burgard, illustrator
Kristen Finn, art director
University of Michigan Medical Center, client

Advance cover article examining minority health care. 19 x 24, charcoal.

3
Philippe Lardy, illustrator
Fred Woodward, art director
Rolling Stone, client

Record review of New Order's album. 6 x 10½, watercolor and ink.

4
Gary Kelley, illustrator
Judy Garlan, art director/designer
Atlantic Monthly, client

Fiction by Garrison Keillor, "Don Giovanni." Figaro and the Don debate marriage at a piano bar in Fargo. 21 x 14, pastel on paper.

2

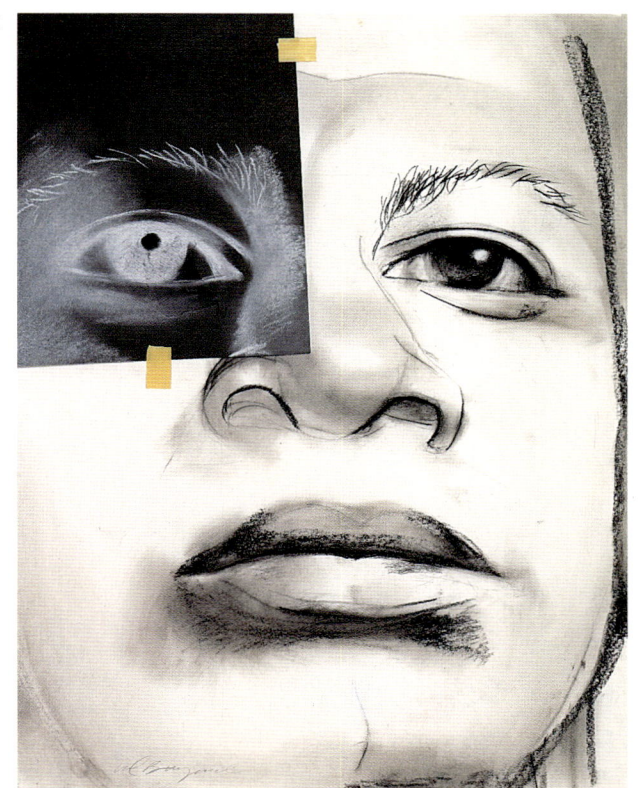

3

4

COMMUNICATION ARTS

EDITORIAL

1
Calef Brown, illustrator
Chris Curry, art director
The New Yorker, client

"Night Life" section. 5½ x 9½, acrylic and oil.

2
Andrea Ventura, illustrator
Chris Curry, art director
The New Yorker, client

Portrait of guitarist David Starobin in the "Goings On About Town" section. 15 x 15, charcoal and acrylic on paper.

3
Robert Crawford, illustrator
Susan McClellan, art director/designer
Harrowsmith/Country Life, client

Article about food co-ops in small towns, "Side Stepping the Supermarket." 12 x 17, acrylic.

COMMUNICATION ARTS 75

1

Editorial

1
Pete Spino, illustrator
Christina Hansen, art director/designer
Alaska Magazine, client

Book excerpt, *Johnny's Girl: A Daughter's Memoir of Growing Up in Alaska's Underworld.* 8½ x 7⅝, gouache and colored pencil.

2
Jeffrey Fisher, illustrator
Linda Brewer, art director
The New York Times, client

Summer Arts section "Events & Festivals." 12¾ x 18, ink on paper.

3
Gary Kelley, illustrator
Andrew Kner, art director
Print, client

Magazine cover art. 16 x 24, pastel on paper.

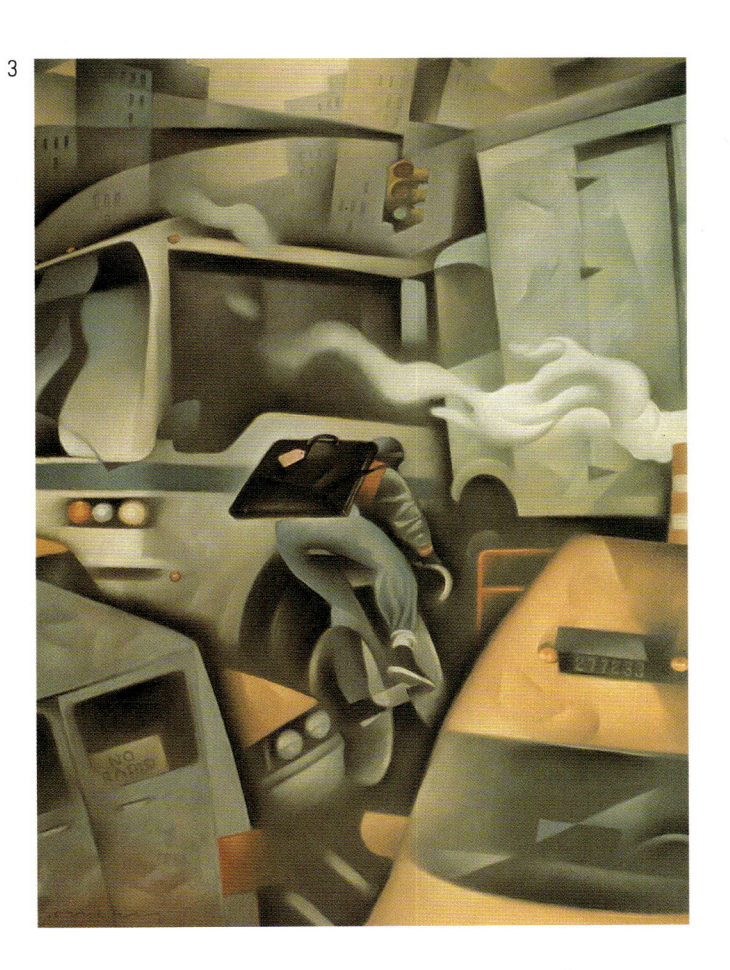

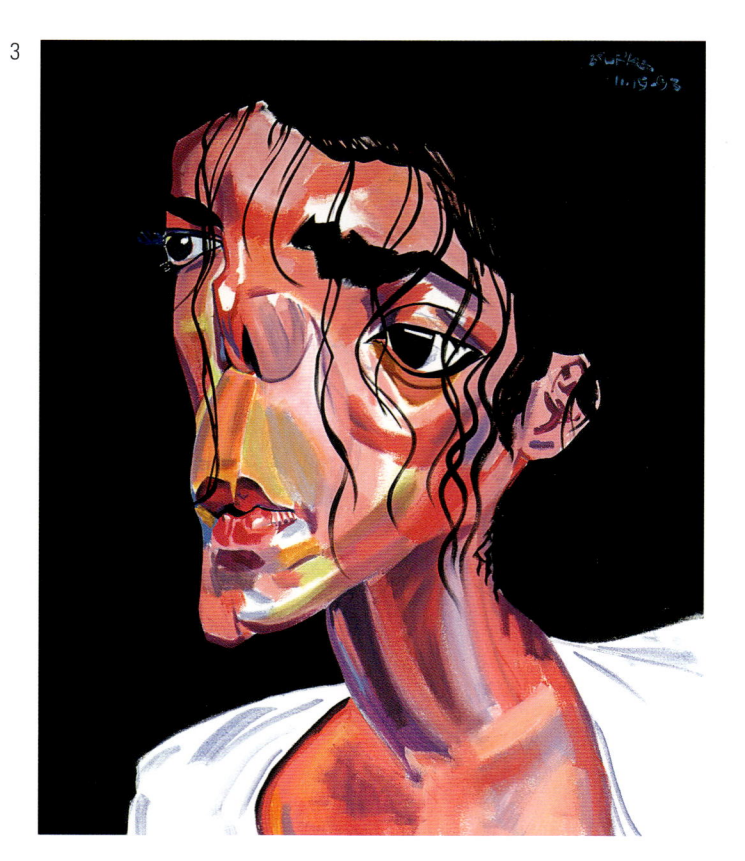

1

2

3

4

Editorial

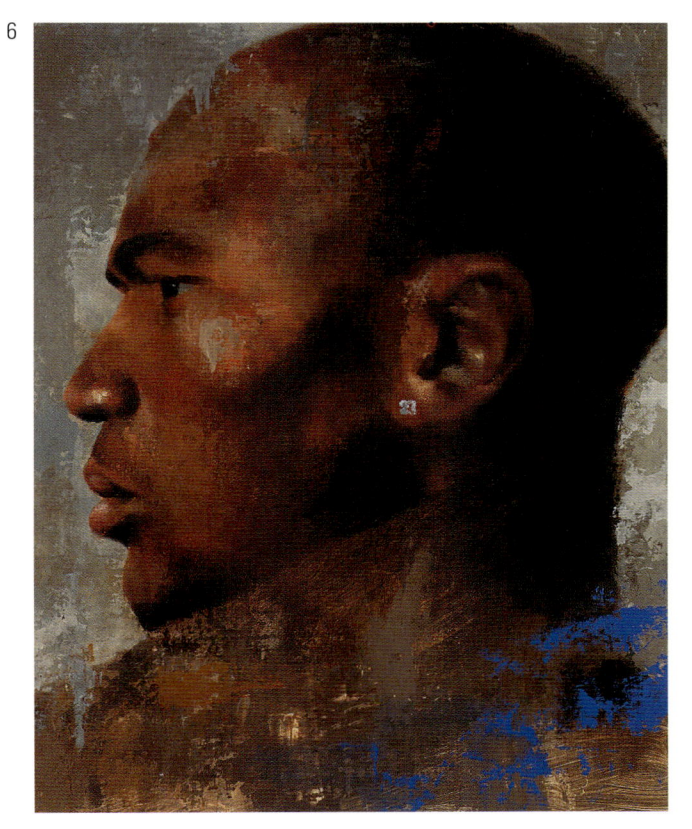

1
Jordin Isip, illustrator
Florian Bachleda, art director
The Village Voice, client

Article, "Shooting an Elephant." 11⅞ x 13½, mixed media.

2
Gary Taxali, illustrator
Kristi Anderson, art director
Utne Reader, client

Article concerning the ethics of giving growth hormones to short youngsters, "Do Short Guys Finish Last?" 19 x 24, alkyd on Masonite.

3
Philip Burke, illustrator
Rudolph C. Hoglund/Kenneth Smith, art directors
Time, client

In the spotlight: Michael Jackson, nowhere to be found and everywhere gossiped about, fights drug addiction and an intensifying probe of sex-abuse charges against him. 30 x 40, oil on canvas.

4
Benoît Van Innis, illustrator
Françoise Mouly, art director
The New Yorker, client

Artist's Easel, "Boo." 11½ x 16, oil.

5
Barry Blitt, illustrator
Rudolph C. Hoglund/Paul Lussier, art directors
Time, client

How a sixteen-year-old stole a train and the hearts of New Yorkers, "The Great A Train Robbery." 2½ x 4, pen, ink and watercolor.

6
Brad Holland, illustrator
Giovanni Russo, art director
Men's Journal, client

"Flying on Empty: The Midcareer Refueling of Michael Jordan." 16 x 20, acrylic on Masonite.

EDITORIAL

1
Peter de Sève, illustrator
Françoise Mouly, art director
The New Yorker, client

Cover. 14 x 17, watercolor and ink.

2
Eric Dinyer, illustrator
Lucy Bartholomay, art director
The Boston Globe Magazine, client

Article titled "Men Who Batter Their Wives." 10 x 12, mixed media, digital.

3
Henrik Drescher, illustrator
D.J. Stout, art director/designer
Texas Monthly, client

Article titled "David Koresh and the Myth of the Alamo." Perhaps the long cult standoff could have happened anywhere, but there are unsettling reasons why it happened in Texas. 12 x 12, collage.

3

1

Editorial

1
Joseph Salina, illustrator
Carmen Dunjko, art director
Scott Gibbs, designer
Joseph Salina Illustrated Inc., design firm
Saturday Night, client

Fiction piece about the social and psychological trauma of a family in postwar Europe, "Family Portrait." 10 x 12¾, acrylic and oil glaze.

2
David Wilcox, illustrator
Tom Staebler, art director
Kristin Korjenek, designer
Playboy, client

Article concerning shutting down the Pentagon and unifying our current military branches into a single service, "Nuke the Pentagon." 20 x 20, casein on hardboard.

3
Mike Benny, illustrator
Tom Staebler, art director
Kerig Pope, designer
Playboy, client

Article, "To Live & Die in L.A." by Ice-T. 18 x 18, acrylic.

FOR SALE

1 (series)
Scott Gustafson, illustrator
Lauren Guttenberg, art director
The Bradford Exchange, client

Series of collector's plates based on Lewis Carroll's *Alice in Wonderland*: Advice From a Caterpillar, A Mad Tea Party, The Queen's Croquet Ground. 26 x 32, oil.

COMMUNICATION ARTS 85

1

For Sale

1
Barbara Banthien, illustrator
The Nature Company, client

Limited edition print and Christmas greeting card. 6 x 10, watercolor and colored pencil.

2
James Gurney, illustrator
David Usher, art director/president
The Greenwich Workshop, Inc., client

Limited edition print. 24 x 36, oil on canvas.

3
Fletcher Sibthorp, illustrator/designer
Phillip Arnott/Fletcher Sibthorp, art directors
Stable Gallery, client

48 x 34, oil and pastel on canvas.

1

For Sale

1 (series)
Mark A. Fredrickson, illustrator
Marna Henley, art director
Mead Products, client

No-Rules portfolio folders for school children.
20 x 30, acrylic.

For Sale

1 (series)
Jan Waddell, illustrator
Malcolm Waddell, designer
Eskind Waddell, design firm
Canada Post Corporation, client

Postage stamp illustrations. 6 x 3½, watercolor, digital manipulation.

2 (series)
Braldt Bralds, illustrator
Rocco Callari, art director
United Nations Postal Administration, design/client

Stamps picturing climate. 28 x 7, oil on Masonite.

2

COMMUNICATION ARTS 91

1

92 ILLUSTRATION ANNUAL 1994

For Sale

1 (series)
Mark Hess, illustrator/designer
Dick Sheaff, art director
Hess Design Works, design firm
United States Postal Service, client

Block of four stamps: Buffalo Bill, Sacagawea, Bill Pickett and Jim Bridger. 4 x 5¼, acrylic and oil on canvas.

2
Gregory Manchess, illustrator
Tricia Manchess, art director
Manchess Illustration, client

"Snow Angel" note card. 26 x 34, oil on canvas.

3
Dugald Stermer, illustrator/designer
Leslee Avchen, art director
Woof Productions, client

Poster for sale to Irish Terrier fanciers. 24 x 36, pencil and watercolor on Arches Paper.

INSTITUTIONAL

1
Becky Heavner, illustrator
Linda Brown/Margaret Georgiann, art directors
Tim Cook, designer
National Institutes of Health, client

Poster announcing a conference on the effect of corticosteroids for fetal maturation on perinatal outcomes. 14 x 20, digital.

2
Rene Milot, illustrator
Tom Lennon, art director
Dorritie Lyons & Nickel, Inc., ad agency
Pfizer Animal Health Group, client

Brochure illustration directed to veterinarians. 20 x 15, oil on canvas.

3
Simón Silva, illustrator
Juan Silverio Gonzalez, art director/designer
Don Juan Productions, design
Mexican American Legal Defense & Education Fund, client

Poster. 20 x 28, gouache.

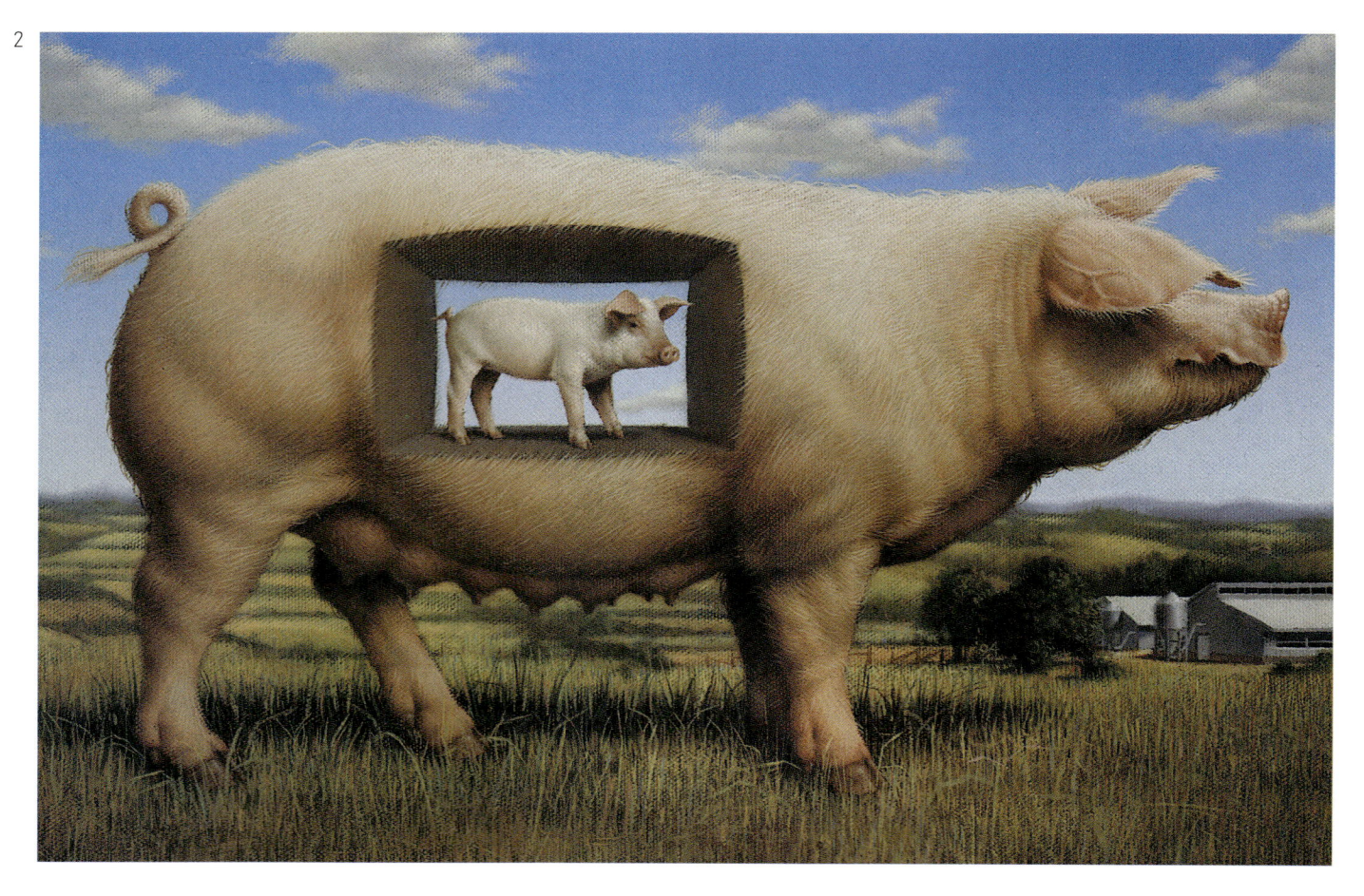

3

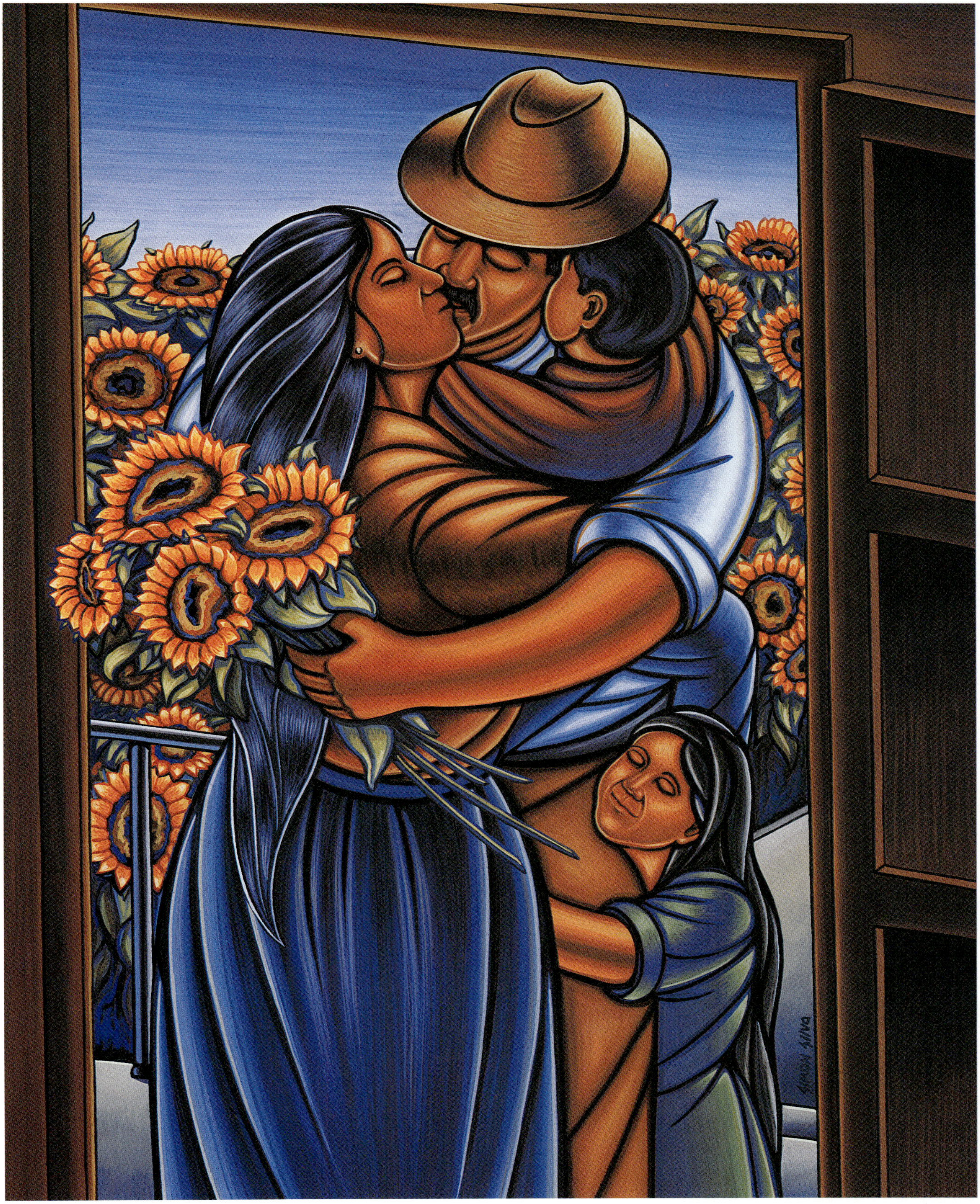

INSTITUTIONAL

1 (series)
R.M. Kato, illustrator
Mary Ruggieri, art director/designer
Joseph A. Wetzel Associates, Inc., design firm
The Florida Aquarium, client

Five from a series of 200 illustrations of the various species in the forested wetlands section of the aquarium. Various sizes, ink.

2
Seymour Chwast, illustrator/designer
Robert Putz, art director
The German Post Office, client

Poster to promote the post office. 15 x 20, Celotak.

3
Albert Rocarols, illustrator/art director/designer
O.E.P.L.I., client

Poster announcing Children's Book Week, 14½ x 19½, acrylic on paper.

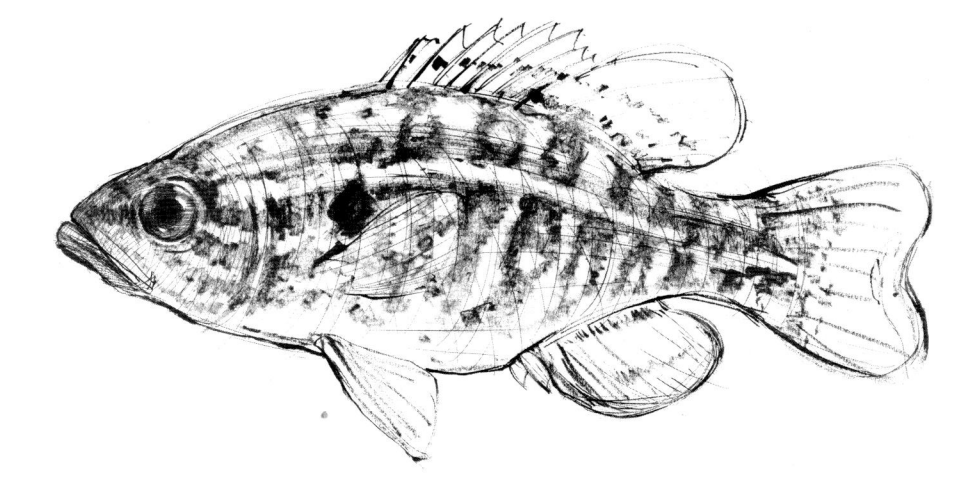

2

3

COMMUNICATION ARTS 97

1

INSTITUTIONAL

1 (series)
Brad Holland, illustrator
Claudia Brambilla, art director
J. Walter Thompson Italia S.p.A., ad agency
Ansaldo, client

Annual report. 11 x 14½, acrylic on Masonite.

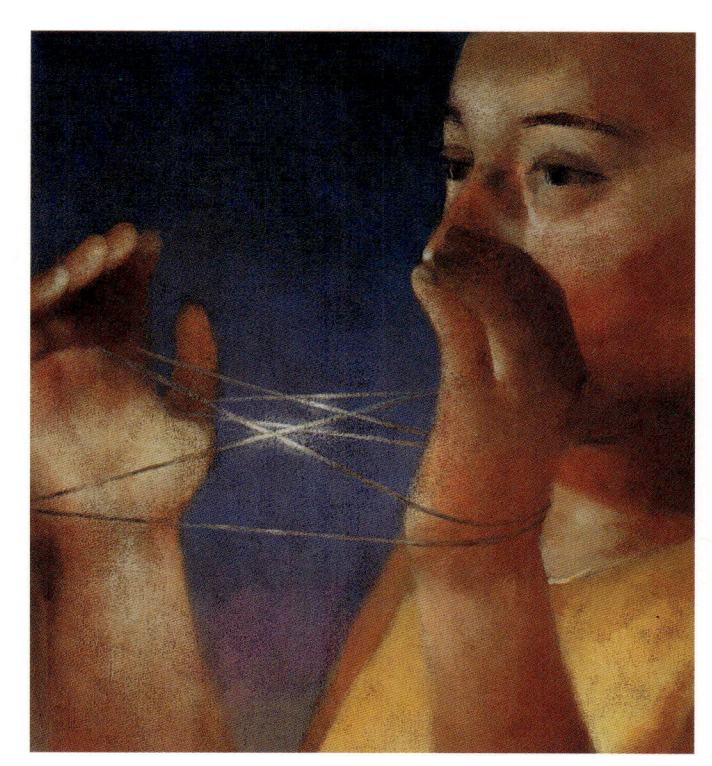

1

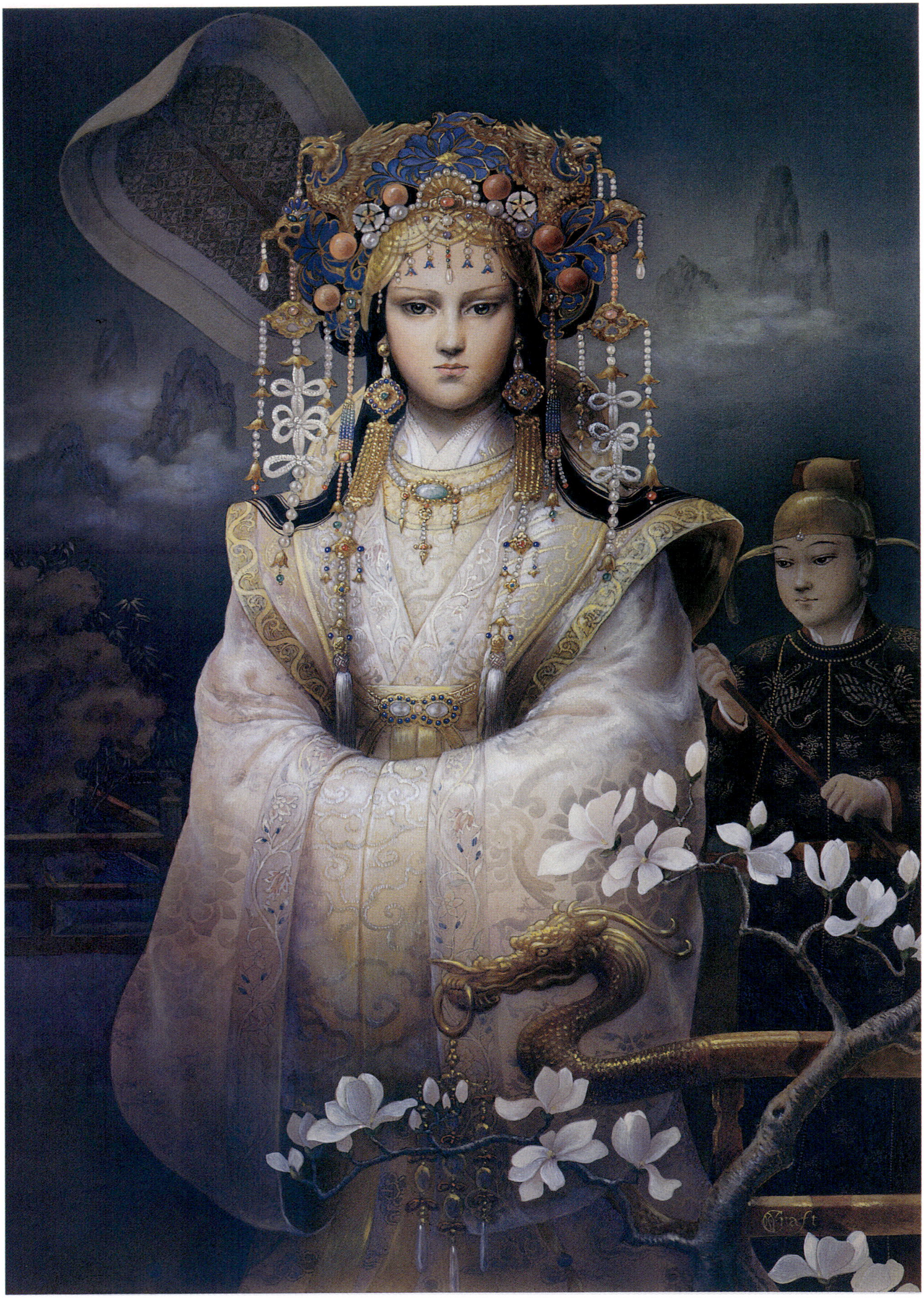

Institutional

1 (series)
Kinuko Y. Craft, illustrator
Douglas May/Clay Freeman, art directors
Clay Freeman, designer
May & Co., Inc., design firm
The Washington Opera Co., client

Promotional brochure and posters showing *Turandot*, *Carmen*, *Manon Lescaut* and *Valentino*. 20 x 25, 18 x 24, 18 x 22, 12½ x 25, watercolor and oil.

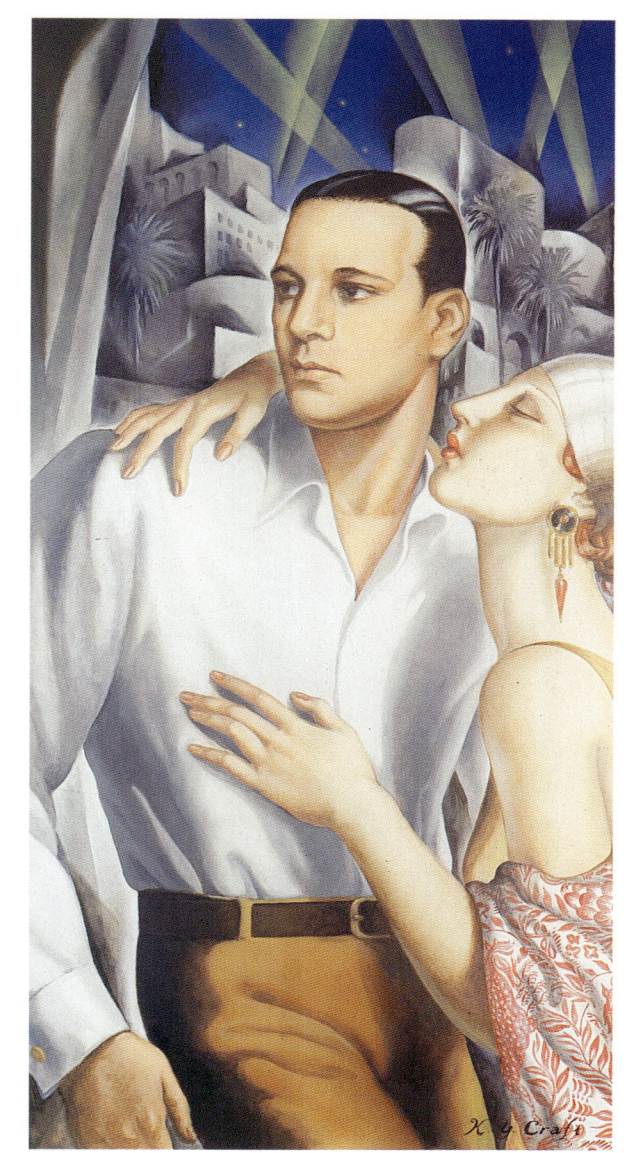

1

Institutional

1 (series)
David Rose, illustrator/designer
Anthony Fortuno, director of marketing/
 communications
Greg Davy, senior communication representative
Metropolitan Transportation Authority Marketing
 Department, agency
Los Angeles County Transportation Authority, client

Documentation of the Los Angeles subway construction. 20 x 15, pen, ink, watercolor and pastel.

Institutional

1
Chris Sheban, illustrator
Joan Body, art director
Studio Grafika, design firm
Charter Medical, client

As a leader in behavioral health care services, Charter Medical explored other strategies to reach new markets and develop new lines of business, hence "less traveled paths." 8½ x 16½, watercolor, pencil and pastel.

2
John Rush, illustrator
Mark Geer, art director
Geer Design, design firm
Texas Children's Hospital Center for Facial Surgery, client

Brochure illustration. 12 x 6, etching and drypoint.

3
Matt Zumbo, illustrator
Steven Wold, art director/designer
Bender Browning Dolby & Sanderson Advertising, ad agency
First Stage Milwaukee, client

Program cover for *James and the Giant Peach*. 9 x 15, acrylic and pastel.

4
Michael Paraskevas, illustrator/art director/designer
Paraskevas Gallery, design
Bide-A-Wee, client

Program cover for a night of comedy to benefit a dog and cat association. 30 x 40, acrylic.

COMMUNICATION ARTS   *105*

1

INSTITUTIONAL

1 (series)
David Johnson, illustrator
Don Owens, art director
Don Owens Visual Communication, design firm
American Jury Trial Foundation, client

Portraits from booklet: Justice Theodore Sedgwick; Patrick Henry; Sir John Fortescue, Chief Justice of the King's Bench; John Dickinson; twelve men and women in the jury box are the cornerstone of the judicial process. Black-and-white, 8 x 11; color, 11 x 14, ink and watercolor.

2
Philippe Weisbecker, illustrator
Ann Harakawa/Brian Sisco, art directors
Dai Nippon, client

Calendar illustration. 15 x 16½, pencil, watercolor on paper.

Institutional

1 (series)
Fletcher Sibthorp, illustrator
Jimmy Yang/Michael Peters, art directors
Jimmy Yang, designer
Identica, design firm
Huhtamaki, client

Five paintings for Huhtamaki's new corporate identity launch brochure. Huhtamaki is the tenth largest conglomerate in Finland and is comprised of three companies: confectionery, pharmaceuticals and food packaging. 32 x 44, mixed media on canvas.

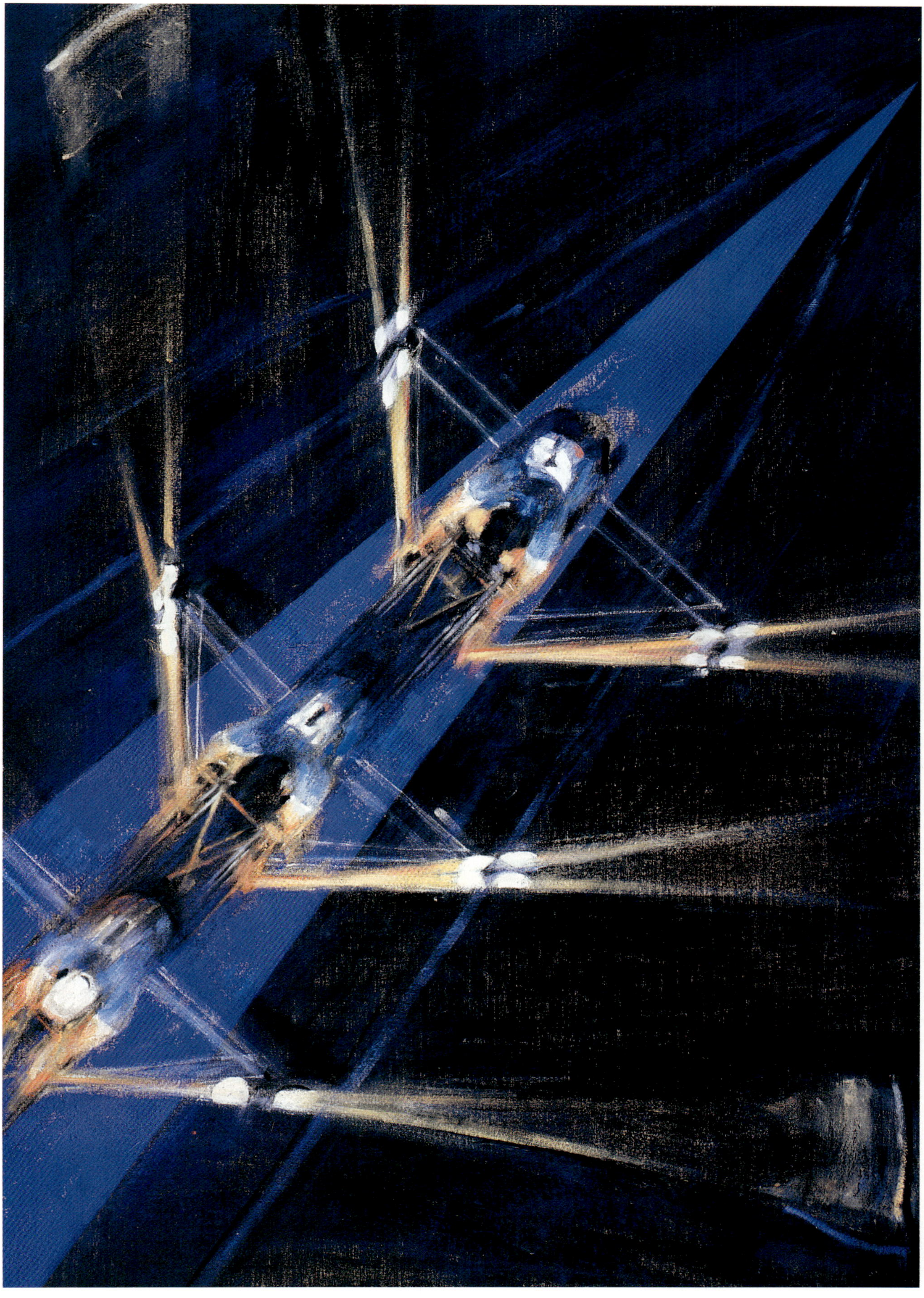

1

Institutional

1
Gary Head, illustrator
Keith Hart, art director
Ed Tel, design
Edmonton Telephone Yellow Pages, client

Cover and poster to show community at another time period.
12 x 14, oil.

2
Harvey Chan, illustrator
Andy Foster, art director
Stratford Festival, client

Cyrano de Bergerac illustration for the theater catalog.
18 x 24, mixed media.

3
Mario Sermoneta, illustrator
Yarom Vardimon, art director/designer
Vardimon Design, design firm
The Tisch Family Zoological Garden in Jerusalem, client

Identification plate. 18½ x 12¾, watercolor.

1

15 Months DTP
12-15 Months
MMR, HIB
6-18 Months
Hepititis B
6 Months
DTP, HIB, OPV
4-6 Years
DTP, OPV, MMR
14-16 Years
TD
4 Months
DTP, OPV, HIB, Hepititis B
2 Months
DTP OPV HIB
0-2 Months
Hepititis B

INSTITUTIONAL

1 (series)
Robert Neubecker, illustrator
Peter Deutsch, art director
Peter Deutsch Design, design firm
Joyce Foundation of Chicago, client

Annual report for a foundation dedicated to funding dialogue and debate on pressing social issues to bring about more creative approaches to solving problems within the culture. 12 x 17¾, ink, watercolor and acrylic.

INSTITUTIONAL

1
Filip Pagowski, illustrator
Jeffrey Keyton, art director
MTV, client

Image on ethnic violence in response to the Bosnian conflict, made for the video music awards presentation. 12⅜ x 16, paint, ink and photocopier.

SELF-PROMOTION

2
Gregory Manchess, illustrator/art director
Richard Solomon, Artists Representative, client

Source book ad, "Lighter Than Air." 13½ x 17½, oil on gesso board.

3
Mark Summers, illustrator/designer
Richard Solomon, art director
Richard Solomon, Artists Representative, client

Source book ad. 9 x 12, scratchboard and watercolor.

4
Nancy Stahl, illustrator/client

6½ x 9¼, digital.

5
Tim O'Brien, illustrator/art director

Source book ad and mailer. 17 x 23, oil on gessoed board.

6
Jim Carroll, illustrator/client

Promotional mailer. 11 x 17, digital.

3

4

5

6

COMMUNICATION ARTS

SELF-PROMOTION

1 (series)
Mark English, illustrator/designer/client
Tim Trabon, art director

Catalog for one-man exhibition. 18 x 24, oil and pastel.

2
Regan Todd Dunnick, illustrator
Chris Hill, art director
Chris Hill/Laura Menegaz, designers
The Hill Group, design firm
Gulf Printing/Regan Todd Dunnick, clients

Poster, "I'm into clowns and circus acts involving pigs."
22 x 18, pastel.

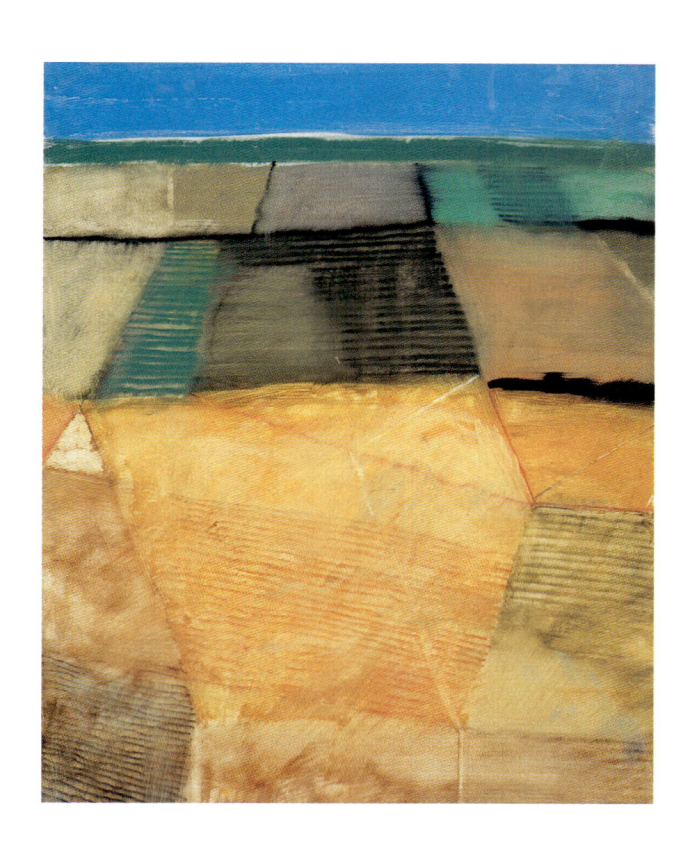

2

COMMUNICATION ARTS 117

1

2

SELF-PROMOTION

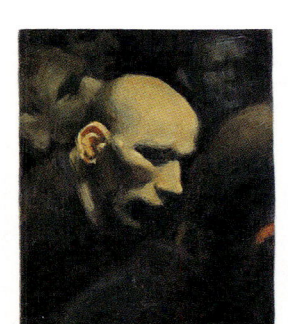

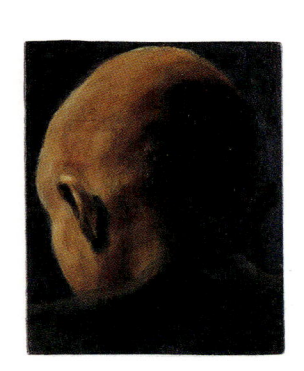

1
David M. Beck, illustrator

Promotional mailer and ad. 18 x 13, mixed media.

2
Regan Todd Dunnick, illustrator
Chris Hill, art director
Chris Hill/Laura Menegaz, designers
The Hill Group, design firm
Gulf Printing/Regan Todd Dunnick, clients

Poster, "I do a really nice rendition of guys goofin' around in '53 Hornets." 22 x 18, pastel.

3
Alan E. Cober, illustrator
Sherri Squires, art director
Denise Olding, designer
Louisville Graphic Design Association, client

Poster. 20 x 16, etching/aquatint.

4
Jaeeun Choi, illustrator
Sunghee Hahn, art director
Jaeeun Choi/Sunghee Hahn, designers
Jae & Hahn Design, design firm
School of Visual Arts, client

Art school poster. 11 x 14, acrylic.

1

SELF-PROMOTION

1 (series)
Martha Anne Booth, illustrator/art director/client

Promotional postcards. Various sizes, oil pastel on paper.

2
Etienne Delessert, illustrator/designer
Albin Uldry, art director
Delessert & Marshall, design firm
Uldry, client

Greeting card for a printer in Switzerland. 20 x 20, egg tempera.

SELF-PROMOTION

1 (series)
Skip Liepke, illustrator/art director
The Eleanor Ettinger Gallery, Inc., client

Artist's catalog. Various sizes, oil.

2
John Collier, illustrator/designer
Richard Solomon, art director
Richard Solomon, Artists Representative, client

Ad, "Ethics in Practice." 24 x 30, pastel.

3
Janelle Cromwell, illustrator

Mailer. 11 x 14, acrylic.

4
Gregory Manchess, illustrator/art director
Richard Solomon, Artists Representative, client

Ad, "Edward Hopper: Notes on Life and Letters." 14 x 19, oil on gesso board.

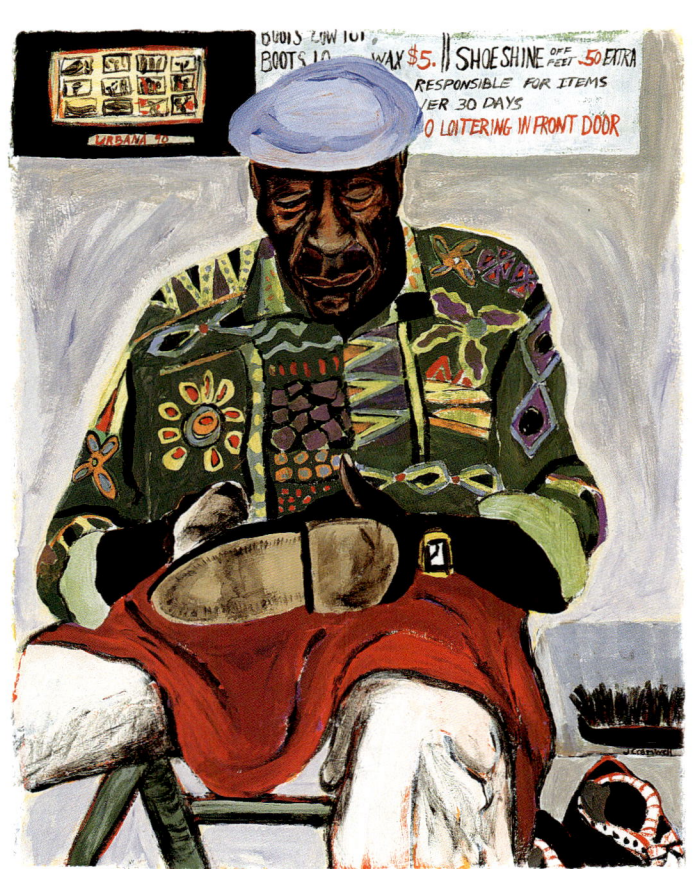

1

2

3

4

COMMUNICATION ARTS 123

1
2
3

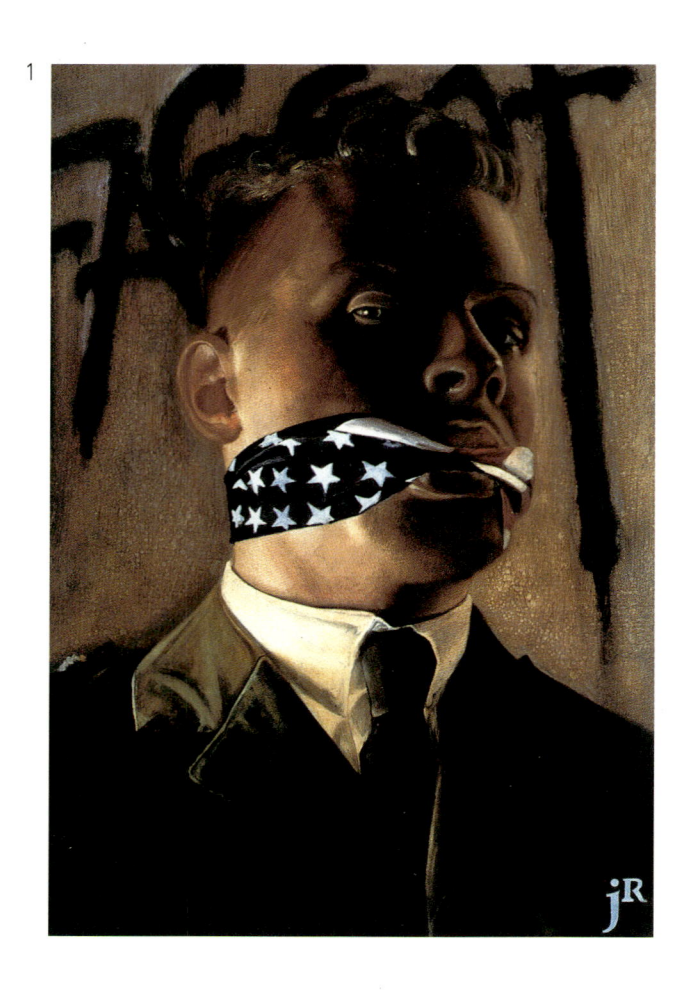

124 ILLUSTRATION ANNUAL 1994

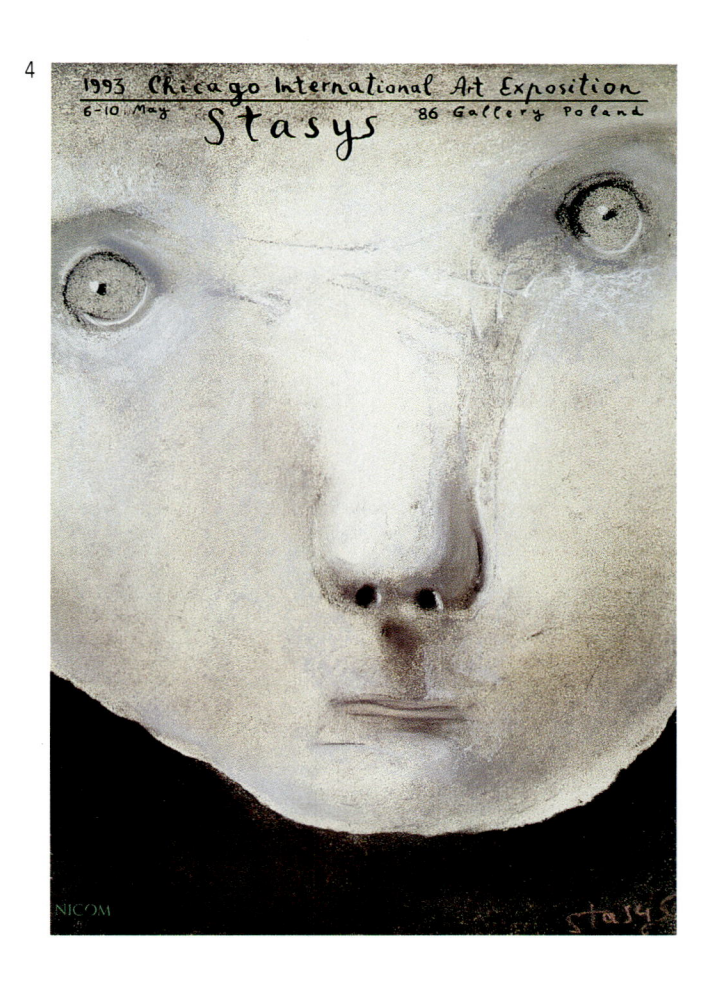

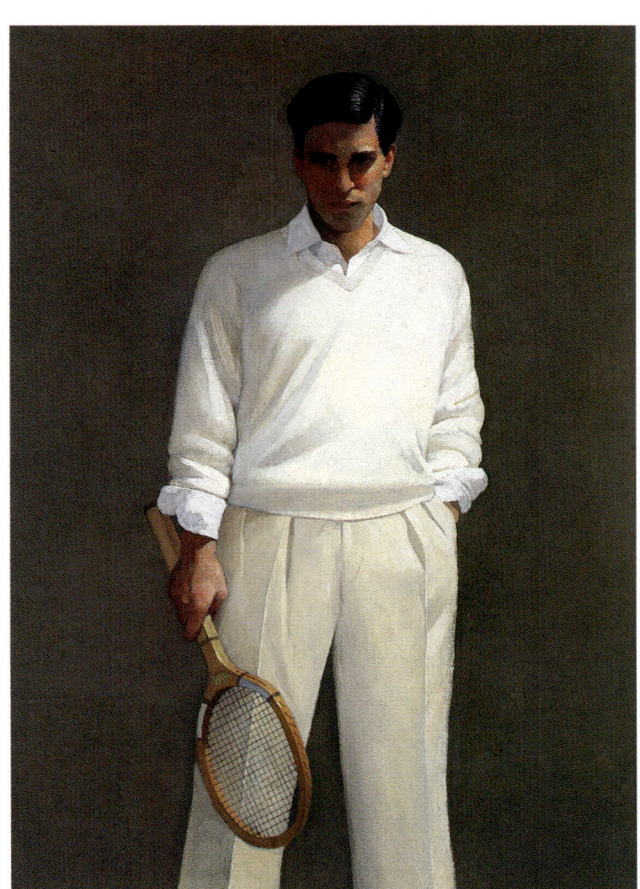

SELF-PROMOTION

1
Jennifer Renshaw, illustrator/art director/designer
Ren Design, design firm/client

Promotional mailer. 10 x 13, oil.

2
Kim Barnes, illustrator

Mailer. Art originally done for the Miniature Art Society of Florida for their art show. 4 x 6, acrylic, pastel and oil.

3
Joseph Lorusso, illustrator

Promotional mailer. 16 x 11, oil.

4
Stasys Eidrigevicius, illustrator
86 Gallery Poland, client

Poster for Chicago International Art Exposition. 18 x 22½, pastel.

5
Daniel Schwartz, illustrator/designer
Richard Solomon, art director
Richard Solomon, Artists Representative, client

Ad, "The Ralph Lauren Look." 36 x 48, oil.

Self-Promotion

1
Wilfredo Rosas, illustrator
Kurt Houser, art director/designer
Silas H. Rhodes, creative director
Visual Arts Press, design
School of Visual Arts, client

Poster, "You Are What You Eat." 8 x 13, oil and crayon on Masonite.

2
C.F. Payne, illustrator
Ben Ross/C.F. Payne, art directors
Ben Ross, designer
Ross Design, design firm
Cincinnati Art Directors Club, client

Poster for the Bad Art Burns & Chili Cookoff. 25 x 14, mixed media.

3
Nanette Biers, illustrator
Vicki Morgan Associates, client

Source book frontispiece for the representative's section. 22 x 28, oil on canvas.

3

SELF-PROMOTION

1
Dugald Stermer, illustrator/designer
Reuben Saunders/Marylynn Oliver, art directors

Source book ad used Sedgwick County Zoo material.
24 x 36, pencil and watercolor on Arches Paper.

2
John Jude Palencar, illustrator
Richard Lebenson, art director
Larry Bode/John Jude Palencar, designers
R.S.V.P., client

Ad. 14 x 14¾, watercolor.

UNPUBLISHED

3
Jack Endewelt, illustrator/art director/designer

12 x 9, oil on board.

© Jack Endewelt 1994

4
Peter Sylvada, illustrator

30 x 20, oil.

© Peter Sylvada 1994

3

4

1

130 ILLUSTRATION ANNUAL 1994

Unpublished

1 (series)
Bill Nelson, illustrator/art director/designer/client

5 x 7, colored pencil.

© Bill Nelson 1994

2
Nancy Stahl, illustrator

3¾ x 5, digital.

© Nancy Stahl 1994

3
Martin Schechter, illustrator

Portfolio piece. 8½ x 11, acrylic.

© Martin Schechter 1994

1

2

Unpublished

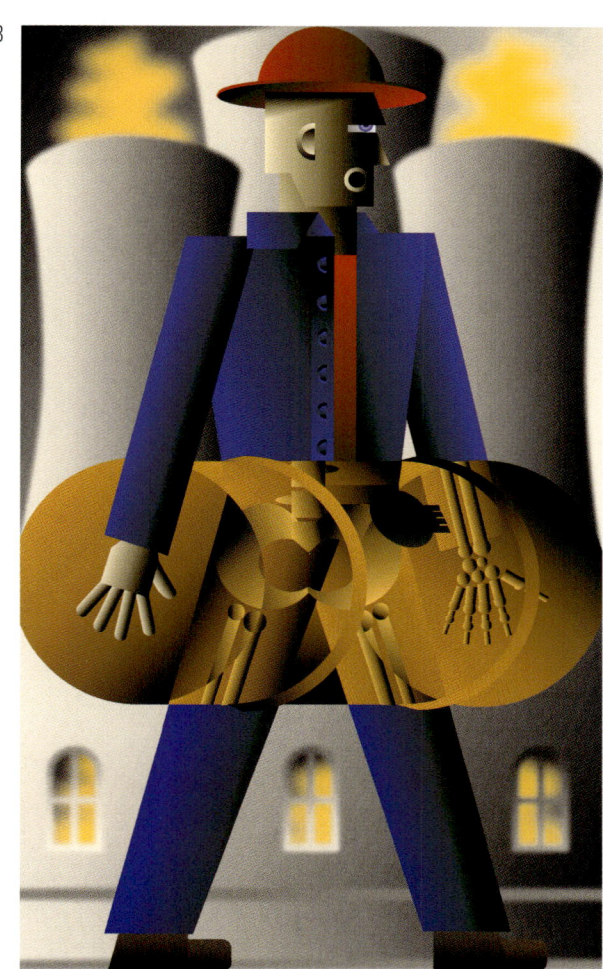

1
David McShane, illustrator

50 x 38½, oil on paper.

© David McShane 1994

2
Paul G. Oxborough, illustrator
The Beard Art Galleries, Inc., client

20 x 18, oil.

© Paul G. Oxborough 1994

3
Don Arday, illustrator
Don Arday, Photocom Inc., client

5 x 8, digital.

© Don Arday 1994

4
Bill Cigliano, illustrator
Joseph Connolly, art director

Experimental piece for a proposed *Boy's Life* article on the blues. 11 x 8, acrylic and oil.

© Bill Cigliano 1994

UNPUBLISHED

1
Simòn Silva, illustrator

24 x 36, oil.

© Simòn Silva 1994

2 (series)
José Ortega, illustrator

Proposed murals for the Metropolitan Transportation Authority to be done as mosaics at the 149th Street and 3rd Avenue subway station in New York. 17 x 6, digital.

© José Ortega 1994

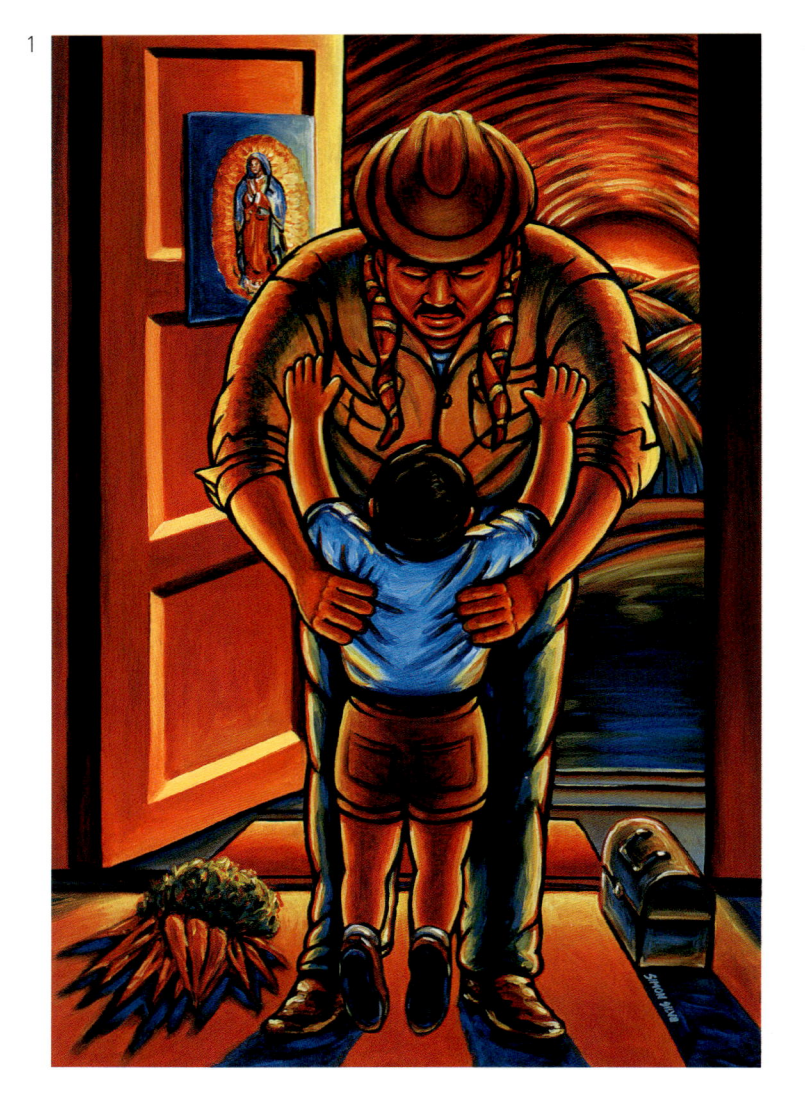

COMMUNICATION ARTS 135

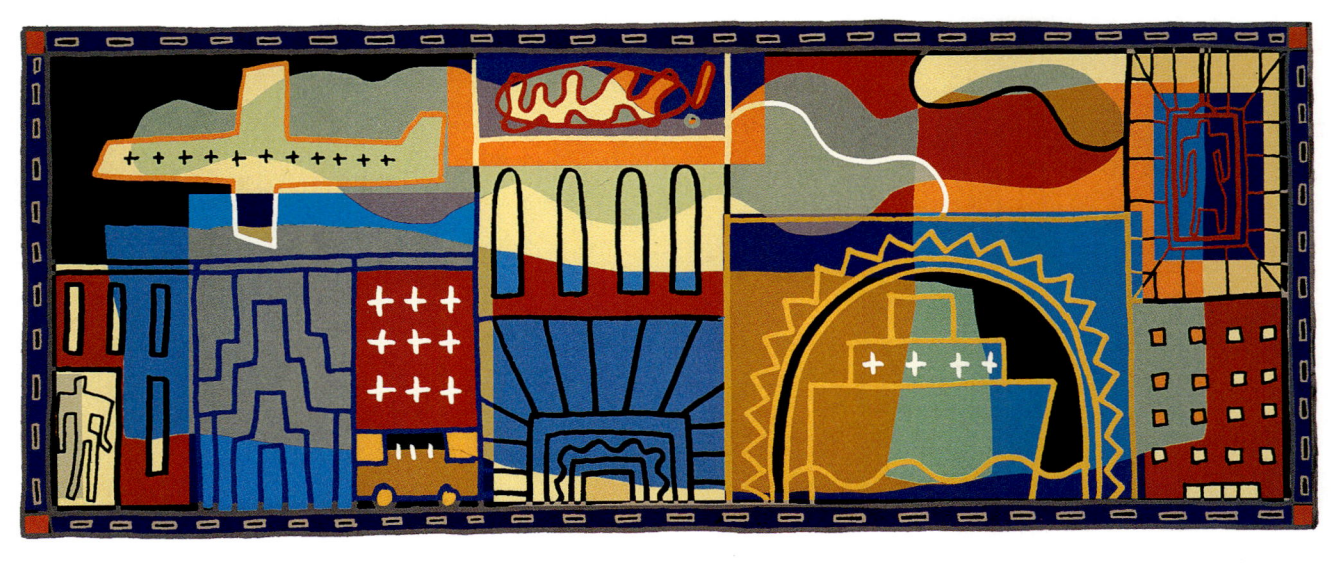

Unpublished

1
Robert G. Steele, illustrator

12 x 15, oil.

© Robert G. Steele 1994

2
Michael Plank, illlustrator
Paul Barker, art director

Hallmark Creative Workshop. 11 x 17, gouache.

© Michael Plank 1994

3
Tristan A. Elwell, illustrator
Ken Kleppert, art director

Unused illustration for a *Runner's World* article on eating insects. 9½ x 8, oil on illustration board.

© Tristan A. Elwell 1994

4
Einat Peled, illustrator

18 x 15, acrylic.

© Einat Peled 1994

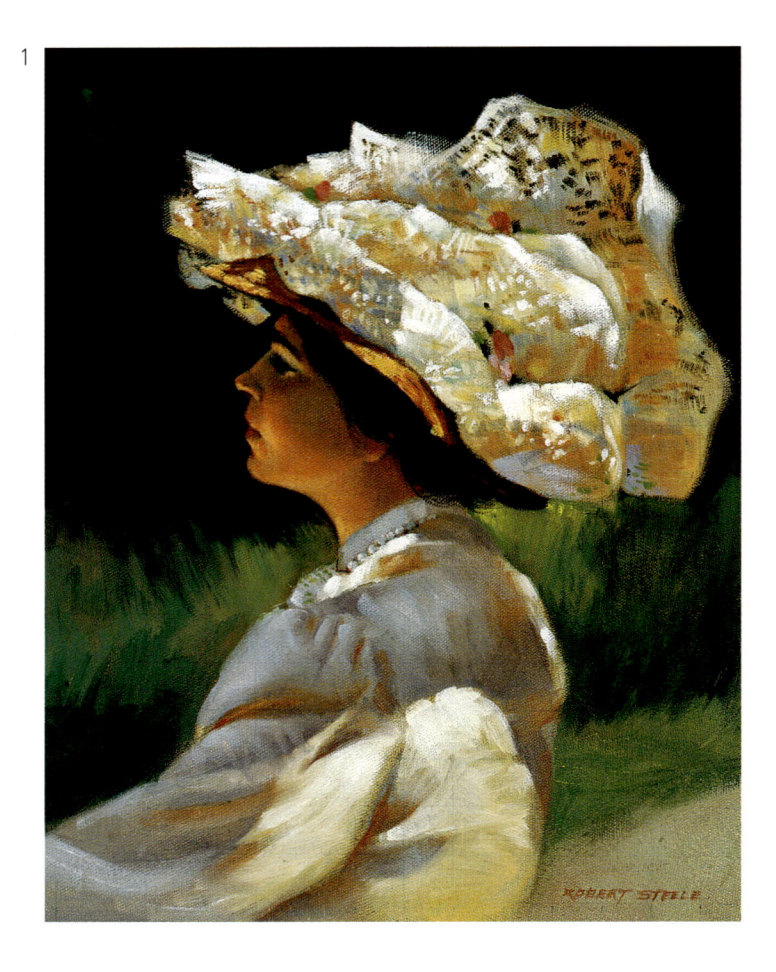

3

4

They continue to work their land

COMMUNICATION ARTS 137

UNPUBLISHED

1
Christopher Baldwin, illustrator

24 x 36, acrylic.

© Christopher Baldwin 1994

2
Robert Jew, illustrator

40 x 36, acrylic on canvas.

© Robert Jew 1994

INDEX

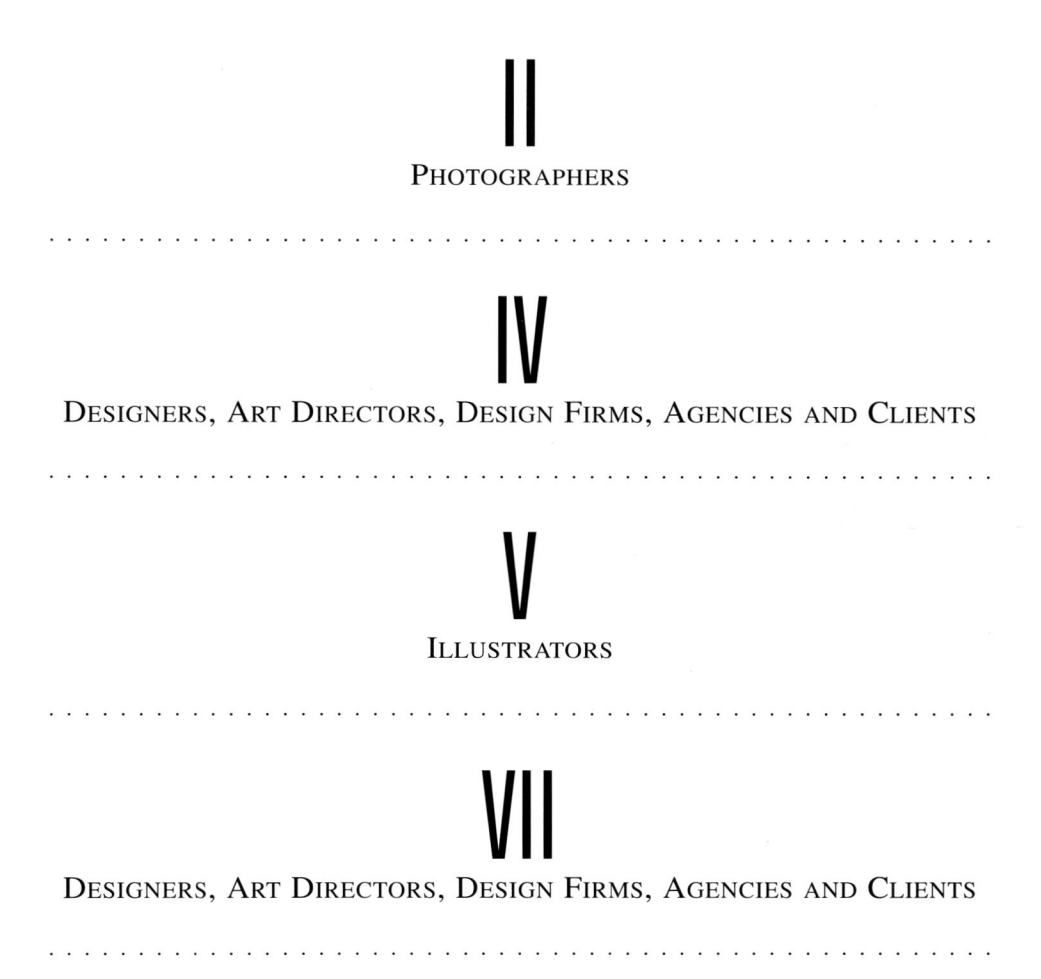

II
PHOTOGRAPHERS

IV
DESIGNERS, ART DIRECTORS, DESIGN FIRMS, AGENCIES AND CLIENTS

V
ILLUSTRATORS

VII
DESIGNERS, ART DIRECTORS, DESIGN FIRMS, AGENCIES AND CLIENTS

Index to Photographers

A

Afanador, Ruven 52, 81
Phone (212) 741-5292
505 W. 23rd Street, #3
New York, NY 10011

Appelbaum, Marcy J. 140
Phone (904) 396-6218
P.O. Box 10083
Jacksonville, FL 32247

Arciero, Anthony 100
Phone (312) 772-7297
1643 N. Milwaukee, #2
Chicago, IL 60647

Aresu, Paul 32
Phone (212) 334-9494
Aresu/Goldring Studio
568 Broadway, #608
New York, NY 10012

Arrabito, James 87
Phone (206) 339-3686
2623 Grand Avenue
Everett, WA 98201

Ashukian, Susan 118
Phone (416) 778-7322
276 Carlaw Avenue, #301
Toronto, Ontario M4M 3L1
Canada

Atkinson, Mark Edward 36
Phone (804) 622-8853
1611-D Colley Avenue
Norfolk, VA 23517

Atkinson, Robert David 131
Phone (718) 836-9335
359 Ovington Avenue
Brooklyn, NY 11209

B

Barrow, Scott 123
Phone (914) 424-4441
Hurst Pierpont Road
Garrison, NY 10524

Belpaire, Christian 70
Phone (416) 696-2630
205 Woodville Avenue
Toronto, Ontario M4J 2R4
Canada

Bennett, Sue 22
Phone (602) 774-2544
107 N. San Francisco, Suite 3
Flagstaff, AZ 86001

Bieber, Tim 114
Phone (312) 463-1921
c/o Mr. Big Productions, Inc.
3312 W. Belle Plaine
Chicago, IL 60618

Blankenship, Bob 136
Phone (404) 872-9145
634 N. Highland Avenue
Atlanta, GA 30306

Borris, Dan 49
Phone (212) 989-6790
40 W. 17th Street
New York, NY 10011

Brandt, David Allan 16
Phone (213) 469-1399
1015 Cahuenga Boulevard,
Studio 14C
Hollywood, CA 90038

Brodēn, Fredrik 91, 136
Phone (214) 720-9019
2912 Maple Avenue
Dallas, TX 75201

Brooks, Ernest H. II 66
Phone (805) 966-3888
Brooks Institute of
 Photography
801 Alston Road
Santa Barbara, CA 93108

Burkey, J. W. 126
Phone (214) 746-6336
1526 Edison Street
Dallas, TX 75207

C

Canavino, Kay 125
Phone (617) 625-1115
1 Fitchburg Street
Somerville, MA 02143

Clement, Michele 88
Phone (415) 695-0100
879 Florida Street
San Francisco, CA 94110

Clifford, Mark 114
Phone (213) 222-7400
600 Moulton Avenue, #102-D
Los Angeles, CA 90031

Cooper, Chip 39
Phone (205) 348-8332
P.O. Box 870144
G-14 Rose Administration
 Building
The University of Alabama
Tuscaloosa, AL 35487

Corbett, Jay 120
Phone (212) 366-1166
352 W. 15th Street, #204
New York, NY 10011

Crowe, Pat 55
Phone (302) 239-5259
4942 S. Raintree Court
Wilmington, DE 19808

Cutler, Craig 7, 109
Phone (212) 473-2892
628-30 Broadway, #403
New York, NY 10012

D

Davidson, Cameron 79
Phone (202) 328-3344
1403-B N. Van Dorn Street
Alexandria, VA 22304

Dazeley, Peter 131
Phone (44) 71-736-3171
The Studios
5 Heathmans Road
Parsons Green, Fulham
London SW6 4TJ
England

De Souza, Daniel 107, 123
Phone (415) 777-3273
185 Clara Street, #202
San Francisco, CA 94107

Dojc, Yuri 97
Phone (416) 366-8081
74 Bathurst Street
Toronto, Ontario M5V 2P5
Canada

Dugan, Joanne 26
Phone (212) 964-6404
8 Thomas Street
New York, NY 10007

Dyer, John 76
Phone (210) 223-1891
107 Blue Star
San Antonio, TX 78204

E

Erickson, Jim 139, 143
Phone (919) 833-9955
117 S. West Street
Raleigh, NC 27603

F

Fawcett, Sarah 146
Phone (415) 824-1565
178 Chattanooga Street
San Francisco, CA 94114

Fehling, Ron 29
Phone (416) 535-1955
Westside Studio
33 Jefferson Avenue
Toronto, Ontario M6K 1Y3
Canada

Ferguson, Scott 125
Phone (314) 241-3811
Ferguson & Katzman
 Photography
710 N. Tucker Boulevard, #512
St. Louis, MO 63101

Forelli, Chip 126
Phone (212) 564-1835
529 W. 42nd Street
New York, NY 10036

Freeman, Don 51
Phone (212) 941-6727
457 Broome Street
New York, NY 10013

G

Gajdel, Edward 87
Phone (416) 535-4773
198 Crawford Street
Toronto, Ontario M6J 2V6
Canada

Garofalo, John Cleveland 132
Phone (703) 368-3861
10743 Lake Forest Drive
Manassas, VA 22111

Gaz, David 30
Phone (33) 1-48-06-3821
14-16 Passage Thiéré
75011 Paris, France
c/o Arlene Soodak
Phone (301) 983-2343
11135 Korman Drive
Potomac, MD 20854

Glentzer, Don 114
Phone (713) 529-9686
3814 S. Shepherd
Houston, TX 77098

Guip, Amy 49
Phone (212) 674-8166
352 Bowery, #2
New York, NY 10012

H

Harbron, Patrick 76
Phone (212) 967-2111
666 Greenwich Street, #746
New York, NY 10014

Hart, Trevor Ray 10
Phone (44) 81-674-2242
c/o Alan Wicks
79 Leonard Street
London, EC2
England

Heimo 118
Phone (415) 621-8260
530 Hampshire, Suite 406
San Francisco, CA 94110

Heumann, Andreas 7, 29
Phone (44) 71-622-3979
35 Larkhall Rise
London SW4 6HU
England

Higgins, Dale 135
Phone (415) 441-1214
1835 Clay Street, #202
San Francisco, CA 94109

Hohmuth-Lemonick, Eileen 92
Phone (609) 924-8346
249 Cherry Hill Road
Princeton, NJ 08540

Huet, John 88
Phone (617) 439-9393
27 Drydock Avenue
Boston, MA 02210

Humphreys, David 139
Phone (504) 924-8075
4624 Hyacinth Avenue
Baton Rouge, LA 70808

Hush, Gary 19
Phone (503) 222-4786
725 N.W. Flanders, #206
Portland, OR 97209

I

Inbar, Limor 57
Phone (212) 529-4219
232 E. 12th Street, Apt. 6B
New York, NY 10003

Iooss, Walter Jr. 44
Phone (718) 601-3232
4730 Independence Avenue
Riverdale, NY 10471

J

Johnson, Curtis 120
Phone (612) 332-5050
c/o Jim Arndt Photography
400 1st Avenue N., #510
Minneapolis, MN 55401

K

Kander, Nadav 14, 21, 30
Phone (44) 71-359-5207
1-7 Britannia Row
London N1 8QH
England

Kashi, Ed 82, 132
Phone (415) 641-4636
824 Florida Street
San Francisco, CA 94110

Kasmauski, Karen 62
Phone (703) 241-7520
2907 Linden Lane
Falls Church, VA 22042

Katzenstein, David 13
Phone (218) 529-9460
23 E. 4th Street, 4th Floor
New York, NY 10003

Katzman, Mark 125
Phone (314) 241-3811
Ferguson & Katzman
 Photography
710 N. Tucker Boulevard,
 #512
St. Louis, MO 63101

Kendrick, Robb 59, 103
Phone (512) 454-7649
703 E. 43rd Street
Austin, TX 78751

Kern, Geof 62
Phone (214) 630-0856
1355 Conant Street
Dallas, TX 75207

Kernan, Sean 117
Phone (203) 481-0213
28 School Street
Stony Creek, CT 06405

Kleinman, Kathryn 42
Phone (415) 456-8544
41 Tamalpais Avenue
San Anselmo, CA 94960

Kohanim, Parish 114
Phone (404) 892-0099
1130 W. Peachtree Street
Atlanta, GA 30309

Kratochvil, Antonin 52, 59, 81
Phone (212) 947-1589
448 W. 37th Street, #69
New York, NY 10013

Kressley, Michael 88, 97
Phone (617) 522-5132
67 Brookside Avenue
Boston, MA 02130

Krist, Bob 22, 79
Phone (201) 445-3259
333 S. Irving Street
Ridgewood, NJ 07450

Krogh, Jennifer 132
Phone (212) 982-4328
522 E. 6th Street, #3
New York, NY 10009

Kuehn, Karen 57, 76
Phone (212) 477-1251
300 E. 4th Street, #1D
New York, NY 10009

Kuhn, Chuck 19
Phone (206) 842-1996
11050 N.E. Seaborn Road
Bainbridge Island
 WA 98110

L

Lacker, Pete 131
Phone (214) 748-7488
1027 Dragon Street
Dallas, TX 75207

Laita, Mark 135
Phone (310) 836-1645
3815 Main Street
Culver City, CA 90232

Lanting, Frans 32
Phone (408) 685-1911
c/o Minden Pictures
24 Seascape Village
Aptos, CA 95003

Lawton, Eric 41
Phone (310) 453-8784
2001 Wilshire Boulevard
Penthouse Suite
Santa Monica, CA 90403

Lloyd, R. Ian 68
Phone (65) 2279600
5 Kreta Ayer Road
Singapore 0208

Lowry, Miles 24
Phone (312) 666-0882
222 S. Morgan, #4A
Chicago, IL 60607

Ludwig, Gerd 57
Phone (213) 882-6999
3472 Oak Glen Drive
Los Angeles, CA 90068
and 1145 17th Street N.W.
Washington, D.C. 20036

Ludwigson, Håkan 62
Phone (46) 31-830438
Sofierogatan 3
412 51 Göteborg
Sweden

M

Mahurin, Matt 75
Phone (212) 691-5115
666 Greenwich Street
New York, NY 10014

Makki, Sari 104
Phone (818) 240-5109
1323 E. Broadway, #302
Glendale, CA 91205

Malaterre, Dominique 123
Phone (514) 844-0294
Tilt, Inc.
231, St-Paul W. Street
Montréal, Québec H2Y 2A2
Canada

Matuschka 59, 66
Phone (212) 722-2131
150 E. 87th Street
New York, NY 10128

Mayo, Scogin 64
Phone (214) 941-0663
413 N. Bishop Avenue
Dallas, TX 75208

Mayor, Randy 97
Phone (205) 933-2818
2007 15th Avenue S.
Birmingham, AL 35205

McArthur, Pete 7
Phone (310) 815-1951
8741 W. Washington
  Boulevard, Suite A
Culver City, CA 90232

McDonald, Michele 70
Phone (617) 646-6926
33 Fountain Road
Arlington, MA 02174

McLeod, William Mercer 52
Phone (415) 550-7576
225 Fair Oaks Street
San Francisco, CA 94110

McNicol, Duncan 145
Phone (44) 71-401-2599
2 Rushworth Studios
63 Webber Street
London SE1 0QW
England

Meeks, Raymond 72, 128
Phone (617) 484-7437
149 Oakley Road
Belmont, MA 02178

Melford, Michael 75
Phone (914) 666-6244
Petersville Farm
Mt. Kisco, NY 10549

Mencher, Eric 135
Phone (215) 854-2871
308 Pemberton Street
Philadelphia, PA 19147

Mendelsohn, David 94
Phone (603) 659-2530
15 Tall Pines Road
Durham, NH 03824

Mermelstein, Jeff 81
Phone (212) 496-9427
172 W. 79th Street, #4C
New York, NY 10024

Meyerson, Arthur 103
Phone (713) 529-9697
2710 Bissonnet
Houston, TX 77005

Miller, Bob 21
Phone (415) 495-1900
c/o Bobbi Wendt
Parallel Universe Creative
152 Mississippi
San Francisco, CA 94107

Morgan, Michael P. 98
Phone (714) 583-0399
23421 Red Robin Lane
Lake Forest, CA 92630

Morgan, Scott 13
Phone (310) 392-1863
711 Hampton Drive
Venice, CA 90291

Morrison, Alistair 66
Phone (44) 71-608-3064
c/o Sue Allatt
30C Great Sutton Street
London EC1V 0DX
England

Mummery, Richard 19
Phone (44) 71-278-7137
16 Rosebery Avenue
London EC1R 4TD
England

Muna, RJ 109, 120
Phone (415) 468-8225
225 Industrial Street
San Francisco, CA 94124

Mutino, Paul 125
Phone (203) 255-6622
Van Gorder Studios
63 Unquowa Road
Fairfield, CT 06430

N

Nachtwey, James 76
Phone (212) 966-9200
Magnum Photos
72 Spring Street, 12th Floor
New York, NY 10012

Nagelmann, Antony 7
Phone (212) 242-8001
29 E. 9th Street, PH1
New York, NY 10003

Neleman, Hans 16, 118
Phone (212) 274-1000
Neleman Studio
77 Mercer Street
New York, NY 10012

Nielsen, Ed 21, 112
Phone (415) 851-3132
303 Highland Terrace
Woodside, CA 94062

Noto, Rino 81
Phone (416) 465-8094
276 Carlaw Avenue, Suite 306
Toronto, Ontario M4M 3L1
Canada

O

Oe, Teiichi 112
Phone (213) 224-8709
Oe/Ueda
618 Moulton Avenue, Studio E
Los Angeles, CA 90031

Ordeñana, Adrian 104
Phone (415) 781-4533
942 Market Street, #508
San Francisco, CA 94102

P

Page, Tim 61
Phone (44) 81-806-9803
Reportage Photos
28 Norcott Road
London N16 7EL
England

Palu, Louie 97
Phone (416) 588-9337
34 Noble Street, Studio 201
Toronto, Ontario M6K 2C9
Canada

Panneton, André 61
Phone (514) 523-3231
4406 Rue Brébeuf
Montréal, Québec H2J 3K9
Canada

Payne, Steve 57
Phone (416) 778-9504
58 Denison Avenue
Toronto, Ontario M5T 2M8
Canada

Price, Larry C. 46
Phone (817) 923-2953
Contact Press Images
2021 Windsor Place
Ft. Worth, TX 76110

Prida, Hector E. 143
Phone (818) 799-6705
1125 Brent Avenue
South Pasadena, CA 91030

R

Richards, Mark 51
Phone (415) 389-8252
61 Sunnyside Avenue
Mill Valley, CA 94941

Robinson, James 91
Phone (212) 580-1793
155 Riverside Drive
New York, NY 10024

Rothfeld, Steven 35
Phone (310) 399-2460
1621 Abbot Kinney
  Boulevard
Venice, CA 90291

Ryan, Tom 85
Phone (214) 651-7085
2919 Canton Street
Dallas, TX 75226

S

Sacha, Bob 49
Phone (212) 749-4128
12 W. 96th Street
New York, NY 10025

Salzano, James 107
Phone (212) 242-4820
29 W. 15th Street
New York, NY 10011

Sanders, Key 100
Phone (713) 621-8393
5637 Cedar Creek
Houston, TX 77056

Schleipman, Russ 100
Phone (617) 292-0055
25 Union Park
Boston, MA 02118

Seaward, Peter 21
Phone (44) 71-608-3249
49 Eagle Wharf Road
London N1 7ED
England

Seliger, Mark 49
Phone (212) 941-6548
96A Grand Street
New York, NY 10013

Sheehan, Chris 10
Phone (612) 874-1999
Parallel Productions
2010 Ist Avenue S.
Minneapolis, MN 55404

Shinn, Chris 94
Phone (713) 526-2623
2411 Bartlett
Houston, TX 77098

Silverman, Hal 109
Phone (315) 434-9121
6515A Basile Rowe
East Syracuse, NY 13057

Simhoni, George 112
Phone (416) 535-1955
Westside Studio
33 Jefferson Avenue
Toronto, Ontario M6K 1Y3
Canada

Sirota, Peggy 79
Phone (805) 494-8877
138 Colt Lane
Thousand Oaks, CA 91361

Slater, Greg 145
Phone (404) 584-6397
141 Mangum Street S.W.
Atlanta, GA 30313

Smith, Rodney 44, 68
Phone (914) 359-3814
P.O. Box 49
Snedens Landing
Palisades, NY 10964

Smith, Sean M. 32
Phone (718) 855-4204
97 Second Place, Apt. 3
Brooklyn, NY 11231

Sugarman, Lynn 110
Phone (214) 748-1019
1019 Dragon Street
Dallas, TX 75207

T

Tanaka, Jamie 136
Phone (415) 648-1122
34 Hill Street
San Francisco, CA 94110

Tilger, Stewart 123
Phone (206) 682-7818
71 Columbia, #206
Seattle, WA 98104

Topelmann, Lars 14, 29
Phone (503) 224-4556
1314 N.W. Irving Street, #214
Portland, OR 97209

U

Ueda, Rick 112
Phone (213) 224-8709
Oe/Ueda
618 Moulton Avenue, Studio E
Los Angeles, CA 90031

V

van Overbeek, Will 32
Phone (512) 454-1501
305 E. Skyview
Austin, TX 78752

Venville, Malcolm 10
Phone (44) 71-436-5191
23 Nassau Street
London W1N 7RF
England

von Renner, Ivo 9
Phone (49) 40-491-7096
Eppendorfer Weg 87 A
20259 Hamburg
Germany

W

Ward, Les 128
Phone (810) 350-8666
21477 Bridge Street, Suite C
Southfield, MI 48034

Wiens, Mark 104
Phone (816) 931-4447
3016 Cherry
Kansas City, MO 64108

Wilby, Dan 106
Phone (212) 929-8231
Wilby Productions
43 W. 24th Street, 11th Floor
New York, NY 10010

Winter, Nita 75
Phone (415) 927-4300
9 Ridge Way
Corte Madera, CA 94925

Winters, Dan 59, 70
Phone (213) 957-5699
6383 Bryn Mawr Drive
Los Angeles, CA 90068

Editor's Note

Every effort has been
made to ensure that
credits accurately comply
with information supplied
to us.

Index to Art Directors, Design Firms, Agencies and Clients

A

Adler Boschetto Peebles & Partners 32
Advanced Computer Communications 21
The University of Alabama, Division of Student Affairs 39
American Red Cross, Birmingham Chapter 97
Anderson, Larry 88
Anderson & Lembke 112
Arimo 9
Armario, David 49, 52, 62
Armus, Jill 87
Jim Arndt Photography 120
Arnold, David 62
Arrabito, James 87
Ashukian, Susan 118
Atkinson, Mark Edward 36
Audi 21
Aur Resources Inc. 97
Aversano, Vince 76

B

BMP DDB Needham Worldwide, Ltd. 10
Babcock, Alice 87
Bailey, Benjamin 91
Baldwin, David 19, 29
Scott Barrow, Inc. 123
Barry, Jennifer 42
Bartle Bogle Hegarty 21
Beadry, Lindsay 70
Beckwith Barrow, Ltd. 123
Beckwith, Karen 123
Beechwood Record Co. 10
Behind the Mask 97
Behnken, Wolfgang 59
Belmont Constructors, Inc. 94
Benson & Hedges 19
Benson, Paula 10
Biagioni, Marcello 68
Bice Design 123
Bice, Luane 123
Bieber, Tim 114
Black, Bill 49, 52, 57, 59, 75, 76, 79, 81
Blankenship, Bob 136
Borders, Brett 14
Bornstein, Eric 97
Boston Globe 70
Brautigan, Doris 66, 81
Breno, Bob 19
British Gas 10
Bruce, Duncan 29
Bryan, Robert 68
Buckley, Stuart 10

C

CKM Press 39
Cabletron Systems 94
Camara, Lia 35
Carbone Smolan Associates 44
Carroll, Alan 79
Centerline 19
Chan, Kinson 16
Chiat/Day/Toronto 29
Children's Television Workshop 75
Chitraker, Raju 92
Chronicle Books 32
Cima, Daniele 9
Clark, John 112
Clarke, Michael 100
Michael Clarke Design 100
Clifford, Mark 114
Mark Clifford Photography 114
Cole & Weber 19, 29
Colle & McVoy, Inc. 10
Collett, Dickenson, Pearce & Partners 19
Collins, Tom 109
CollinsPublishers San Francisco 42, 44
Comex Communications Exponents 92
Condé Nast Traveler 62
Condé Nast Vanity Fair 7
Conner, Al 32
Context 100
Cousineau, Phil 41
Covenant House 100

D

Davis, Dale 92
Dayton Hudson, Department Store Division 13
Dazai Advertising 21
De Souza, Daniel 107, 123
Dean, Chris 112
Dearwater, Andy 103
Dearwater Design 103
deJori, Charlene 66
Design Thing 120
Devers, Wade 32
DiLorenzo, Lou 49, 52, 57, 59, 75, 76, 79, 81
Dimick, Dennis 59
Discover 49, 52, 62
Domer, Jennifer 44
Doubleday 44
Doyle Advertising and Design Group 88
Drace, Matthew 72, 128
Drummond, Stacy 13
Dunjko, Carmen 76
Dunn, Mary 52, 59, 66, 70, 79, 81, 87
Du Pont 22

E

Eakins, Warren 30
Eastman Kodak Company 97
Echave, John 82
Elle Québec 61
Elliott, Alice 97
Entertainment Weekly 52, 59, 66, 70, 79, 81, 87
Evans and Associates 91
Evans, Tim 91

F

Ferguson, Scott 125
Forelli, Chip 126
Form 10
Forster, Philip 19
Fox, Bert 46
Frankfurt Balkind Partners 91
Freedman, Dennis 68
French Vogue 51
Friend, David 61
Froelich, Janet 66
Fucinato, Bob 109

G

Gala Bingo Clubs 29
Gap Advertising 14, 21
Gap Boots USA 14, 21
Gap, Inc. 16
Gap Shoes 16
Garneau, Philippe 29
The Globe and Mail 57, 81
Goebel, Bob 100
Graves, Bill 59
Green Art 30
Gregory, Jeff 97
Griffin, David 57
Grossman, Michael 8

H

HG Design 104
Halis, Monte 22
Halis/Russo 22
Hall, Steve 22
Hanna, Leslie 104
Haraldsson, Gudrun 57, 81
HarperSan Francisco, Division of HarperCollins Publisher 41
Heimo Inc. 118
Herman Hospital 103
Herman, Rebecca 75
Hilgars, Lisa 51
Hoffman York & Compton 7
Art Directors Club of Houston 114
Humphreys, David 139
Hurley, Brianne 88
Hyland, Marie 94
Hyland, Terry 94

I

Imagic 21, 112
Impact Italia 9
Inside Sports 76

J

Jacobson, Mark 59, 70, 79
Johnson, Curtis 120
Jorgensen, Conrad 8

K

Katzman, Mark 125
Kavre Community Based Rehabilitation Project Team 92
Keiffer, Antoine 51
Helen Keller International 92
Kennedy, Tom 57, 59, 79
Kerbow, Michael 21, 112
Kernan, Sean 117
Sean Kernan, Inc. 117
Kleinman, Kathryn 42
Kohanim, Parish 114
Parish Kohanim Studio 114
Kraft, Theresa 123
Kressley, Michael 97
Krogh, Jennifer 132
The Kuester Group 100
Kuester, Kevin 100

L

LaGuardia, Diana 62
Laita, Mark 135
Lamboy, Patrick 30
Lecourt, Ariane 30
Left Brain Creative 14
The Leith Agency 29
Lemon, Ann 26
Life 61
Liska & Associates 114
Liska, Steve 114
Live Communications, Ltd. 16
London Underground International 19, 29
Looking 112
Loucks Atelier 14
Loucks, Jay 114
Lussier, Paul 57, 75, 76

M

Malaterre, Dominique 123
Mangiacotti, Michele 88
Marr, Bill 62, 82
Martin, Jean-Marc 61
McMillan Associates 44
McMillan, Michael 44
McMillen, Nancy 64, 85
McQuiston, Rick 21
Meek, John 76
Men's Journal 128
Mendelsohn, David 94
Mi, Patty H.P. 7
Microsoft 7
Mikich, Tripp 51
Mintz & Hoke Inc. 19
Money, Shawn 104
Morgan, Michael P. 98
Morgan, Tim 21
Morin, Tom 100
Muna, RJ 109, 120
Mutino, Paul 125

N

The Nashville Network 32
National Geographic 57, 59, 62, 79, 82
Nepal Association for the Welfare of the Blind 92
Art Directors Club of the Netherlands 118
Netten, Larae 10
The New York Times Magazine 66, 81
Nichols, Harvey 7
Nighswander, Larry 79
Nike, Inc. 21
Nike International 30

O

Ocean Realm 66
Oe/Ueda 112
Ogilvy & Mather 22
Ogilvy & Mather Direct 7
Ooka, Diane 51
Operation Smile International 36
Otto Visual Arts 36
Outdoor & Travel Photography 55
Outlook Eyewear Co./Bausch & Lomb Inc. 98
Overseas Shipholding Group 103
Owen, William 36

P

PC Magazine 32
Pagano, Schenck & Kay, Inc. 32
Parenting 51
Parkinson, Jon 107
Partners III 112
Paulini, Barb 7
Paws 14
Pellikaan, Hans 97
Penna, Detta 41
Pentagram 110
Perry, Harper & Perry 97
Pettit, Scott 24
Pfeiffer + Company 125
Phelps, Connie 79
Philadelphia Inquirer Magazine 46
Phillips, Ken 131
Photo Life 68
Postcards 26
Pro Passport 97
Public Relations Society of America 104

R

RCA Records/Cowboy Junkies 32
Ramsey, Russell 21
Rathe, Joanne 70
Redman, Kevin 14, 16, 21
Reifschneider, Kurt 14
Reprox Printing of St. Louis 125
Resound 88
Rhea & Kaiser 24
Rhône-Poulen 24
Richer, Paul 75
Rietta, Terry 32
Rigsby Design 94
Rigsby, Lana 94
Rolling Stone 49
Rumrill Hoyt 22
Russo, Rich 22
Ryan, Kathy 81

S

Said, Carmel 19
Saks, Arnold 103
Arnold Saks Associates 103
San Francisco AIDS Foundation 104
Saturday Night 76
Saucony Athletic Shoes 88
Scher, Paula 110
Schorp, Cheryl 66
The Seagram Company Ltd. 91
Sesame Street Magazine 75
Shands, Joe 19, 29
Sheen, Mike 29
Hal Silverman Studio, Inc. 109
Simhoni, George 112
Simmons, Margaret Staats 49, 52, 57, 59, 75, 76, 79
Skarratt, Julie 66
Slater, Greg 145
Smith, Sean M. 32
SmithKline Beecham Animal Health 10
Smolan, Leslie 44
Sony Music 13
Stephenson, Michele 57, 75, 76
Stern 59
Steven, Robert 76
Stevens, Terence 29
Stockman, Matthew 76
Stout, D. J. 64, 85
Stratagem Marketing and Design 97
Studio 2 88
Sugarman, Lynn 110
Syrop, Stephanie 49, 52, 57, 59, 75, 76, 79, 81

T

Talese, Nan A. 44
Tenazas Design 32
Tenazas, Lucille 32

Schwab, Michael 14
Phone (415) 331-7621
80 Liberty Ship Way, #7
Sausalito, CA 94965

Schwartz, Daniel 125
Phone (212) 533-0237
48 E. 13th Street
New York, NY 10003
c/o Richard Solomon
Artists Representative
Phone (212) 683-1362

Sealock, Rick 9
Phone (403) 276-5428
112 C 17th Avenue N.W.
Calgary, Alberta T2M OM6
Canada

Sermoneta, Mario 111
Phone (972) 3-5445010
Shderot Motzkin 23
Tel Aviv 62288
Israel

Sheban, Chris 104
Phone (312) 271-2720
1807 W. Sunnyside, #1G
Chicago, IL 60640

Sibthorp, Fletcher 87, 108
Phone (212) 741-2539
c/o Jaqueline Dedell, Inc.
58 W. 15th Street
New York, NY 10011

Silva, Simón 94, 134
Phone (909) 883-7901
3197 North G Street
San Bernardino, CA 92405

Sorren, Joe 65
Phone (503) 295-3670
2125 N.W. Glisan, #101
Portland, OR 97210

Spalenka, Greg 53
Phone (818) 992-5828
21303 San Miguel Street
Woodland Hills, CA 91364

Spino, Pete 77
Phone (619) 225-9476
3050 Kellogg Street
San Diego, CA 92106

Stahl, Nancy 114, 131
Phone (212) 362-8779
470 West End Avenue, #8G
New York, NY 10024

Steele, Robert G. 136
Phone (415) 923-0741
14 Wilmot Street
San Francisco, CA 94115

Stermer, Dugald 93, 128
Phone (415) 777-0110
600 The Embarcadero, #204
San Francisco, CA 94107

Summers, Mark 114
Phone (416) 689-6219
12 Milverton Close
Waterdown, Ontario
LOR 2H0
Canada
c/o Richard Solomon
Artists Representative
Phone (212) 683-1362

Sweeny, Glynis 53
Phone (810) 548-4381
346 W. Webster
Ferndale, MI 48220

Swierzy, Waldemar 19
Phone (212) 289-5514
c/o Marlena Torzecka
Artist Representative
211 E. 89th Street, Suite A-1
New York, NY 10128

Sylvada, Peter 128
Phone (619) 436-6807
2026 #D Montgomery
Avenue
Cardiff, CA 92007

T

Taxali, Gary 79
Phone (905) 625-1079
1589 Lovelady Crescent
Mississauga, Ontario
L4W 2Y9
Canada

Thompson, John 39
Phone (201) 865-7853
118 Parkview Avenue
Weehawken, NJ 07087

Thompson, Richard 60
Phone (703) 516-0354
3504 N. 21st Avenue
Arlington, VA 22207

Toelke, Cathleen 10, 51
Phone (914) 876-8776
P.O. Box 487
Rhinebeck, NY 12572

Turgeon, Pol 46
Phone (514) 273-8329
5187 Jeanne-Mance, #3
Montréal, Québec H2V 4K2
Canada

U

Unruh, Jack 57, 69
Phone (214) 871-0187
2706 Fairmount
Dallas, TX 75201

V

Van Innis, Benoît 79
Phone (212) 989-8770
c/o Riley Illustration
155 W. 15th Street, #4C
New York, NY 10011

Ventura, Andrea 63, 74
Phone (212) 932-0412
2785 Broadway, #5l
New York, NY 10025

Ventura, Marco J. 21
Phone (39) 2-89409784
Via Bergognone, 31
Milan 20144
Italy

W

Waddell, Jan 90
Phone (416) 762-3961
6 Yule Avenue
Toronto, Ontario M6S 1E8
Canada

Weisbecker, Philippe 107
Phone (212) 989-8770
c/o Riley Illustration
155 W. 15th Street, #4C
New York, NY 10011

White, Eric 63
Phone (415) 821-3839
1142 Castro Street
San Francisco, CA 94114

Wilcox, David 83
Phone (215) 297-0849
5955 Sawmill Road
Doylestown, PA 18901

Wolff, Ashley 41
Phone (415) 826-7345
98 Cortland Avenue
San Francisco, CA 94110

Y

Yang, James 63
Phone (212) 807-6627
c/o The David Goldman
Agency
41 Union Square W.
Suite 918
New York, NY 10003

Yardley, Joanna 33
Phone (413) 586-9253
48 Ward Avenue
Northampton, MA 01060

Z

Zumbo, Matt 104
Phone (414) 277-9541
301 N. Water, 5th Floor
Milwaukee, WI 53202

Editor's Note

Every effort has been made to ensure that credits accurately comply with information supplied to us.

INDEX TO ART DIRECTORS, DESIGN FIRMS, AGENCIES AND CLIENTS

A

Accordino, Michael 30, 46
Actors Theater of Louisville 21
Adobe Systems, Inc. 25
Alaska Magazine 77
Alexander, Alex 63
Alexander, Gunta 35
Allison, Herb 28
American Jury Trial Foundation 107
Anderson, John Jr. 69
Anderson, Kristi 79
Anema, Andy 9
Anheuser-Busch 30
Ansaldo 99
Arlow, Arnold 26
Armario, David 65
David Armario Design 65
Arnott, Phillip 87
Artefact 30
Atlantic Monthly 72
Australian Penthouse 70
Avchen, Leslee 93

B

Bachleda, Florian 79
Ballantine Books 51
Banker's Trust 10
Barker, Paul 136
Barrick, Marty 60
Bartels & Company 10, 30
Bartels, David 10, 30
Bartholomay, Lucy 80
Baseman, Gary 10
The Beard Art Galleries, Inc. 133
Bender Browning Dolby & Sanderson Advertising 104
Bide-A-Wee 104
Bikini 65
Bishop, Debra 53
Black Vinyl Records 9
Bode, Larry 128
Body, Joan 104
Booth, Martha Anne 121
Borge, Rich 9
Borowsky, Doris 30
The Boston Globe Magazine 80
Boy's Life, Boy Scouts of America 57
Bozell, Inc. 6
Bradbury, Patricia 57
The Bradford Exchange 84
Brambilla, Claudia 99
Brewer, Linda 77
Brower, Steve 49
Brown & Caldwell 28
Brown, Linda 94
Burger King Corp. 21

C

CKS Partners 26
Callari, Rocco 90
Canada Post Corporation 90
Carabetta, Michael 51
Carillon Importers, Ltd. 26
Carol Publishing 49
Carroll, Jim 114

Carson, Bill 13
Carson, David 10
David Carson Design 10
Central City Opera 28
Chambers, Tony 70
Charter Medical 104
Chiang, Albert 69
University of Chicago Press 39
Choi, Jaeeun 119
Chomowicz, Lucille 30
Chronicle Books 51
Chwast, Seymour 96
Cincinnati Art Directors Club 126
Clum, Scott 65
Cobb, Linda 13
Collier, John 122
Connolly, Joseph 57, 133
Cook, Tim 94
Coors Brewing Company, Killian's Red Beer 26
Cory, Michael 13
Counihan, Claire B. 39
Creative Editions 44

D

Dai Nippon 107
Davis, Paul 22
Paul Davis Studio 22
Davy, Greg 103
Dayton Hudson, Department Store Division 19
De Barros, Jim 16
Delessert, Etienne 121
Delessert & Marshall 121
Dell Publishing 33
Destination Discovery 53
Deutsch, Peter 113
Peter Deutsch Design 113
Dizney, Joe 67
Don Juan Productions 94
Donnelan, Tim 70
Dorritie Lyons & Nickel, Inc. 94

Cuccurito, David 58
Curry, Chris 63, 74
Cutler, Nancy 67
Czeczko, Terry 33

D

Dai Nippon 107
Davis, Paul 22
Paul Davis Studio 22
Davy, Greg 103
Dayton Hudson, Department Store Division 19
De Barros, Jim 16
Delessert, Etienne 121
Delessert & Marshall 121
Dell Publishing 33
Destination Discovery 53
Deutsch, Peter 113
Peter Deutsch Design 113
Dizney, Joe 67
Don Juan Productions 94
Donnelan, Tim 70
Dorritie Lyons & Nickel, Inc. 94

Duckworth, Nancy 53
Dunjko, Carmen 83
Dunnick, Regan Todd 116, 119
Dutton Children's Books 41

E

Eberhard Faber 21
Ed Tel 111
Edmonton Telephone Yellow Pages 111
86 Gallery Poland 125
Eller, Matt 19
Emerge 63
Endewelt, Jack 128
English, Mark 116
Eskind Waddell 90
The Eleanor Ettinger Gallery, Inc. 122
Eugenio Fabozzi Onoranze Funebri 16
Evans, Shane W. 6

F

Fehrs, Rick 30
Fili, Louise 44
Louise Fili Ltd. 44
Finn, Kristen 72
First Stage Milwaukee 104
Fitzpatrick, Wayne N. 63
The Florida Aquarium 96
Foote Cone & Belding 22, 26
Foote Cone & Belding/Technology 25
Fortuno, Anthony 103
Foster, Andy 111
Frank, Laura 63
Frankfurter Allgemeine Magazin 54
Freeman, Clay 100
Frere-Jones, Sasha 25
Fritzson, Howard 16
Full Moon Creations, Inc. 21
Fuzanbo 42

G

Gallagher, James 25
Garlan, Judy 72
Gault, Alison 25
Geer Design 104
Geer, Mark 104
Georgiann, Margaret 94
Geringer, Laura 46
The German Post Office 96
Gibbs, Scott 83
Gonzalez, Juan Silverio 94
Governing 54
Gravity Workshop 9
Greenberg, Gary 26
The Greenwich Workshop, Inc. 87
Grinley, Mike 67
Gulf Printing 116, 119
Guttenberg, Lauren 84
Gwinn, Aubyn 22

H

Hadley, David 21
Haffner, Bill 14
Hahn, Sunghee 119
Hansen, Christina 77
Harakawa, Ann 107
HarperCollins Publishers 41, 46
Harrington, Glenn 30
Harrowsmith/Country Life 74
Hart, Keith 21
Heiden, Jeri 9
Hemiola Records 25
Henderson, Hayes 26
Henderson Tyner Art Co. 26
Henley, Marna 89
Hess Design Works 93
Hess, Mark 93
Hill, Chris 116, 119
The Hill Group 116, 119
Hoglund, Rudolph C. 79
Houser, Kurt 126
Huhtamaki 108
Hunter, David 25

I

IMS America 10
Identica 108
Iowa City Magazine 65
Islands 69

J

Jae & Hahn Design 119
Jewett, Doris 57
Joyce Foundation of Chicago 113

K

KSK Communications, Ltd. 21
Kaizer Communications 28
Kane, Nelson 10
Keyboard 54
Keyton, Jeffrey 114
Klein, Howard 33
Kleppert, Ken 136
Kner, Andrew 77
Korjenek, Kristin 83
Krenitsky, Nick 41
Kushnirsky, Julia 49

L

Ralph Lauren, Polo 30
Lebenson, Richard 128
Leeds, Richard 54
Leleu-Gingras, Lisa 21
Lennon, Tom 94
Liepke, Skip 122
Litwhiler, Woody 6
Lord Fletcher's Restaurant 14
Los Angeles County Transportation Authority 103
Los Angeles Times Magazine 53
Louisville Graphic Design Association 119
Lucas Management Systems 21
Lussier, Paul 79
The Lyric Players Theatre, Belfast 2

M

MTV 114
Manchess, Gregory 114, 122
Manchess Illustration 93
Manchess, Tricia 93
Marino, Guy 10
Marshall, Rita 44
Martin, Allison 63
May & Co., Inc. 100
May, Douglas 100
McCaffrey & Company 19
McClellan, Susan 74
McClellen, Ron 65
Mead Products 89
Men's Journal 79
Menchin, Scott 49
Menegaz, Laura 116, 119
Merck Group, Astra 19
Mercury House 42
Merkley, Newman, Harty 10
Metropolitan Transportation Authority Marketing Department 103
Mexican American Legal Defense & Education Fund 94
Michelman, Fran 22
University of Michigan Medical Center 72
Rodney Miller Associates 25
Minolta 6
Mires Design 6
Mobil 22
Vicki Morgan Associates 126
Morrissey, Georgia 51
Motichka, Dolores 69
Mouly, Françoise 69, 79
Movieline 63
Murphy, John 9

N

National Institutes of Health 94
The Nature Company 87
Neuhaus, David 30
The New York Times 77
The New Yorker 63, 69, 74, 79, 80
NewMedia 67
Newsweek 57
Noli, Suzanne 41
Not Drowning, Waving 13
Nuttal, Ted 28

O

O.E.P.L.I. 96
O'Brien, Tim 114
Odds & Ends 6
Ogilvy & Mather 9
Olding, Denise 119
Oliver, Marylynn 128
Owens, Don 107
Don Owens Visual Communication 107
Oxford University Press 49

P

Pacelli, Mike 28
Palencar, John Jude 128
Pallas Advertising 28
Pallas, Kristine 28
Paraskevas Gallery 104
Paraskevas, Michael 104
Paredes, Alfredo 30
Payne, C.F. 126
Peninsula YMCA 6
Penthouse 58
Peters, Michael 108
Pfizer Animal Health Group 94
Philomel Books 33, 35, 36
Piedmont Guitar Society 26
Playboy 60, 83
Plunkett, John 57
Porter, J. 69
Pospischil, Hans-Georg 54
Clarkson N. Potter, Inc. Publishers 33
Print 77
Promotrak Software 10
Putz, Robert 96

R

R.S.V.P. 128
Ralston Purina 13
Random House 51
Ray Gun 10
Reggio, Agostino 16
Reggio del Bravo Pubblicita 16
Reinhard, Matt 26
Ren Design 125
Renshaw, Jennifer 125
Reynolds, Sara 41
Rhodes, Silas H. 126
ride design 65
Hal Riney & Partners 13
Robie, Kevin 63
Rocarols, Albert 96
Roditski, Greg 19
Rolling Stone 53, 60, 72
Rose, David 103
Ross, Ben 126
Ross Design 126
Rossin Greenberg Seronick 26
Ruggieri, Mary 96
Russo, Giovanni 79

S

Saatchi & Saatchi 21
Saint Louis Zoo 10
St. Martin's Press 30, 46
Sakuma, Yumiko 42
Joseph Salina Illustrated Inc. 83
Sanford, John Lyle 53
Saturday Night 83
Saturn Corp. 13
Saunders, Reuben 128
Savini, Jill 26
Schiedt, David 28
Scholastic Inc. 39
School of Visual Arts 119, 126
Michael Schwab Design 14
Schwartz, Daniel 125
Scoble, Gretchen 51
Scripto-Tokai, Inc. 14
Seacat, Jimmy 21
Sears, Roebuck & Company 9
Serrano, José 6
Sheaff, Dick 93
Sibthorp, Fletcher 87
Simon & Schuster 30
Sisco, Brian 107
SmartMoney 67
Smith, Kenneth 79
Smith, Sharon 42
Sharon Smith Design 42
Software Marketing Association 28
Richard Solomon, Artists Representative 114, 122, 125
Sommers, Joan 39
Joan Sommers Design 39
Sony Music 16
Soteropulos, Connie 19
Spelling Films International 28
Art Spikol, Inc. 10
Squires, Sherri 119
Stable Gallery 87
Staebler, Tom 60, 83
Stahl, Nancy 114
Stanford Medicine 65
Steadham, Richard 54
Stermer, Dugald 93, 128
Stevenson, Nanette 33, 36
Stout, D.J. 80
Stratford Festival 111
Stratus Computer, Inc. 26
Levi Strauss & Company 22
Stucki, Ron 63
Studio Grafika 104
Summers, Mark 114
The Sunday Times Magazine 70
Swierzy, Waldemar 19
Sztuki, Galeria 19

T

TBWA Advertising 26
Terry, Keith 21
Texas Children's Hospital Center for Facial Surgery 104
Texas Monthly 80
Third Matinee 9
Thomas & Perkins 28
J. Walter Thompson Italia S.p.A. 99
Time 79
The Tisch Family Zoological Garden in Jerusalem 111
Trabon, Tim 116
Tran, David 49
Tsujimura, Masuro 42

U

UI 25
Uldry 121
Uldry, Albin 121
United Nations Postal Administration 90
United States Postal Service 93
Usher, David 87
Utne Reader 79

V

Vardimon Design 111
Vardimon, Yarom 111
The Village Voice 79
Visual Arts Press 126

W

Waddell, Malcolm 90
Walking Magazine 67
Warner Books 49
Warner Bros. Records 9, 13
The Washington Opera Co. 100
The Washington Post 60, 69
The Washington Times 69
Joseph A. Wetzel Associates, Inc. 96
Wired 57
Wold, Steven 104
Wolff, Ashley 41
Woodward, Fred 53, 60, 72
Woof Productions 93
Wordperfect Publishing 63
World Monitor 63

Y

Yang, Jimmy 108
Yankee Magazine 69
Yardley, Joanna 33
Young & Associates 28

Z

The Zipatoni Company 13

Editor's Note

Every effort has been made to ensure that credits accurately comply with information supplied to us.

Texas Monthly 64, 85
Thermo Cardio 88
Thorburn, Bill 13
Thunen, Michaele 42
Thurman, Chuck 114
Stewart Tilger Photography 123
Tilt Inc. 123
Time 57, 75, 76
Toronto Magazine 70
Toshiba of Canada Ltd. 29
Travel & Leisure 22
Travel & Leisure, American Express Publishing 72

Travel Holiday 49, 52, 57, 59, 75, 76, 79, 81

U

United Technologies 100

V

Valcourt, Christiane 61
Van Der Paardt, Bas 118
Vendetti, Dan 7
Vieceli, John 44
Voluntary Hospitals of America 91
Von Ulrich, Mark 120

W

W, Fairchild Publications 68
Walden University 100
Walsh, Dick 61
Walsh, Reneé 125
Weather Shield Manufacturing Company, Visions 2000 7
Welchman, Susan 57
Jeffery West Footwear 16
West, Paul 10
Wetherby, Kara 118
Wieden & Kennedy 21
Wieden & Kennedy-Amsterdam 30
Winkelman, Craig 55
Woelfel-Madison, Laura 39
Wolf, Hans 118
Wood Design 109
Wood, Tom 109
Woodward, Fred 49
Workman Publishing Company, Inc. 35
Worrell, Mary 57, 75

X

Xavier, Jessica 98

Editor's Note

Every effort has been made to ensure that credits accurately comply with information supplied to us.

INDEX TO ILLUSTRATORS

A

Arday, Don 133
Phone (214) 223-6235
616 Arbor Creek Drive
De Soto, TX 75115

Arisman, Marshall 60
Phone (212) 662-2289
314 W. 100th Street
New York, NY 10025

Asmussen, Don 69
Phone (619) 298-0414
3975 Hortensia Street, #E6
San Diego, CA 92110

B

Baldwin, Christopher 138
Phone (206) 284-8553
601 Valley Street, #309
Seattle, WA 98109

Banthien, Barbara 87
Phone (415) 381-0842
127 Leland Way
Tiburon, CA 94920

Barnes, Kim 125
Phone (410) 544-4644
735 Cypress Road
Severna Park, MD 21146

Bartalos, Michael 16
Phone (415) 863-4569
30 Ramona Avenue, #2
San Francisco, CA 94103

Baseman, Gary 10
Phone (718) 499-9358
443 12th Street, #2D
Brooklyn, NY 11215

Baviera, Rocco 35
Phone (905) 570-0004
41 King William Street
Suite 210
Hamilton, Ontario L8R 1A2
Canada

Beck, David M. 119
Phone (513) 741-1228
4042 Appletree Court
Cincinnati, OH 45247

Benny, Mike 83
Phone (916) 677-9142
2773 Knollwood Drive
Cameron Park, CA 95682

Biers, Nanette 126
Phone (415) 927-1531
123 Willow Avenue
Corte Madera, CA 94925

Blitt, Barry 79
Phone (203) 622-2988
34 Lincoln Avenue
Greenwich, CT 06830

Booth, Martha Anne 121
Phone (415) 728-8332
P.O. Box 208
990 Acacia Street
Montara, CA 94037

Borge, Rich 9
Phone (704) 251-1795
124 Maney Avenue
Asheville, NC 28804

Bralds, Braldt 10, 26, 90
Phone (203) 868-7577
P.O. Box 1145
Washington, CT 06793

Braught, Mark 13
Phone (404) 373-7430
767 N. Parkwood Road
Decatur, GA 30030

Brown, Calef 74
Phone (818) 986-6361
15339 Camarillo Street
Sherman Oaks, CA 91403

Buchanan, Nigel 70
Phone (305) 576-0142
c/o Tonal Values Inc.
111 N.E. 42nd Street
Miami, FL 33137

Burgard, William 72
Phone (313) 971-3014
2785 Heather Way
Ann Arbor, MI 48104

Burke, Philip 72, 79
Phone (716) 297-0345
1948 Juron Drive
Niagara Falls, NY 14304

Bustamante, Gerald 6
Phone (619) 234-8803
2400 Kettner Boulevard, #226
San Diego, CA 92101

C

Carroll, Jim 114
Phone (518) 794-8803
Box 233, Albany Turnpike
Old Chatham, NY 12136

Chan, Harvey 111
Phone (416) 533-6658
2 Clinton Place
Toronto, Ontario M6G 1J9
Canada

Chan, Ron 25
Phone (415) 389-6549
24 Nelson Avenue
Mill Valley, CA 94941

Choi, Jaeeun 119
Phone (718) 237-0216
70 Clark Street, #6C
Brooklyn, NY 11201

Chwast, Seymour 54, 96
Phone (212) 674-8080
215 Park Avenue S.
Suite 1300
New York, NY 10003

Cigliano, Bill 133
Phone (312) 973-0062
1525 W. Glenlake Avenue
Chicago, IL 60660

Cober, Alan E. 60, 119
Phone (914) 941-8696
95 Croton Dam Road
Ossining, NY 10562

Collier, John 122
Phone (214) 324-2879
8329 San Leandro
Dallas, TX 75218
c/o Richard Solomon
Artists Representative
Phone (212) 683-1362

Cousineau, Normand 70
Phone (514) 672-6940
870 Oak Avenue
Saint-Lambert, Québec
J4P 1Z7
Canada

Cox, Paul 33, 67
Phone (44) 55-382-9313
Old Rectory Tilney All Saints
Kingslynn, Norfolk PE3 44SJ
England
c/o Richard Solomon
Artists Representative
Phone (212) 683-1362

Craft, Kinuko Y. 100
Phone (203) 542-5018
83 Litchfield Road
Norfolk, CT 06058

Craig, John 53
Phone (608) 872-2371
Tower Road
Rt. 2, Box 2224
Soldiers Grove, WI 54655

Crawford, Robert 74
Phone (203) 266-0059
123 Minortown Road
Woodbury, CT 06798

Cromwell, Janelle 122
Phone (213) 882-6011
1151 N. Fuller Avenue, #3
Los Angeles, CA 90046

Curry, Tom 69
Phone (915) 837-2311
901 W. Sul Ross
Alpine, TX 79830

D

Davidson, Colin 25
Phone (44) 232-815313
76 Greystown Avenue
Belfast BT9 6UL
Northern Ireland

Davis, Paul 22
Phone (212) 420-8789
14 E. 4th Street
New York, NY 10012

Day, Rob 57
Phone (317) 253-9000
6095 Ralston Avenue
Indianapolis, IN 46220

Delessert, Etienne 121
Phone (203) 435-0061
Box 1689
Lakeville, CT 06039

Denise, Christopher 36
Phone (203) 657-4419
1060 Mott Hill Road
South Glastonbury, CT 06073

de Sève, Peter 69, 80
Phone (718) 398-8099
25 Park Place
Brooklyn, NY 11217

Dinyer, Eric 49, 80
Phone (816) 363-4795
5510 Holmes Street
Kansas City, MO 64110

Downs, Richard 65
Phone (909) 677-3452
24294 Saradella Court
Murrieta, CA 92562

Drescher, Henrik 80
Phone (510) 883-9616
2434 California Street
Berkeley, CA 94703

Dunnick, Regan Todd 116, 119
Phone (813) 351-1957
1345 University Parkway, #1
Sarasota, FL 34234

E

Eidrigevicius, Stasys 21, 125
Phone (212) 289-5514
c/o Marlena Torzecka
Artist Representative
211 E. 89th Street, Suite A-1
New York, NY 10128

Elwell, Tristan A. 136
Phone (212) 734-3353
188 E. 80th Street, #3B
New York, NY 10021

Endewelt, Jack 128
Phone (212) 877-0575
50 Riverside Drive
New York, NY 10024

Index to Photographers

English, Mark 116
Phone (817) 781-0056
512 Lakeside Court
Liberty, MO 64068

Evans, Shane W. 6
Phone (816) 756-1534
4152 McGee Street, #3N
Kansas City, MO 64111

F

Fiedler, Joseph Daniel 16
Phone (212) 929-5590
41 Union Square W.
New York, NY 10003

Field, Ann 22
Phone (310) 450-6413
2910 16th Street
Santa Monica, CA 90405

Fisher, Jeffrey 67, 77
Phone (212) 989-8770
c/o Riley Illustration
155 W. 15th Street, #4C
New York, NY 10011

Fraser, Douglas 19
Phone (403) 244-6636
1742 10th Avenue S.W.
Calgary, Alberta T3C 0J8
Canada

Fredrickson, Mark A. 89
Phone (602) 722-5777
853 S. Pantano Parkway
Tucson, AZ 85710

G

Gall, Chris A. 28, 41, 49
Phone (602) 299-4454
4421 N. Camino del Santo
Tucson, AZ 85718

Gallagher, James 25
Phone (718) 857-5958
462 Bergen Street, #3
Brooklyn, NY 11217

Garns, Allen 28
Phone (602) 835-5769
209 W. First Avenue
Mesa, AZ 85210

Gazsi, Edward S. 46
Phone (813) 844-3482
7930 Sycamore Drive
New Port Richey, FL 34654

Goodrich, Carter 54
Phone (800) 992-4552
1798 Main Road
Westport Point, MA 02791

GrandPré, Mary 33
Phone (612) 645-3463
475 Cleveland Avenue N.
Suite 222
St. Paul, MN 55104

Granner, Courtney 54
Phone (209) 892-2973
328 N. Fifth Street
Patterson, CA 95363

Gurney, James 87
P.O. Box 693
Rhinebeck, NY 12572

Gustafson, Scott 84
Phone (312) 725-8338
4045 N. Kostner Avenue
Chicago, IL 60641

H

Harrington, Glenn 30
Phone (610) 294-8104
329 Twin Lear Road
Pipersville, PA 18947

Head, Gary 111
Phone (816) 363-3119
6023 Wyandotte
Kansas City, MO 64113

Heavner, Becky 94
Phone (703) 683-1544
202 E. Raymond Avenue
Alexandria, VA 22301

Henderson, Hayes 26
Phone (910) 748-1364
815 Burke Street
Winston-Salem, NC 27101

Hess, Mark 93
Phone (914) 232-5870
88 Quicks Lane
Katonah, NY 10536

Hewgill, Jody 41
Phone (416) 601-0301
17 Bellwoods Place, Studio 2
Toronto, Ontario M6J 3V5
Canada

Holland, Brad 10, 79, 99
Phone (212) 226-3675
96 Greene Street
New York, NY 10012

I

Ilić, Mirko 63
Phone (212) 645-8180
652 Hudson Street, #3W
New York, NY 10014

Isip, Jordin 79
Phone (718) 624-6538
44 4th Place, #2
Brooklyn, NY 11231

J

Jew, Robert 138
Phone (818) 797-6141
1770 E. Sonoma Drive
Altadena, CA 91001

Johnson, David 107
Phone (203) 966-3269
299 South Avenue
New Canaan, CT 06840
c/o Richard Solomon
Artists Representative
Phone (212) 683-1362

K

Kato, R.M. 96
Phone (818) 356-9990
638 S. Marengo Avenue, #1
Pasadena, CA 91106

Keleny, Earl 30
Phone (203) 222-7740
20 Nordholm Drive
Weston, CT 06883

Kelley, Gary 19, 44, 65, 72, 77
Phone (319) 277-2330
301 1/2 Main Street
Cedar Falls, IA 50613

Kiuchi, Tatsuro 42
Phone (212) 781-7845
c/o Pesha Rubinstein
Artists Representative
37 Overlook Terrace, #1D
New York, NY 10033

Klanderman, Leland 13
Phone (314) 781-7377
c/o Ceci Bartels Associates
3286 Ivanhoe
St. Louis, MO 63139

L

Lardy, Philippe 57, 72
Phone (212) 473-3057
478 W. Broadway, #5A
New York, NY 10012

Leer, Rebecca J. 30
Phone (212) 595-5865
440 West End Avenue, #12E
New York, NY 10024

Leister, Bryan 28
Phone (703) 683-1544
202 E. Raymond Avenue
Alexandria, VA 22301

Liepke, Skip 58, 122
Phone (212) 724-5593
30 W. 72nd Street, Suite 2B
New York, NY 10023
c/o Richard Solomon
Artists Representative
Phone (212) 683-1362

Lofaro, Jerry 6, 28
Phone (212) 941-7936
57 Laight Street, 4th Floor
New York, NY 10013

Lorusso, Joseph 125
Phone (816) 756-5723
4600 J.C. Nichols Parkway, #403
Kansas City, MO 64112

Lyhus, Randy 69
Phone (301) 986-0036
4853 Cordell Avenue, #3
Bethesda, MD 20814

M

Manchess, Gregory 26, 30, 93, 114, 122
Phone (513) 439-5990
7910 C Moulins Drive
Dayton, OH 45459

Marsh, James 21
Phone (44) 71-622-9530
21 Elms Road
London SW4 9ER
England

Mattos, John 26
Phone (415) 397-2138
1546 Grant Avenue
San Francisco, CA 94133

Mayer, Bill 14
Phone (404) 378-0686
240 Forkner Drive
Decatur, GA 30030

McShane, David 133
Phone (609) 858-1567
12 Lees Avenue
Collingswood, NJ 08108

Melani, Daniele 16
Phone (39) 2-8372626
c/o Arcoquattro
via Pietro Custodi 16
Milan 20136
Italy

Menchin, Scott 49
Phone (212) 673-5363
640 Broadway
New York, NY 10012

Milot, Rene 94
Phone (416) 425-7726
49 Thorncliffe Park Drive
Suite 1604
Toronto, Ontario M4H 1J6
Canada

N

Nakamura, Joel 13
Phone (818) 301-0177
221 W. Maple Avenue
Monrovia, CA 91016

Nelson, Bill 131
Phone (804) 783-2602
107 E. Cary Street
Richmond, VA 23219

Neubecker, Robert 113
Phone (212) 219-8435
c/o Brigham Young University
Design Department, 210 B.R.M.B.
Provo, UT 84602

Niklewicz, Adam 30
Phone (203) 270-8424
26 Great Quarter Road
Sandy Hook, CT 06482

O

O'Brien, Tim 114
Phone (718) 832-1287
480 13th Street
Brooklyn, NY 11215

Olbinski, Rafal 21
Phone (212) 532-4328
142 E. 35th Street
New York, NY 10016

Ortega, José 134
Phone (212) 772-3329
524 E. 82nd Street
New York, NY 10028

Oxborough, Paul G. 133
Phone (612) 544-5345
8133 Julianne Terrace
Minneapolis, MN 55427

P

Pagowski, Filip 114
Phone (212) 662-3601
113 W. 106th Street, #4B
New York, NY 10025

Palencar, John Jude 128
Phone (216) 774-7312
249 Elm Street
Oberlin, OH 44074

Paraskevas, Michael 104
Phone (516) 287-1665
157 Tuckahoe Lane
Southampton, NY 11968

Parker, Robert Andrew 63
Phone (212) 989-8770
c/o Riley Illustration
155 W. 15th Street
New York, NY 10011

Pastrana, Robert M. 67
Phone (818) 548-6083
473 A Riverdale Drive
Glendale, CA 91204

Payne, C.F. 26, 126
Phone (513) 821-8009
758 Springfield Pike
Cincinnati, OH 45215
c/o Richard Solomon
Artists Representative
Phone (212) 683-1362

Peled, Einat 136
Phone (718) 275-6549
c/o Schneidman
62-28 Cromwell Crescent
Rego Park, NY 11374

Plank, Michael 136
Phone (913) 631-7021
5833 Monrovia
Shawnee, KS 66216

Porfirio, Guy 30
Phone (602) 881-7708
4101 E. Holmes
Tucson, AZ 85711

R

Renshaw, Jennifer 125
Phone (215) 546-0833
1521 Spruce Street, #203
Philadelphia, PA 19102

Rocarols, Albert 96
Fax (34) 3-451-2251
Rosselló 148 5° 2ª
08036 Barcelona
Spain

Rosas, Wilfredo 126
Phone (201) 854-8142
60 63rd Street, #3A
West New York, NJ 07093

Rose, David 103
Phone (213) 876-0038
1623 N. Curson Avenue
Los Angeles, CA 90046

Rush, John 104
Phone (708) 869-2078
123 Kedzie Street
Evanston, IL 60202

Ryden, Mark 9
Phone (818) 303-3133
541 Ramona Avenue
Sierra Madre, CA 91024

S

Sadowski, Wiktor 39
Phone (212) 289-5514
Marlena Torzecka
Artist Representative
211 E. 89th Street, Suite A-1
New York, NY 10128

Salina, Joseph 83
Phone (416) 699-4859
2255 B Queen Street E.
P.O. Box 321
Toronto, Ontario M4E 1G3
Canada

Schechter, Martin 131
Phone (914) 232-7267
34 Bedford Road
Katonah, NY 10536

Schumaker, Ward 42, 51
Phone (415) 398-1060
466 Green Street
San Francisco, CA 94133